MW00605270

25th ANNIVERSARY ISSUE
1974-1999

The Journal
of
Christian
Reconstruction
Volume XVI

edited by

P. Andrew Sandlin

CHALCEDON FOUNDATION
VALLECITO, CALIFORNIA 95251

Copyright 2000

by

Chalcedon Foundation

Printed on acid-free paper.

All rights reserved

No part of this book may be
reproduced in any form without
permission in writing from the publisher.

ISBN # - 1-891375-04-0

Printed in the United States of America

Published by Chalcedon Foundation
P. O. Box 158
Vallecito, CA 95251

Table of Contents

Introduction
by P. Andrew Sandlin

Since its inception in 1964, Chalcedon has stood unwaveringly for the relevance of the Bible and the Christian Faith to the modern world. Since 1974, the *Journal of Christian Reconstruction* has been a principal organ of articulating that relevance in a scholarly format. The *Journal* has steered a course midway between a popular magazine whose substance is sometimes wanting and an academic journal whose relevance is sometimes missing. The *Journal* has provided often profound and always relevant essays on topics as crucial though varied as creation, the arts, English and Russian literature, the American and French Revolutions, the Biblical translation controversy, Satanism, and much else. The goal has always been to articulate an explicitly Biblical Christianity that meets the immediate needs of the culture.

During something of a heyday for Christian anti-intellectualism, the *Journal of Christian Reconstruction* summoned the church to a rationally defensible and intellectually rigorous expression of the Faith. "Rational" and "intellectual" not in terms of man's wisdom—but in terms of an uncompromising commitment to using all of one's mental faculties in the service of the Word of God in advancing Christ's kingdom. This Silver Anniversary issue of the *Journal of Christian Reconstruction* contains articles of particular relevance culled from the *Journal's* pages over the past two and a half decades. They represent the best of Chalcedon's scholarship and their uncompromisingly Biblical premise offers a persuasiveness few dedicated Christians can elude and few dedicated humanists can ignore. These essays, as relevant today as they were when first written (and in some cases, more relevant), demonstrate to one degree or another and in one discipline or another, the utter bankruptcy of humanism and all other anti-Christian systems of thought and action. The essays are reprinted here with the prayer and hope that they will kindle the flame of uncompromising orthodoxy and kingdom-advancing Christianity in the hearts of a new generation of believers.

Vol. 9, Nos. 1 & 2, 1982-83

The Vision of Chalcedon
by Rousas John Rushdoony

The vision of Chalcedon began with a personal note and, before that, a family fact. When Armenia was converted to Christianity in c. A.D. 301, many of the nobility and previous royal dynasties were also converted. Each such family dedicated itself to the Lord, swore to full obedience to the Lord's every word, and promised to provide continuously for the support of a pastor from their own house. More than a few families were faithful to this promise; sometimes son succeeded father, at other times a nephew or a cousin, but always someone from the house became a pastor. In my own case, I am the eighth in a father and son line, and a long line from the early 300s.

With the Turkish massacres, that world ended. Previously, my paternal grandfather, a pastor, had first been blinded by the Turks and later killed (as was my maternal grandfather, and many relatives). In all, one and a half million Armenians were killed. My brother of eight months, Rousas George, died shortly before the flight into Russia. I was born on April 25, 1916, not too long after my parents arrived in the United States. Before my birth, while still in Russia, my father prayed that I would serve the Lord in the ministry of the word. From my earliest days, before I could say more than a few words, my father echoed Hannah's words (*1 Sam. 1:27-28*) and constantly reminded me that I had been given to the Lord, and I was not my own. I was very young when my father's commitment became my own. I had been prayed for!

John L. Dagg, D.D., the great American Baptist leader, prayed earnestly that his descendents would become believers and join him in heaven. Just yesterday morning, a sixth generation descendent of J. L. Dagg, Beth Sutton of Georgia, a strong Christian, left us after a wonderful visit. Dagg's prayers are being answered to the sixth generation at least! More parents need to pray for their children, and for their unborn descendents.

Very early, two facts impressed me. *First*, almost everyone in the farm community (in California) where we lived went to a church. Even in my high school years, much later, only one of these many churches was known to be somewhat modernistic. *Second*, in spite of this, both our community and the world left much to be desired in terms of being Christian. (Things are dramatically worse now, but they still left much to be desired then.) A *third* fact struck me forcibly as a boy. An elderly saint in the neighborhood, called "Grandfather" by all of us, was somewhat blind and rather feeble. He exercised daily around the two walls of the barn which were not included in the corral. He would tap the side of the barn with his cane, until he came to the end, and would then turn to the other side, all the while praying, reciting Bible verses, and the like. We boys always said "Hello" to him, and shook his hand. In 100° weather, his hands were still cold, even though he wore his winter underwear through the summer. His heart, we were told, was tired and thus would not pump blood to his extremities, and hence they were cold, a sign of creeping death. Years later, as a university student, I read a book which compared the 20ᵗʰ century church to an old man, no longer able to pump blood effectively to the extremities. This illustration struck me with especial force. It also helped set my Christian calling. The healing blood of Christ must be "pumped" to the extremities by the living church, both to carry the good news of salvation, and also to extend Christ's royal dominion over all things.

Towards this end, I began my ministry (ordained as an evangelist) among Chinese Americans and American Indians. I preached, during those years (twelve years in all) in the open air, in the streets on occasion, in prisons, and visited the hospital bed by bed, and so on. At the same time, I thought, prayed, and planned in terms of a theological ministry to set forth the whole word of God for the whole of life.

I had begun to write articles (in 1948, I believe), and had three books published, before we finally established Chalcedon, with no money whatsoever, simply by faith. In 1965, an opportunity arose when some people, whom I had not previously known, asked me to move to the Los Angeles area and teach them the word of God systematically. Thus, in September, 1965, the first, one-page *Chalcedon Report* was published. It now goes to every continent. We have five full-time and two part-time staff members, and our secretary, and will add more as funds permit. Also, our unpaid trustees are working with us, and two plan to be in residence here soon. We are hoping and praying for funds to develop a study center.

Our goal is to bring every area of life and thought into captivity to Jesus Christ. We believe that the whole word of God must be applied to all of life.

It is not only our duty as persons, families, and churches to be Christian, but it is also the duty of the state, the school, our callings, the arts and sciences, economics, and every other sphere to be under Christ our King. Nothing is exempt from his dominion. Like the Puritans, we seek to assert the "Crown Rights of Christ the King" over all of life.

We believe in the necessity for the total surrender of our whole life and world to the dominion of Jesus Christ; he is not simply a life and fire insurance salesman but our Lord and Savior. Our salvation is only and exclusively by his atoning blood, and our sanctification is by his law-word, by which his spirit gives us power and grace to live by; as the Lord's covenant people, we must live by his word, not our own. He is the only way.

Our sinful world lies under the burden of guilt and the sentence of death. The churches too often are like an old man whose dying heart cannot pump blood to the extremities. We must strive to reach the inner and the outer city, places near and far, church, state, school, and all other areas of life and thought with the saving power of Christ and his sanctifying law-word. We are plainly told that, "without shedding of blood is no remission" of sins (*Heb. 9:22*). Christ's blood has been shed, and ours is now the task of proclaiming his salvation, dominion, and victory unto all the world. Our Lord tells us very plainly that the very "gates of hell shall not prevail (or, hold out) against" his church (*Mt. 16:18*). John tells us what this means: "For whatsoever is born of God overcometh the world: and this is the victory that overcometh the world, even our faith" (*1 Jn. 5:4*). In fact, Paul tells us, whatever the persecution or battle, "we are *more* than conquerors through him that loved us" (*Rom. 8:37*). Having such assurance, we dare not retreat, nor think of defeat. We belong to the Lord: he made us, and we are his property; he redeemed us, and thereby made us doubly his possession. Our Lord, as the Adam of the redeemed and new humanity, said, "Lo, I come to do thy will, O God" (*Heb. 10:9*), and we must follow his example of obedience or faithfulness in all our ways. We must rebuild the walls of our Jerusalem and say with Nehemiah, "The God of heaven, he will prosper us: therefore we his servants will arise and build" (*Neh. 2:20*). In that task of reconstruction, the joy of the LORD is our strength (*Neh. 8:10*).

Vol. 1, No. 1, 1974

The Doctrine of Creation and Christian Apologetics

by Cornelius Van Til

When the apostle Paul preached to the Athenians on Mars Hill, he challenged them to become Creator-worshippers, instead of creature-worshippers (*Ac. 17*). It is this that all other believers, since the time of Paul, have also done. To realize why Paul did this, we must go back to Adam.

Adam disobeyed the command of God with respect to the tree of the knowledge of good and evil; he became a creature-worshipper instead of a Creator-worshipper. He declared his independence from God. He did not want God to tell him who he was and what he should do. Adam tried to shake off that which Satan had told him was an unwholesome and unbearable harness placed on him by "God." He wanted to be his own law-giver (autonomy).

To escape the punishment God had said would follow upon his disobedience to God, Adam sought to make himself believe that the world is not under God's control at all, that is, that God did not create the world and that therefore he cannot control it. Adam tried to make himself believe that Satan was right when he said that God was himself only a part or aspect of the world. If you are to be really free, that is, independent of God, Satan suggested to Adam, you must think of the whole world, including God, as having come into existence by chance. Then everybody has equal rights and an equal chance to make his own fortune.

The result of Adam's choice actually meant slavery and death, not only for himself, but also for all his descendants. All men, Paul tells us, have sinned in Adam (*Rom. 5:12*). All men are fallen (apostate) in and with him. All men in Adam have adopted Satan's hypothesis about man and his world. All men are, therefore, subject to the wrath of God.

All men know that they are created by God and that, therefore, Satan was wrong in what he told Adam (*Rom. 1*). All men are like the prodigal son in the parable of Jesus. The prodigal knew that he was the son of his father. He knew that the change he jingled in his pocket had come from the father. But he had pasted a mask on his face which no one, not even he himself, was able to remove. He made himself and others believe that all his wealth came from his own gold mines. Where were those gold mines? He did not know. The only think he "knew" was that they *did not* belong to his father. The prodigal hated the father and the father's house. It was this hatred of his father that controlled his view of the world. Only God's grace could unpaste the mask, the mask which had only anti-father lenses cemented in the eyeholes.

The Greeks as Followers of Satan

The Greeks to whom Paul preached exhibited the same attitude that Adam, after he listened to Satan, displayed. The Greeks did not prove; they could not prove; they just assumed that they were not image-bearers of God and that the universe about them was not created by God at all, but was "just there."

The Greeks simply assumed: (a) that all things are at bottom One, (b) that infinite plurality of things they saw in the space-time world about them eternally ooze out of this One, and (c) that this same plurality is also from all eternity being reabsorbed into this One. Thales said that *All* is water. Anaximander said that *All* is indefinite. Anaximanes said that *All* is Air. Parmenides said that *All* is static, and Heraclitus said that *All* is flux. The important point here is not the differences among them as to the nature of the *All* but the fact that all of them said that *all* reality is of one substance. They all assumed that God's being is not different from man's being and that man's being is not different from God's being. They all assumed that there has not been a creation out of nothing at the beginning of time. This is the philosophy of *monism*.

To say what Paul said, that God is the self-sufficient triune being and that man's existence is derivative because this God had created him "out of nothing," that is, by mere expression of his will, was nonsense to the Greeks.

Parmenides and Paul

Parmenides expressed that attitude of all the Greeks in his classic phrase to the effect that "Being and Thought are Identical" because they *must* be identical. Only that which I can think without contradiction, said Parmenides, can exist; creation out-of-nothing is against the law of contradiction and therefore impossible. Man's autonomous mind is therefore the ultimate standard of reality.

We can imagine Paul and Parmenides having a quite talk one evening. They would not have argued about details. Neither of them would have argued that his position is more "in accord with logic" and/or more "in accord with fact" than that of the other. Each would have claimed that only his position, rather than that of the other, was "thinkable" at all. Spinoza said in effect what Parmenides has said: "The order and connection of things is identical with the order and connection of ideas." We may put the matter in more modern terms. Parmenides and Spinoza might have said that only on the presupposition that all reality *is*, in Parmenides' sense of the term, can anything intelligible be said about anything. Man's mind *must* conform to the reality that *is*, by definition— man's definition.

Creation and the Philosophy of History

To make this point clear, we must understand that for Paul the idea of creation was but the beginning of a philosophy of history. This philosophy includes such teaching as the resurrection of Christ and his return from heaven to judge the living, and judging according as they have or have not accepted Christ as their king before their death. Moreover, the notion of creation as an aspect of this view of reality as a whole is taken from the Scriptures of the Old and New Testaments as the word of the Christ who identified himself as the way, the truth, and the life (*Jn. 14:6*). Paul *proclaims* his philosophy of history to the Greeks, in the name of and by the absolute authority of Jesus, the Christ who had appeared to him from heaven on his way to Damascus, where he intended to destroy those who were of that *Way*, the Way of Jesus Christ. "Saul, Saul, why persecutest thou me?" Jesus had said to him. In other words, "Why have you repressed the Truth speaking to you in nature, in your conscience, and in the Scriptures?"

From this time forth, Paul preached Christ, whom before he had persecuted, as the only light and life of men. All men, he said, are spiritually dead; without the life-giving power of the Holy Spirit, who takes the things of Christ and gives them unto men, they keep going down the staircase that ends in eternal futility— intellectually, morally, and spiritually—until they join Satan in eternal separation from the God of love. "Hath not God made foolish the wisdom of the world, for after that the world by wisdom knew not God it pleased God through the foolishness of preaching to save those that believe" (*1 Cor. 1:20-21*).

"Parmenides, my friend," Paul might have said, "you have assumed that you are not created but ultimate, and that your thought is not that of a creature but instead is creative or legislative in the way that God's thought is creative and legislative. We both have pre-interpreted 'fact' and 'logic' in terms of our comprehensive and mutually exclusive views. I once held to a view basically similar to yours. I now see that 'logic' and 'fact' must be what alone they can be according to the 'gospel' of creation and redemption in Christ. They *are* because they must be *what they are said to be* in the total configuration of history, from creation to judgment portrayed in Scripture, and what I now, in the name of Christ, declare them to be. Having seen this, I no longer do what I formerly did, that is, try to penetrate exhaustively the relation of the triune Creator-Redeemer God to myself and the created; I merely seek to make as much order as I can relating the facts of the space-time cosmos to one another and to God, thus forming a 'system' of knowledge. I am always mindful that this 'system' of mine is true because it is based on God's revelation to me in Christ, but it nevertheless remains subject to further development because I am only a creature using the laws of the Creator. My thinking is not originally constructive but recreatively reconstructive of the revelation of God."

Plato and Paul

The principle of Parmenides has been called "the adequacy of thought to begin." It affirms the capacity of man's mind to comprehend the universe. Plato used this principle in his philosophy. But in his later life, he realized that he could not think through the space-time world exhaustively by means of his power of conceptualization. In his later dialogues, Plato's *non-being* of his earlier dialogues changed into *"otherness of being."* In the *Timaeus* dialogue, this "otherness of being" appears as an anti-being—a restraining force to the effort of the demurrage to make a perfect world. How can the best of sculptors make a perfect statute if the marble he has to work with is marred? Plato's "creator" was not omnipotent. The "stuff" of existence—matter—endlessly resists the "efforts" of impersonal forms to shape it.

Paul's gospel of any original, perfect man, who had disobeyed the known will of God, and as such was subject to the wrath of God, could not be conjoined with the life and worldview of Plato. Paul challenged the Greeks to reject their Satanically inspired impersonal form-matter scheme as being internally meaningless and hateful in the sight of their Creator to whom they owed allegiance.

Plotinus

Plotinus developed this form-matter scheme of the Greeks into his notion of the *scale of being*. In this scale of being, Plotinus has room for everything except for the Creator-Redeemer God of Scripture. In the philosophy of Plotinus, the Greek apostate, the spirit—the Greek *paideia*—challenges to a duel the Biblical scheme of creation, fall, and redemption through Christ. The concept of some universal scale of being that fuses God's being to the creation's being is a monistic concept—the heritage of Adam's rebellion. God becomes merely one aspect of being in general: crucial, but not *that* crucial! This was the intellectual challenge of Plotinus, the Greek.

Augustine

Augustine accepted this challenge. As Paul had been changed by the grace of Christ from being a persecutor of Jesus to his greatest apostle, so Augustine gradually emerged from the disfiguring detritus of Platonism and of Greek philosophy to the glorious vision of his creation and redemption by the triune God of the Scriptures. The Creator is also the Savior.

In his later writings, Augustine worked out the implications of the Biblical teaching on creation by opposing the self-salvation idea in the Greek notion of man as inherently participant in God. This Greek notion had been insinuated into the Christian church by such men as Pelagius. For a brief time, Augustine won the day. But at an evil hour Pseudo-Dionysius and John Scotus Erigena brought back the Plotinian scale-of-being idea into the church. They did so by allegorizing the creation narrative. Before them Plato had already spoken of creation as a myth. If creation is mythical, God is mythical.

Thomas Aquinas

Following in this line of thinking the medieval theologians, and notably Thomas Aquinas, accommodated the Biblical idea of creation to the Greek idea of slenderness of being. Man is free because he has being, but only a little being. Following the Greeks, and more particularly Aristotle, "the Philosopher," the Council of Trent rejected Protestant theology as heresy, since Protestantism is grounded in the idea of man's freedom as that of the creature of the triune God, accomplishing his task as a prophet, priest, and king unto God. The theology of the Reformation, based on the simple teaching of Paul about creation, sin, and redemption, was anathematized as heretical in the name of a Christianized Greek philosophy. (The attempt by Roman Catholic scholars such as Hans King and their Protestant counterparts to minimize the differences between the Council of Trent and Protestantism is grounded on a modernized, Kantian reinterpretation of Christian categories and language.)

Immanuel Kant

In modern times, Immanuel Kant developed the Satanic notion of human autonomy more consistently than anyone before him.

On the surface, Kant's position is quite diverse from that of Parmenides and Plato. Whereas for Parmenides reality—*true* reality—is exhaustively eternal, for Kant it is exhaustively temporal. Even so, as Parmenides needed the idea of ultimate contingency as a foil to his notion of utterly timeless being, so Kant needed the idea of timeless logic and being as being a foil to his notion of time or contingency.

All apostate philosophy is constituted by correlative interaction between rationalist-determinism and irrationalist-indeterminism. Such philosophies are based on the notion of human autonomy.

What Herman Dooyeweerd calls the "freedom-nature" scheme of post-Kantian thought and what he calls the "form-matter" scheme of Greek thought are but two forms of apostate thought, and both are *dialetical.*[1] Modern thought merely works out the implication of Greek thought to the effect that (a) all reality is at bottom One, (b) all temporal reality is working itself back into the One, that is, the notion that God and man develop together as aspects of one being. In the place of the Biblical idea of God as Creator and man as his creature, all apostate thinking has equally ultimate forces of form and matter eternally striving against one another.

Recent Evolutionary Thinking

In recent times, evolutionary thinking has carried on the apostate man's notion that all being is one. Working along the lines of Kant, recent science, recent philosophy, and recent theology have taken for granted that there is not and cannot be any such thing as creation out of nothing.

When in 1859 Charles Darwin published his *Origin of Species,* he thought he was "proving" that man has come from an animal ancestry by self-existent cosmic forces. The evolution hypothesis in science involves the idea of cosmic evolution. Cosmic evolution, which Kant argued for a century before Darwin, necessarily preceded "scientific" evolution. There is no possibility of carrying to a conclusion an argument between those who believe in biological evolution and those who believe in creation, unless this argument be seen to be but an aspect of two mutually exclusive views of reality as a whole.

Modern biological evolution theory *assumes* that all reality is flux. It does this together with modern science in general.

It might appear that in modern evolutionary thinking, Heraclitus' idea that *all is flux* has won out over the Parmenidean idea that *all is static.* Yet no one can say anything about "all being as flux." How can a whitecap on a bottomless and shoreless ocean of chance say, "*Here I am*"? There is no possibility of man identifying either himself or any fact in his environment in a universe of *pure* chance. As long as he holds that all is flux, he cannot even get under way to ask a question about *anything,* let alone giving any answers to any questions he might ask.

Yet the modern scientist simply asserts or assumes that there cannot be any such thing as creation out of nothing, and he ignores the consequences of what his denial entails for the question of the philosophy of history. In other words, modern science stands on the surface of a bottomless ocean of chance as it announces that Christianity *cannot* be true. The Heraclitean idea of all reality as being *pure flux* needs the support of the Parmenidean idea of all reality as *purely static* in order to justify "autonomous" science's assumption that creation cannot have taken place in the past and that there cannot be any such thing as a coming judgment by Christ, in and by whom all things are and were created (*Rev. 4:11*).

When Darwin's theory of evolution was first presented, there was great rejoicing among those who were anxious to see the historic Christian faith discredited. At last it had been "proved" by the "facts" that man had not been created by the self-sufficient God of the Scriptures. By now it should be clear for all to see that the very idea of space-time fact is utterly unintelligible on the basis of reality as total flux. By now it should also be clear that a combination of the idea of pure irrationalist indeterminism and the idea of pure rationalist determinism is meaningless. A great philosopher of science, Morris Cohen, says that science needs the idea of a universe that is both *wholly* closed and *wholly* open. This idea of the *pure correlativity* of pure staticism and pure flux underlies all modern evolutionary science. No one could say anything intelligible on such a foundation.

Modern Philosophy

We have come from the philosophy of Kant, with its notion that *time* or chance is ultimate, to the idea of science built on chance. We must turn for a moment to a brief look at the philosophical positions developed by men who lived after biological evolution had been "discovered."

In his book on *The Limitations of Science*, J. W. N. Sullivan writes that "we shall never reach a set of concepts in terms of which all the phenomena can be described. The entities used in science are abstractions from experience" (105). In other words, according to Sullivan, the pure fluidity of chance must be frozen by the pure conceptual determinism of pure staticism. In order to have science at all, purely fluid sense-experience must be, yet cannot be, exhaustively expressed by an abstract, timeless conceptualization process. And when the "facts" are thus discovered and seen for what they really are, they are seen as never having been originated and as never possibly coming to be. Thus, a pure dualism between conceptualization and sensuous experience is turned into a monism of pure negation: no past or future is allowed.

A. N. Whitehead's philosophy is often called a process-philosophy. Whitehead rejects the older static view of science. He aims to develop a "higher concept" of science, a concept that will include the notion of human freedom as well as of impersonal necessity. "We must start," says Whitehead, "with the event as the ultimate unit of natural occurrence."[2] Taking the idea of the event "as a process whose outcome is a unit of experience" enables Whitehead, as he thinks, to enthrone freedom above all forms of necessity that one might find in reality.

The idea of event as a "unit of experience" also enables Whitehead to avoid paying "metaphysical compliments" to God.[3] As with Kant, Whitehead makes room for faith, that is, for *a faith other than the historic Christian faith*. The historic Christian faith would, argues Whitehead, be deterministic. True religion is, for Whitehead, "the vision of something which stands beyond, behind, and within, the passing flux of immediate things; something which is real, and yet waiting to be realized; something which is a remote possibility, and yet the greatest of present facts; something that gives meaning to all that passes, and yet eludes apprehension; something whose possession is the final good, and yet is beyond all reach; something which is the ultimate ideal, and the hopeless quest."[4]

Modern Theology

Modern theology as well as modern philosophy agrees with modern science in building its structure on the assumption that historic reality is not created by the self-sufficient, self-contained triune God of Scripture.

The prince of modern theologians is Karl Barth. His entire philosophy is built on the assumption that the Genesis account of the origin of man and his world must be allegorized. To be sure, Barth insists that theology needs the idea of creation. Creation is the foundation of the covenant, and the covenant is the essence of the relation of God to man. God *is* Christ, and Christ is his work of the saving of all men. There are *not* two natures, the divine and the human, that are genuinely united in Christ but without mixture. That was the Confession of Chalcedon. But we must "actualize Chalcedon." We must say that it is God's very nature to turn into the opposite of himself and then take all men back up into participation with his own self-existence. "In Jesus Christ it comes about that God takes time to Himself; that He Himself becomes temporal; that He is present for us in the form of our own existence and our own world, not simply embracing our time and ruling it, but submitting Himself to it, and permitting created time to become and to be the form of His eternity."[5]

The Kingdom of Man

It is thus that modern process theology, building on modern process philosophy and modern process science, is leading men into the "dust of death." Senior demon Screwtape, in his second letter to his nephew Wormwood, points out that "one of our great allies at present is the Church itself." Not the invisible church, but the "sham Gothic" building and its ordinary looking members. He might also have included its "sham orthodoxy."

Jesus said that the last days would be like those of the time of Noah. Long before Socrates came upon the scene, Lamech scorned the idea that he was guilty because he was breaking the ordinances of God, especially the ordinance of monogamous marriage. And the children of Seth had joined the children of Cain in rejecting the creation-ordinances of God.

So now, as Jesus predicted, leading theologians are led by leading philosophers and scientists in assuming that there cannot be any such thing as a clear and finished revelation of God to man in history. Leading theologians are saying, "Lo here is Christ, or there" (*Mt. 24:23*). Believers in Christ now see the modern equivalent of the "abomination of desolation, spoken of by Daniel the prophet, standing in the holy place" (*Mt. 24:15*).

The main target of attack on the part of the theologians of the kingdom of man is the traditional Protestant view of Scripture and its content. It is the "literalism" of and the "determinism" of the reformers and their followers that the "free man" of modern apostate thinking cannot tolerate. Just as Dionysius the Aereopagite and John Scotus Erigena allegorized the entire narrative of Scripture in terms of the flux theory of reality, so men like Paul Tillich have in our day demythologized the creation story and all that goes with it. To be sure, Tillich speaks of a final revelation in Jesus Christ. But, for Tillich, revelation is finally only "if it has the power of negating itself without loosing itself."[6] His thought, like that of the Greeks, is dialectical.

In Tillich's view, "Adam" was quite right in following Satan's advice to seek for freedom independently of the creation-redemption ordinances of God. Orthodox literalism is absurd. We must seek for a "cosmic myth" behind the Genesis story. This myth probably has "Orphic roots....It received a Christian form by Origen, a humanistic one by Kant, and is present in many other philosophies and theologies of the Christian Era. All have recognized that existence cannot be derived from within existence, that it cannot be derived from an individual event in time and space. They have recognized that existence has universal dimension."[7]

As for modern Roman Catholic theology, can one think of it as lagging behind in adopting the idea of biological and cosmic evolution? The great scientist-theologian Tielhard de Chardin tells the story of the emergence of Christ from the amoebae with great enthusiasm. How glorious the process of final victory of man over nature and over himself is now seen to be![8]

As for Roman Catholic philosophy, we may take Jacques Maritan as an illustration. Maritan too speaks of the great freedom that man has in terms of the *Philosophia Perrennis*. This philosophy is bound to be the philosophy of the future. It has taken into its bosom all the progress made by modern evolutionary scientific thought, while yet it holds to the permanence imbedded in Aristotle's thinking. The "Christian Aristotelianism of Albert the Great and particularly of St. Thomas Aquinas" offers us a truly "objective outlook on reality, and, at the same time looks upward in accordance with the theology of the church."[9] Such theologians as Hans Küng and Yves Congar take a position similar to that of Martian.

Vatican II has followed the lead of these and similar theologians of flux. Its notorious assertion to the effect that there is no salvation outside the church (*extra ecclesia nulla salus*) is no barrier to the idea of universal salvation. The "church" now includes all men of good will.

Thus we find that leading Protestant theologians and leading Roman Catholic theologians join hands in terms of modern evolutionary thinking. But the end is not yet. The Master Historian of World History, Arnold J. Toynbee (cf. vol. 27 of *Wisdom*) invites us to see that Christianity and all other higher religions "have addressed themselves to Humanity in general in an *élan* of love."[10] In the course of biological cosmic evolution, creative personalities have sprung forth who have sought to transfigure their fellowmen into living in accord with the "law of love."[11]

Jesus was one of these creative personalities: Buddha was another. Jesus exhibited the cosmic principle already expressed by Aeschylus, to the effect that all suffering sanctifies. Toynbee makes certain that no one who makes special redemptive claims for Jesus should be allowed citizenship in the universal kingdom of man. The historian "will be suspicious *a priori*," says Toynbee, "of any presentation that goes on to assert that a *unique* and *final* revelation has been given by God to *my* people in *my* time on *my* satellite of *my* sun in *my* galaxy. In this self-centered application of the thesis that God reveals Himself to His creatures the historian will espy the Devil's cloven hoof."[12]

The Christian's Answer

This may suffice to indicate the fact that evolutionary philosophy is generally accepted by leading scholars in all fields of inquiry today. This may also suffice to indicate that the acceptance of the notion of evolution as a substitute for that of creation in the Biblical meaning of the term is not something to which open-minded men were led by the evidence of fact and the probative force of logic. On the contrary, the evolution doctrine is accepted in spite of the fact that it is inherently destructive of the possibility of all meaningful human speech and action. The evolution hypothesis is a view of reality by which the natural man, following Adam, seeks freedom from the laws of his Creator-

God, and is caught in the dialectical net of having to interpret himself and his world in terms of the interaction between pure impersonal rationalistic determinism and pure impersonal irrationalistic indeterminism. This philosophy shows men's hatred of the God who is understood, deep in the heart of each man, to be the Creator. This hatred makes men cling, in defiance to God's revelation, to a worse-than-meaningless view of themselves and the world.

What, then, are Christian believers to do in this situation? They are not to seek to answer evolutionary theory by means of a theology or philosophy that is itself based in part on the same false idea of "human freedom as autonomy" that underlies the evolution view. This excludes the use of Roman scholasticism or neo-scholasticism, for both are largely built upon the Aristotelian notion of the *analogy of being*, and this notion ultimately rests on the impossible correlatively of pure Parmedian staticism and pure Heraclitean flux.[13] The analogy of being seeks to supply the "objectivity" that man needs for this thought by means of the notion of "being" inherent in the consciousness of man.

In the second place, it is equally impossible to reply successfully to evolutionary thinking by means of Protestantism's traditional Butler-analogy method of apologetics, with its supposedly logical proofs of God.[14] Furthermore, there is no hope in the concept of objectivity offered by the evangelical thinker, C. S. Lewis—the notion of a universal *Tao* (way) taught by all higher religions.[15] This *Tao* is itself a projection of the would-be-autonomous man as he emerges from his hypothetical animal life to his equally hypothetical divinity.

The only way in which evolutionary thinking can be answered is by following the method of the Apostle Paul. Paul tells apostate man that all the facts of the entire world of space and time clearly manifest the creative, controlling, redeeming work of God. Paul tells apostate man that his attempt to interpret the world in terms of himself as "free" from God is clearly the effort of one who is involved in the fall of Adam, and represents the same sort of hostility to God that Adam manifested when he listened to Satan. Accordingly, apostate man's activity of thought and behavior is not only futile but God-insulting. Accordingly, the wrath of God rests and will rest forever upon the "children of disobedience" unless they repent and believe in Christ and his resurrection.

Paul tells apostate man that he himself is not in himself any wiser or better than they. He has been taken out of the depth of intellectual chaos and moral corruption by the substitutionary death for him by Christ on the cross and by the application of the significance of this death for him by the regenerating and enlightening work of the Holy Spirit.

Such being the case, says Paul, I now see that the facts and the laws of the created universe in relation to one another are what they are because of God's purpose in creating and redeeming a people for himself which should proclaim his praise. Only if man takes his interpretative efforts to be that of reinterpretation (as a redeemed creature) of God's original interpretation—given to him in Christ—as the way, the truth, and the life, will he have light and freedom.

If the Christian is deeply convinced that he himself was formerly caught in the clutches of the god of this world, he will speak with deep sympathy to those who are "outside" the freedom with which Christ has made them. "Your freedom," he will say to his friend, "is, in reality, nothing but slavery. Flee to Christ for true freedom. Pray to the Holy Spirit to enable you to repent and believe.

"Yes, to say this is apparently contradictory. But the only alternative to it is freedom in a vacuum and the wrath of God remaining upon you."

----

[1] Herman Dooyeweerd, *In the Twilight of Western Thought* (n. p., 1960), chap. 2.

[2] A. N. Whitehead, *Science and the Modern World* (n. p., 1925), 103.

[3] *ibid.*, 179.

[4] *ibid.*, 191.

[5] Karl Barth, *Kirchliche Dogmatik II*, ii, 694, Eng. Tr. 616.

[6] Paul Tillich, *Systematic Theology I* (n. p., n. d.) 148.

[7] *ibid.*, II, 40, 41.

[8] c.f., C. Van Til's study, *Pierre Teihard de Chardin.*

[9] John S. Zybura, ed., *Present Day Thinking and the New Scholasticism* (n. p., 1926), 402.

[10] Arnold J. Toynbee, *A Study in History, III* (n. p., n. d.) 232.

[11] *ibid.*, 236.

[12] _____, *An Historian's Approach to Religion* (n. p., n. d.) 135.

[13] cf. C. Van Til. "Analogia Entis," in Edwin Palmer, ed., *The Encyclopedia of Christianity I*, (n. p., n., d.), 200-201.

[14] c. f. C. Van Til, *The Defense of the Faith* (n. p., 1963).

[15] C. S. Lewis, *The Abolition of Man* (n. p., 1947).

Volume 1, No. 1, 1974

Basic Implications of the Six-Day Creation
By Gary North

Introduction

Christian churches seldom lack an issue that can serve as a means of internal disruption and conflict: the mode of baptism, age of one's first communion, the form of government, the role of the institutional church in non-church realms. Surprisingly—and contrary to the impression given by popular textbooks—the conflict between evolution and creation has not been one of these major and continuing sources of contention within the vast majority of Christian churches. Prior to 1800, the concept of biological evolution had not been widely considered; a few secular philosophers—for example, Immanuel Kant—had argued for some form of cosmic evolution, but Christians were generally uninformed about, or unimpressed by, such speculation. Yet after 1900, outside of a few so-called fundamentalist groups, the question of the time and mode of God's creation was no longer considered intellectually or ecclesiastically respectable as a topic of fundamental importance. Men are expected to "agree to disagree" as Christians; specifics concerning creation are officially relegated into the realm of *adiophora*, that is, things indifferent to salvation or the life of the church. "Theistic evolution" or the "gap theory" or "progressive creation" or the "literary framework hypothesis" serve as popular alternatives to the six-day creation within those circles that still concern themselves with the question of Biblical inerrancy. Outright Darwinism has been adopted readily by everyone else.

Since the turn of the century, we have witnessed a strange phenomenon inside the evangelical churches. Pastors have been dismissed by their congregations or their hierarchical superiors for mismanaging budgets, changing their minds about the mode of baptism, softening their views concerning the Sabbath, or disrupting the autonomy of the choir director. But a heresy trial for a pastor who holds to some variant of theistic evolution would be unthinkable in most evangelical churches today. As a means of institutional confrontation, the choir is a far more potent issue than the doctrine of creation. So powerful have been the forces of religious syncretism, philosophical pragmatism, and academic respectability inside the churches, that this crucial foundation of the Faith has become operationally secondary—or less.

If the pastors, clutching desperately at their advanced academic degrees from accredited colleges, have abandoned the defense of the Faith, why should the layman think that he has any right to call the churches to repentance? How can a layman challenge the official expertise of certified scholarship and ordained respectability? This was Moses' question to God, basically, in Exodus 4:10. God's answer was straightforward: "Who hath made man's mouth? or who maketh the dumb, or deaf, or the seeing, or the blind? have not I the LORD?" (*Ex. 4:11*). God is the source of all valid theories and all valid footnotes, not the geology department of Harvard University. His revelation of himself in the Bible is the standard of accuracy, not the latest discovery (which will be refuted in five years by someone else) of hypothetically neutral science. If intelligent, devoted, and necessarily self-taught laymen do not make use of the services of the various creation research organizations in their efforts to call Christians back to the explicit revelation of the Bible and the historic faith of the orthodox churches, then a major battle will have been lost. The status quo in the churches today is our defeat; orthodoxy demands reconstruction. Assistance from the pastors in this struggle would be appreciated, but as it stands today, the laymen are necessarily the strategists and generals.

Why make the stand here? Why is creation the rallying issue? First, because it is the one issue which has established itself in the minds of many orthodox Christians as a necessary and legitimate area of confrontation between apostate science and Christianity. Men who would not be confident in challenging secular thought in the realms of psychology, politics, economics, or other academic disciplines, nevertheless do understand the false nature of the claim of scientific neutrality concerning evolution. As a result, the intellectual division of labor is greater in the areas of biology and geology than in any other Christian academic endeavors. More men are already involved in the battle. Thus, it is tactically a solid place to make a stand. More important than tactics, however, is the centrality of the doctrine of creation to Christian faith. Langdon Gilkey, a neo-orthodox theologian who does not believe in the verbal, plenary inspiration of the Bible, has nonetheless seen the issue more clearly than most supposedly evangelical theologians. His *Maker of Heaven and Earth* announces forthrightly:

> It is quite natural, of course, that Christian devotion and Christian thought should concern themselves most with God's redeeming activity in Jesus Christ, for upon this our knowledge of God as Loving Father, and so our hope for salvation, most directly depends. Nevertheless, the centrality of God's redeeming activity to our life and thought should not blind Christians to the divine work of creation, which, if not so close to our hearts, is just as significant for our existence and just as important if we are to think rightly about God. Through God's redeeming works we know that He is supremely righteous and supremely loving. But when we ask *who* is supremely righteous and loving, the answer comes in terms of God's original activity, creation: the Creator of heaven and earth, the Lord, is He who judges and redeems us. The transcendent "Godness" of God, what gives Him deity and so ultimate significance to our lives, is most directly manifested to us through His creative activity as the transcendent source of all being and of all existence. Without this transcendent aspect of "deity," the judgment and love of God would be ultimately unimportant to us, and the redemption promised by them impossible for God. The idea of creation, therefore, provides the most fundamental, if not the most characteristic, definition of God in the Christian faith. Among all the activities of God, creation is that activity or attribute which sets him apart as "God." (83-84)

The doctrine of the Trinity—the eternal, infinite, self-revelation and communion of the holy God who is three persons—is the starting point of Christian theology. But insofar as he has any relationship with men, the doctrine of creation is absolutely central. The fact that Gilkey, who is not orthodox, can see this, and evangelicals do not, testifies to the disastrous effects of syncretism. Christianity and antitheism cannot be successfully fused without destroying Christianity.

Creation Defined

The Bible testifies to the fact that a personal God created all things—matter and energy, structure and motion—out of nothing: *creatio ex nihilo*. The opening words of the Bible are concerned with the question of origins: "In the beginning God created the heaven and the earth" (*Gen. 1:1*). God repeats this fact to us again and again: "Yea, before the day was I am he; and there is none that can deliver out of my hand: I will work, and who shall let it?" (*Is. 43:13*). We read in the New Testament concerning God the Son: "For by him were all things created, that are in heaven, and that are in earth, visible and invisible, whether they be thrones, or dominions, or principalities, or powers: all things were created by him, and for him: and he is before all things, and by him all things consist" (*Col. 1:16-17*). There is no more comprehensive statement in Scripture concerning the creation. Christ our Savior is identified with God the Creator; were he not the Creator, he would not be the Savior. We would still be dead in our sins (*Eph. 2:5*). The Gospel of John, the most explicitly evangelistic of the gospels (*Jn. 20:30-31*), begins with the affirmation that Christ, the Word of God, is the Creator: "All things were made by him; and without him was not any thing made that was made" (*1:3*). God precedes all things: "Before the mountains were brought forth, or ever thou hadst formed the earth and the world, even from everlasting to everlasting, thou art God" (*Ps. 90:2*). He is therefore sovereign over all things: "Thou turnest man to destruction; and sayest, Return, ye children of men" (*Ps. 90:3*).

No knowledge of God as Creator could penetrate the minds of rebellious men sufficiently to bring them to repentance were it not for God's gracious self-revelation in the Bible, by means of the Holy Spirit. Men willfully hold back the knowledge they have of God as Creator (*Rom. 1:18-23*). The saving knowledge of God comes only by means of his special revelation and special grace to his people. Therefore, men are required to believe that God is the Creator, and not the creator devised by the rebellious human imagination, but the Creator as revealed in the Bible. Any old kind of creation will not do; we are not to adopt a doctrine of creation in the same way as we select salads in a cafeteria. The words of Genesis 1 inform us of the fact that God created all things in six days. This is repeated in the Decalogue (Ten Commandments): " . . . in six days the LORD made heaven and earth, the sea, and all that in them is, and rested the seventh day . . . " (*Ex. 20:11*). The creation was out of nothing, in response to the sovereign word of God: "By the word of the LORD were the heavens made; and all the host of them by the breath of his mouth . . . For he spake, and it was done; he commanded, and it stood fast" (*Ps. 33:6, 9*). Therefore, the Apostle Paul writes: "For of him, and through him, and to him, are all things: to whom be glory for ever. Amen" (*Rom. 11:36*).

Modern translators of the Bible have sometimes sought to revive the theology of the pagan ancient world, since a similar theology undergirds all modern apostate rationalism. They have translated Genesis 1:1-2 as follows: "When God began to create the heaven and the earth—the earth being unformed and void, with darkness over the surface of the earth. . . . "[1] The language, while grammatically possible, is theologically perverse. The translation is governed by the premises of apostate man rather than by the explicit teaching of the Bible. It is the Bible, not the presuppositions of rebellious men, which is to interpret the verbal revelation of God (*2 Tim. 3:16; 2 Pet. 1:20*). Modern translators believe, far too often, in the coexistence of the material (or energetic) universe with the being of God. This assumption of the ancient cosmologies, contemporary "primitive" cosmologies, ancient philosophy (Aristotle, *Physics*, VIII), and modern evolutionism, is erroneous. When this pagan god began to mold the eternally existing "stuff" of the universe, he found that he was not sovereign over it, because he had not created it. He, like the "stuff" in front of him, behind him, above him, and beneath him, was governed by the independent laws of probability and chance. Lots of luck, there, God! We're pulling for you!

In contrast to this stands the Creator of the Bible. At best, the pagan god is Dr. God, while we humans are only Misters. But the book of Hebrews testified of another God altogether: "And, thou, Lord, in the beginning hast laid the foundation of the earth; and the heavens are the works of thine hands: They shall perish; but thou remainest; and they all shall wax old as doth a garment; And as a vesture shalt thou fold them up, and they shall be changed:

but thou art the same, and thy years shall not fail" (*Heb. 1:10-12*). God dwells in eternity (*Is. 57:15*); he creates the new heaven and new earth (*Is. 65:17-18; 2 Pet. 3:9-13, Rev. 21:1*). The Creator is the Savior: "Lift up your eyes to the heavens, and look upon the earth beneath: for the heavens shall vanish away like smoke, and the earth shall wax old like a garment, and they that dwell therein shall die in like manner: but my salvation shall be for ever, and my righteousness shall not be abolished" (*Is. 51:6*). He who dares to tamper with the doctrine of creation compromises the revelation of the Creator concerning his own activity. He who distorts the testimony of God as to his creative activity simultaneously calls into question the testimony of God to his saving activity. If the latest finding of science—based, as it is, on the oldest antitheistic philosophy of creation—should be permitted to undermine the explicit revelation of God concerning one aspect of his relationship to his creation, there is no logical reason to draw back in horror when science also undermines the doctrine of salvation. Without the doctrine of creation there can be no doctrine of salvation— not, at least, an orthodox doctrine.

God is eternal and unchanging (*Mal. 3:6*). His words shall not pass away (*Mt. 24:35*); his counsel is immutable (*Heb. 6:17*). "The LORD by wisdom hath founded the earth; by understanding hath he established the heavens" (*Pr. 3:19*). God's wisdom founded the world; the fallen world's wisdom cannot accept this. God's wisdom is foolishness to the world (*1 Cor. 1:20*), and God warns his people not to be beguiled by the vanity of apostate philosophies (*Col. 2:4-9*). God is the standard of reference, the unchanging measure of all truth. Thus, the Bible rejects the pagan idea of creation through self-generated *process*, and it affirms the *fiat* creation by the word of God. Creation was a discontinuous event—*the* discontinuous event prior to Christ's incarnation. Process theology is the remnant of Adam's thought; by stressing the continuity between man's truth and God's truth, it relativizes God's truth. The shifting opinions of scientists replace the verbal revelation of God. *Time*, not God, becomes the framework of creation; *chance*, not God's eternal word, becomes the creative force in history. Evolution, the most consistent and most dangerous form of process theology, cannot be made to fit the categories of Christian faith.

Providence

The definition of creation goes beyond the concept of the original creation which ended on the sixth day. It simultaneously affirms the *sustaining hand* of God in time. It is Christ, "who being the brightness of his glory, and the express image of his person, and upholding all things by the word of his power" (*Heb. 1:3*), maintains the earth and the stars. "He hath made the earth by his power, he hath established the world by his wisdom, and hath stretched out the heaven by his understanding. When he uttereth his voice, there is a multitude of waters in the heavens; and he causeth the vapours to ascend from the ends of the earth: he maketh lightnings with rain, and bringeth forth the wind out of his treasures" (*Jer. 51:15-16*). Psalm 104 is a lengthy presentation of God's creative, sustaining providence in history. This applies equally to matters spiritual and physical: "Fear thou not; for I am with thee: be not dismayed, for I am thy God: I will strengthen thee; yea, I will help thee; yea, I will uphold thee with the right hand of my righteousness" (*Is. 41:10; cf. 42:5-6*). The doctrine of providence reveals the total sovereignty of God.

Creator-Creature Distinction

Is God wholly removed from the world, as an eighteenth-century deist would have argued? Is God wholly identified with the world, as the pantheists have argued? As far back as we have written records, men have answered both ways. Sometimes, as in the case of the philosopher Plato and the neo-orthodox theologian Barth, secularists have held both positions simultaneously.[2] Aristotle's "thought thinking itself," deism's watchmaker god, or Plato's Forms or Ideas are all wholly transcendent, wholly aloof gods. Eastern religious monism and Western pantheism are examples of the god who reveals himself wholly in his creation. The first god has no point of contact with life and change; the second god cannot be distinguished from life and change. Neither is therefore truly personal.

The Bible affirms the existence of a *personal* Creator who is simultaneously transcendent and immanent. This is not held, as in the case of neo-orthodoxy, on the basis of modern philosophical dualism, but rather on the basis of a personal God's verbal and therefore understandable revelation of himself to those creatures made in his image. God is not to be identified with his creation, yet the creation testifies to his existence. There is no uniform Being that in some way links God and the creation—some ultra something that both God and creation participate in. There is no scale of Being between the devil and God, with God as the possessor of more Being than anyone else, and the devil drifting into non-Being. The God of the Bible is personal and sovereign, unlike the secular transcendent God (who is too different or too removed to care about the world) or the secular immanent God (who is too similar and too close to the world to influence it). We are informed by Psalm 90:1-2 that God is our dwelling place (immanence), yet he existed before the foundation of the world (transcendence). The universe is therefore personal; in contrast to all forms of paganism, at bottom a personal God controls all his creation. Christianity affirms *cosmic personalism*.

1. *Transcendence.* "For thou, LORD, art high above all the earth: thou art exalted far above all gods" (*Ps. 97:9; cf. 135:5; Is. 46:9*). The Psalms are filled with the language of transcendence. "The LORD is great in Zion; and he is high above all the people" (*Ps. 99:2*). "Be thou exalted, O God, above the heavens: and thy glory above all the earth" (*Ps. 108:5*). While we do not need to accept the conclusions of the so-called higher criticism of the Bible, that is, the multiple authorship of many individual books of the Bible, there is no doubt that Isaiah 40-66 does stress the idea of the transcendence of God far more than Isaiah 1-39. Perhaps the crucial verses in the Bible dealing with God's transcendence are Isaiah 55:8-9: "For my thoughts are not your thoughts, neither are your ways my ways, saith the LORD. For as the heavens are higher than the earth, so are my ways higher than your ways, and my thoughts than your thoughts." Yet God's transcendence is not impersonal; he is on high, but he cares for his people: "For thus saith the high and lofty One that inhabiteth eternity, whose name is Holy; I dwell in the high and holy place, with him also that is of a contrite and humble spirit, to revive the spirit of the humble, and to revive the heart of the contrite ones" (*Is. 57:15*). This same link between transcendence and mercy is found in Jeremiah 32:17-18. But the most comprehensive statement of God's absolute

transcendence is presented in Job, chapters 38-41. No created being can challenge the creative hand of God. It was the unwillingness of the devil to respect this limitation that brought his downfall (*Is. 14:12-15*), as it also was in the case of Adam and Eve.

It is therefore insufficient to argue merely for the separation of God and the creation. As Cornelius Van Til writes:

> The transcendence concept of theism is not clearly stated, if it is merely said that God is independent of the world. According to the ordinary use of the word, that would not exclude the possibility that the world would also be independent of God. And it is this dependence of the world upon God that a theist is interested in as much as the independence of God apart from the world. In fact God would not be truly independent of the world unless the world were dependent upon God. No one is absolutely independent unless he alone is independent.[3]

The doctrine of creation prevents the appearance of a deistic view of transcendence, for the Bible's account of creation also teaches the doctrine of providence. God sustains the world. It is only in terms of his eternal decree that the world has existence or meaning.

2. *Immanence.* The transcendence of God the Creator implies his immanence. "But will God indeed dwell on the earth? behold, the heaven and heaven of heavens cannot contain thee; how much less this house that I have builded?" (*1 Kin. 8:27*). God is omnipresent; he cannot be contained in heaven alone. He dwells throughout his creation and far beyond infinity. Psalm 139:7-8 is the archetype passage: "Whither shall I go from thy spirit? or whither shall I flee from thy presence? If I ascend up into heaven, thou art there: if I make my bed in hell, behold, thou are there." God asks Jeremiah: "Am I a God at hand, saith the LORD, and not a God afar off? Can any hide himself in secret places that I shall not see him? saith the LORD. Do I not fill heaven and earth? saith the LORD" (*Jer. 23:23-24*). Near and far, God is present. "For what nation is there so great, who hath God so nigh unto them, as the LORD our God is in all things that we call upon him for?" (*Dt. 4:7*). God's words are very clear in this regard. As Paul proclaimed before the pagans in Athens, "For in him we live, and

move, and have our being . . ." (*Ac. 17:28a*). Our physical bodies serve as the temple of the Holy Spirit (*1 Cor. 6:19; 2 Cor. 6:16*).

Man is made in the image of God (*Gen. 1:26-27*). Man's inner being calls him to repentance and worship. Man's environment also calls him to worship the Creator: "The heavens declare the glory of God; and the firmament sheweth his handywork" (*Ps. 19:1*). Therefore, concludes Paul, every man is totally without excuse:

> For the invisible things of him from the creation of the world are clearly seen, being understood by the things that are made, even his eternal power and Godhead; so that they are without excuse: Because that, when they knew God, they glorified him not as God, neither were thankful; but became vain in their imaginations, and their foolish heart was darkened. Professing themselves to be wise, they became fools, And changed the glory of the uncorruptible God into an image made like to corruptible man, and to birds, and fourfooted beasts, and creeping things. Wherefore God also gave them up to uncleanness through the lusts of their own hearts, to dishonour their own bodies between themselves. Who changed the truth of God into a lie, and worshipped and served the creature more than the Creator, who is blessed for ever. Amen. (*Rom. 1:20-25*)

There is no escape from God's revelation of himself; the whole creation proclaims his majesty. There is not sufficient natural revelation to save men from destruction, but there is natural revelation sufficient to condemn them for all eternity. The "work of the law" is written in every man's heart, "conscience also bearing witness" to his own evil nature (*Rom. 2:15*). Men seek desperately to escape this testimony. Again, quoting Van Til:

> The main point is that if man could look anywhere and not be confronted with the revelation of God then he could not sin in the Biblical sense of the term. Sin is the breaking of the law of God. God confronts man everywhere. He cannot in the nature of the case confront man anywhere if he does not confront him everywhere. God is one; the law is one. If man could press one button on the radio of his experience and not hear the voice of God then he would always press that button and not the others.

But man cannot even press the button of his own self-consciousness without hearing the requirement of God.[4]

In short, "Psychologically there are no atheistic men; epistemologically [knowledgeably] every sinner is atheistic."[5] For this reason, the evil man Dives asked to be allowed to return from hell to warn his lost brothers—not because he had a trace of goodness or compassion for the lost, but because if he could get God to admit that his revelation to the brothers was not sufficient to warn them, then God would have no cause to judge any man, including Dives. God, understandably, turned the request down flatly: though one rose from the dead (Jesus Christ), they would not be persuaded (*Lk. 16:27-31*). The problem is not their lack of revelation; it is their willful rebellion against that revelation. God's creation reveals him.

The Sovereignty of God

Job 38-41 is an important testimony to the sovereignty of God. God, who created all things and sustains all things, rules all things. Nothing happens outside the decrees of God; Satan had to ask permission in order to harass Job, and God set limits to everything he did (*Job 1:12, 2:6*). Everything is known to God beforehand, of course: "Known unto God are all his works from the beginning of the world" (*Ac. 15:18*). But in Isaiah 45 we learn of the extent of God's total direction of all events:

> I form the light, and create darkness: I make peace, and create evil: I the LORD do all these things. Drop down, ye heavens, from above, and let the skies pour down righteousness: let the earth open, and let them bring forth salvation, and let righteousness spring up together; I the LORD have created it. Woe unto him that striveth with his Maker! Let the potsherd strive with the potsherds of the earth. Shall the clay say to him that fashioneth it, What makes thou? or thy work, He hath no hands? ... I have made the earth, and created man upon it: I, even my hands, have stretched out the heavens, and all their host have I commanded. (*Is. 45:7-9, 12*)

God is not the author of confusion (*1 Cor. 14:33*), yet he

controls and directs all things. There is no solution to this seeming intellectual dilemma in terms of the logic of autonomous man.

The image of the potter and his workmanship is a recurring one in the Bible. "But now, O LORD, thou art our Father; we are the clay, and thou our potter; and we all are the work of thy hand" (*Is. 64:8*). Jeremiah 18, God's confrontation with Israel, is constructed upon this analogy: "O house of Israel, cannot I do with you as this potter? saith the LORD. Behold as the clay is in the potter's hand, so are ye in mine hand, O house of Israel" (*Jer. 18:6*). But in Romans 9, the great chapter in the New Testament dealing with the total predestination of the world by God, Paul uses the potter analogy to stifle the apostate and illegitimate conclusion of those who would argue that God's predestination is opposed to human responsibility. Paul's use of the potter analogy has no meaning except in terms of such an illegitimate use of human logic; he answers that issue, and only that issue, in these words:

> Therefore hath he mercy on whom he will have mercy, and whom he will he hardeneth. Thou wilt say then unto me, Why doth he yet find fault? For who hath resisted his will? Nay but, O man, who art thou that repliest against God? Shall the thing formed say to him that formed it, Why hast thou made me thus? Hath not the potter power over the clay, of the same lump to make one vessel unto honour, and another unto dishonour? [vv. 18-21]

God therefore sets explicit limits on the exercise of human logic. God is good, and he created all things good in the beginning, yet he uses evil and rebellion to fulfil his plan of history. Man is totally predestined by the Creator (*Rom. 8:28-30; Eph. 1*), yet man is wholly responsible for his actions. We are required to affirm both points. We are the vessels; God, the Creator, is the potter. Men are reminded that "The secret things belong unto the LORD our God: but those things which are revealed belong unto us and to our children for ever, that we may do all the words of this law" (*Dt. 29:29*). Creatures are not permitted knowledge as exhaustive as God's is, whether of outward affairs or of the heart (*1 Sam. 16:7*). Godly humility requires every Christian to submit to the sovereignty of God, acknowledging his total predestination as well as man's total responsibility. Anything less than this affirmation—any quibbling concerning possible zones of human autonomy to make decisions respecting anything, including their salvation—involves men in outward rebellion. "The king's heart is in the hand of the LORD, as the rivers of water: he turneth it whithersoever he will" (*Pr. 21:1*). "A man's heart deviseth his way, but the LORD directith his steps" (*Pr. 16:9*).[6]

Meekness and Dominion

Since God is sovereign over the creation which exists only because of God's decree, and since man is made in the image of God, man therefore has a legitimate, though subordinate, right of dominion over the creation. This is man's *cultural mandate*. "And God said, Let us make man in our image, after our likeness: and let them have dominion over the fish of the sea, and over the fowl of the air, and over the cattle, and over all the earth, and over every creeping thing that creepeth upon the earth. So God created man in his own image, in the image of God created he him; male and female created he them. And God blessed them, and God said unto them, Be fruitful, and multiply, and replenish the earth, and subdue it: and have dominion over the fish of the sea, and over the fowl of the air, and over every living thing that moveth upon the earth" (*Gen. 1:26-28*). This cultural mandate was reaffirmed with Noah and his sons (*Gen. 9:1*). Man's meekness before a Creator God is the foundation of man's inheritance of the earth, for the meek shall inherit the earth (*Mt. 5:5*). Christ, who claimed to be meek (*Mt. 11:29*), was the one who drove the money-changers from the temple (*Mt. 21:12*) and called the Pharisees sons of the devil (*Jn. 8:44*). It is *meekness before God* which gives man *dominion over nature*.

> When I consider thy heavens, the work of thy fingers, the moon and the stars, which thou hast ordained; What is man, that thou art mindful of him? and the son of man, that thou visitest him? For thou hast made him a little lower than the angels, and hast crowned him with glory and honour. Thou madest him to have dominion over the works of thy hands; thou hast put all things under his feet: All sheep and oxen, yea, and the beasts of the field; the fowl of the air, and the fish of the sea, and whatsoever

passeth through the paths of the seas. O LORD our LORD, how excellent is thy name in all the earth! (*Ps. 8:3-9*)

Now we are made a little lower than the angels, but not forever. "Know ye not that we shall judge angels? how much more things that pertain to this life?" (*1 Cor. 6:3*). Christians who retreat from the affairs of this world are, by their very actions, acknowledging the devil's view of God's sovereignty: man does not have legitimate rule because God, in whose image man is made, does not have legitimate sovereignty. It should come as no surprise that as the doctrine of evolution has invaded the churches, the idea of meekness before God has departed; with it has departed the idea of man's legitimate rule over earthly affairs. Christians today are in full retreat almost everywhere.

We have noted that God is transcendent to, yet immanent to, his creation. Man, created in God's image, occupies an analogical position in the creation. He is under many of nature's laws, yet he is simultaneously above nature as God's subordinate sovereign. Gilkey, the neo-orthodox theologian, has called attention to this dual position of man:

> History takes on meaning, then, when man not only sees himself as a creature in a "good" nature, but, more importantly, has distinguished himself from nature. He must realize that he alone among God's creatures is not completely dominated by nature; he must become conscious of his own unique capacity for self-direction and meaning, and therefore of being in some sense transcendent to the repetitive natural order in which he participates ... If man is understood as totally out of relation to nature because he is regarded as purely soul or mind, or if man is understood as totally immersed in nature and so as purely creature, then no understanding of history arises. Greek idealism lost a sense of history because it could not understand the value of the natural world and of time [pure transcendence—G. N.]; Greek naturalism never achieved historical consciousness because it understood existence only in terms of the cycles of natural life [pure immanence—G. N.][7]

The tool of man's dominion over nature is law. God has established patterns of regularity in the mind of man (logic) and in the creation (natural law). He has also established ethical and social laws by his revealed word. Rebellious man cannot acknowledge the fact that God's sovereign word undergirds natural law, human logic, and ethical (revealed) law. The self-proclaimed autonomous man cannot even explain the relationship between the logic of his own mind—especially mathematical logic—and the external universe he perceives, although his science demands that such a relationship exist.[8] The works of the law are in men's hearts (*Rom. 2:15*). God established his covenant with men, and his ordinances are continual (*Jer. 33:25-26; Heb. 8:10-12; 10:15-17*). Our universe is orderly (*Pr. 30:24-28*). It is orderly because God is its Creator (*Ps. 136:6-9; Pr. 8:22-31*). Therefore, he calls us to repentance: "Now therefore hearken unto me, O ye children: for blessed are they that keep my ways" (*Pr. 8:32*). "Let us hear the conclusion of the whole matter: Fear God, and keep his commandments: for this is the whole duty of man" (*Ec. 12:13*).

This is God's universe; he does as he pleases with it. Here is the primary lesson from the book of Job. Yet men are to gain power over earthly affairs through the godly exercise of Biblical law (*Dt. 8*). God covenants with men in terms of his law; though men violate his statutes, yet he still shows mercy to many, as chapters 5-8 of the epistle to the Romans indicate. God's covenant, through grace, is sure, for man can trust in God's word. Because of Christ's sacrifice on the cross, God's wrath is placated (*Rom. 5:8*). Men can therefore subdue the earth in confidence through God's law (*Gen. 9:1-7*), for "the earth hath he given to the children of men" (*Ps. 115:16*).

Fall and Restoration

By breaking the law of God, Adam brought destruction to humanity (*Rom. 5:12-21*). Deny this historic event, and you deny the doctrine of original sin. Deny the doctrine of original sin, and man is left without an understanding of his desperate plight. He will think that his own efforts can bring him eternal life. Without a comprehension of the effects, both in time and eternity, of the ethical rebellion of man, it becomes impossible to appreciate the extent of Christ's atoning sacrifice on the cross. Theological modernism, so closely linked with an evolutionary cosmology, has produced precisely this state of disbelief.[9]

The ethical rebellion took place in time and on earth. The death and resurrection of Christ took place in time and on earth. The firstfruits of the new heaven and new earth are now manifested and will continue to manifest themselves in time and on earth. As men subdue their own hearts in terms of God's law, they work out their gift of salvation (*Phil. 2:12*). God's gift of sanctification, personal and social, is added unto his great gift of personal justification. God gives the increase (*1 Cor. 3:7*). Every good gift is from God (*Jas. 1:17*). The possibility of the restoration of the external world is set before God's people (*Dt. 8, 28; Is. 2, 65, 66*).

The fall of man involved a false claim of divinity on the part of man. Man, following the devil's lead, came to the conclusion that his own word, rather than God's, is ultimately creative. He made himself the judge of the reality of God's word. He would stand between God and the devil to test which one was telling the truth. He made his own hypothetical neutrality as the standard of judgment. He wanted to determine good and evil (*Gen. 3:5*), for knowledge is always preliminary to the exercise of power. This was the devil's sin of pride (*Is. 14:12-15*). Such a path leads to destruction (*Is. 14:16-23*). Man is supposed to think God's thoughts after him, not attempt to be an autonomous creature. When man becomes humble in all his ways before God, victory is within his grasp, in time and on earth: "And it shall come to pass, if thou shalt hearken diligently unto the voice of the LORD thy God, to observe and to do all his commandments which I command thee this day, that the LORD thy God will set thee on high above all nations of the earth: And all these blessings shall come on thee, and overtake thee, if thou shalt hearken unto the voice of the LORD thy God" (*Dt. 28:1-2*). Or, in other words, "But seek ye first the kingdom of God, and his righteousness; and all these things shall be added unto you" (*Mt. 6:33*). Christ is given all power (*Mt. 28:18*).

Time and Development

"And as it is appointed unto men once to die, but after this the judgment: So Christ was once offered to bear the sins of many; and unto them that look for him shall he appear the second time without sin unto salvation" (*Heb. 9:27-28*). History has meaning; it determines the place of each man in eternity: "Every man's work shall be made manifest: for the day shall declare it, because it shall be revealed by fire; and the fire shall try every man's work of what sort it is. If any man's work abide which he hath built thereupon, he shall receive a reward. If any man's work shall be burned, he shall suffer loss: but he himself shall be saved; yet so as by fire" (*1 Cor. 3:13-15*). History had a beginning (*Gen. 1:1*), and the fallen earth shall have an end (*1 Cor. 15*). Therefore, in absolute opposition to ancient pagan philosophies, the Bible teaches that time is *linear*. It is also *limited*. Only after the final judgment shall the burden of time be removed from this fallen world (*Rev. 10:6*). God is the ruler of time.

Sanctification in a personal sense is a progressive process, once God has imputed the perfect sanctification of Christ to the regenerated man. Paul speaks of running the good race (*1 Cor. 9:24*) and fighting the good fight (*2 Tim. 4:7*). As with the individual who strives against sin in his own life (*Eph. 6:10-18*), so it is with Christian institutions and nations. The earth is to be subdued to the glory of God, not just in eternity, but in time— not just after the final judgment, but before it, when sinners are still alive on earth (*Is. 65:20*). History has purpose, direction, and meaning, precisely because God's decree controls all events. Ours is a personal universe, not an impersonal, chance multiverse. Ours is a providential world. As Gilkey writes: "Now in a world created by a transcendent and purposive God, such an ultimate coherence and significance is possible . . . . The belief that existence finds its ultimate origin in God sets each creaturely life in a context of coherence and significance impossible on any other terms . . . . And the sole basis for such a faith is the knowledge of the Creator. Without such knowledge, there is no basis for this context of coherence and significance, and without that context the meaning of life quickly evaporates."[10] If a neo-orthodox theologian can see this so clearly, why is the doctrine of creation so neglected in the pulpits of the supposedly evangelical churches? It is this optimism concerning God's decree in history which made modern science possible.[11] Without a faith in the possibility of progress, science loses meaning. By destroying the faith in creation, apostate science has almost entirely eroded the foundation of its own existence.[12]

Because God's eternal decree undergirds time, and because in his grace he assures his people that "all things work together for good to them that love God, to them who are the called according to his purpose" (*Rom. 8:28*), Christians need not fear time. Time brings with it the curses imposed by God as punishment for the rebellion of man, and not until death is finally subdued and the new heavens and new earth appear, will time lose all of its characteristic burdens, but Christians are not time's prisoners. Our citizenship is in heaven (*Phil. 3:20*). Unlike the pagans, whose chaos festivals like Mardi Gras and Carnival have symbolized a desperate attempt to escape time,[13] Christians are told to walk circumspectly, redeeming the time, that is, buying it back, prolonging it, conserving it, and using it diligently (*Eph. 5:16*). It is a tool for one's calling, a gift of God to his people. It is a resource to be used efficiently for the glory of God, and not a burden to be escaped by means of ritual debauchery or bloody revolution.[14] Time is therefore a means of production, not the justification for destruction.

Knowledge and Interpretation

We have already noted the scriptural instruction concerning God's wisdom as the foundation of the creation (*Pr. 3:19-20*). The revelation of God to man is the source of all human wisdom. Psalm 119, the longest chapter in the Bible, stands as the great passage dealing with the close relationship between wisdom and God's holy law: "Thy word is a lamp unto my feet, and a light unto my path" (*Ps. 119:105*). "Deal with thy servant according unto thy mercy, and teach me thy statutes. I am thy servant; give me understanding, that I may know thy testimonies" (*Ps. 119:124-125*). But it is in Job that we find most succinctly stated the basis of our knowledge: "But there is a spirit in man: and the inspiration of the Almighty giveth them understanding" (*32:8*). Elihu, the youthful fourth companion who has come to visit Job, challenges both Job and the other three "comforters" for their failure to consider the ways of a totally sovereign God. Apart from God the sovereign Creator, no knowledge is possible. He has made all things, directed all events, and he comprehends all facts. We, as God's images, are to think God's thoughts after him: "Behold, I am according to thy wish in God's stead: I also am formed out of the clay" (*33:6*). It is only by God's grace, Elihu announces, that we are given knowledge: "Why dost thou strive against him? for he giveth not account of any of his matters. For God speaketh once, yea twice, yet man perceiveth it not. In a dream, in a vision of the night, when deep sleep falleth upon me, in slumbering upon the bed; Then he openeth the ears of men, and sealeth their instruction, That he may withdraw man from his [man's] purpose, and hide pride from man" (*33:13-17*). God, through his gracious revelation, restrains the hands of evil men who are bent on destruction. He is not compelled to do so; his mercy is unearned.

God finally replies to Job as Elihu had, announcing that he alone possesses original knowledge. He drives this point home by referring back to the creation; he is God the Creator!

> Where wast thou when I laid the foundations of the earth? declare, if thou hast understanding. Who hath laid the measures thereof, if thou knowest? or who hath stretched the line upon it? Whereupon are the foundations thereof fastened? or who laid the cornerstone thereof; When the morning stars sang together, and all the sons of God shouted for joy? ... Hast thou perceived the breadth of the earth? declare if thou knowest it all. Where is the way where light dwelleth? and as for darkness, where is the place thereof, That thou shouldst take it to the bound thereof, and that thou shouldest know the paths to the house thereof? ... Knowest thou the ordinances of heaven? canst thou set the dominion thereof in the earth? Canst thou lift up thy voice to the clouds, that abundance of waters may cover thee? Canst thou send lightnings, that they may go, and say unto thee, Here we are? Who hath put wisdom in the inward parts? or who hath given understanding to the heart? (*Job 38:4-7, 18-20, 33-36*).

The lessons of these latter passages in the book of Job are repeated by Paul: "For who hath known the mind of the Lord? or who hath been his counselor? Or who hath first given to him, and it shall be recompensed unto him again? For of him, and through him, and to him, are all things: to whom be glory for ever. Amen" (*Rom. 11:34-36*). As the Creator, he controls; as the Redeemer, he reveals. All things are known to him: "I will praise thee; for I am fearfully and wonderfully made: marvelous are thy works; and that my soul knoweth right well. My substance was not hid from thee, when I was made in secret, and curiously wrought in the lowest parts of the earth. Thine eyes did see my substance, yet being unperfect; and in thy book all my members were written, which in continuance were fashioned, when as yet there was none of them" (*Ps. 139:14-16*). He knows all things because he created all things; his book sets forth what is or is not possible and actual. And in grace he redeems: "He that chastiseth the heathen, shall not he correct? he that teacheth man knowledge, shall not he know? The LORD knoweth the thoughts of man, that they are vanity. Blessed is the man whom thou chastenest, O LORD, and teachest him out of thy law; That thou mayest give him rest from the days of adversity, until the pit be digged for the wicked" (*Ps. 94:10-13*). God has revealed himself preeminently through his Son (*Jn. 1*). "Father, I will that they also, whom thou hast given me, be with me where I am; that they may behold my glory, which thou hast given me: for thou lovedst me before the foundation of the world" (*Jn. 17:24*).

Men are not autonomous from God, they are analogous to God. Their knowledge should therefore be analogical to God's knowledge, that is, in conformity to his revelation concerning himself, man, and the creation. Men are told that they are not the source of knowledge because they are not the source of the creation. They have knowledge only to the extent that they think God's thoughts after him. Even in their rebellious thought, sinners can be said to see the world only in terms of borrowed capital. To use Van Til's analogy, the child must sit on his father's lap in order to slap his face. Thus, he writes, "Christianity is the only reasonable position to hold. It is not merely as reasonable as other positions, or a bit more reasonable than other positions; it alone is the natural and reasonable position for man to take."[15] Apart from God's revelation, all men are blind. God, in fact, deliberately blinds the minds of some men so that they will not see the truth and be converted; Christ specifically said that this is why he spoke in parables (citing *Is. 6:9-10; Mt. 13:10-15*). Sinful men want to believe lies, so God sends them lies (*Ez. 14:9-11; 2 Thes. 2:11-12*).

"All scripture is given by inspiration of God, and is profitable for doctrine, for reproof, for correction, for instruction in righteousness: That the man of God may be perfect, thoroughly furnished unto all good works" (*2 Tim. 3:16-17*). In all true knowledge there is grace. God the Redeemer is God the Creator. What he reveals is true because he created and sustains all things. Were he not the Creator, he could not be the Redeemer; his revelation could always be suspect—another possible interpretation in a random multiverse. In fact, his revelation of what he is and does would have to be false, since it is not compatible with a random multiverse. A God who is not the Creator is not the God of the Bible.

Ownership and Stewardship

God, as Creator, is owner of the universe. This is stated throughout the Bible, but especially in the Psalms. "The earth is the LORD's, and the fulness thereof; the world, and they that dwell therein. For he hath founded it upon the seas, and established it upon the floods. Who shall ascend into the hill of the LORD? or who shall stand in his holy place?" (*Ps. 24:1-3*). "The heavens are thine, the earth also is thine: as for the world and the fulness thereof, thou hast founded them" (*Ps. 89:11*). Perhaps most famously: "For every beast of the forest is mine, and the cattle upon a thousand hills" (*Ps. 50:10*). This being true, then man, as God's image-bearer, possesses subordinate ownership: "The heaven, even the heavens, are the LORD's: but the earth hath he given to the children of men" (*Ps. 115:16*). The foundation of ownership on earth is God's creation of the earth.

God places limitations on the exercise of the rights of property. Secularists, whether Marxists, libertarians, or anarchists, do not acknowledge these restrictions. God requires a system of tithes, and the whole book of Malachi is devoted to an exposition of the ethical and social impact of tithe-rejection. In the Old Testament economy, God placed restrictions on the practice of lending money, prohibiting the taking of interest from a poverty-stricken fellow believer (*Ex. 22:25-27*). There is no indication that this restriction is no longer binding.[16] During the time that Israel served God as his throne, containing the tabernacle and the Holy of Holies, it was also illegal to sell the family's land for a period longer than forty-nine years; in the jubilee year, all land was to revert to the original owner or his family (*Lev. 25:23-28*).[17] "The land shall not be sold for ever: for the land is mine; for ye are strangers and sojourners with me" (*Lev. 25:23*). With the rending of the veil of the temple, which had separated the Holy of Holies, at the point of Christ's death (*Mt. 27:50-51*), this unique position of the land of Israel departed from God's economy, but the general ownership of the whole earth by God still holds true. Ownership is never autonomous. It is always covenantal.

Ownership thus involves personal stewardship. The use of property is bounded by the laws of the various possessors: individuals, civil governments, private corporations, families, churches. Each has its own rules and regulations set by the Bible. None can ever be the exclusive owner, for no human or earthly sphere of life is exclusively divine. As Proverbs 10 through 29 indicate, men are to be charitable, industrious, honest, just; in short, they are to be faithful stewards of the goods God loans or leases to them. Each institution or individual has some legitimate rights of ownership that may not be infringed upon by another human sovereignty. Ahab was not acting legally when he killed Naboth to steal his vineyard (*1 Kin. 21:18-19*), even though he was the king. It is God who is the source of all wealth, not men, states, churches, or the devil (*Dt. 8:18; Jas. 1:17*). Thus, when the devil offered Christ the world in return for Christ's worship of him, he was making an impossible offer (*Mt. 4:9*). It was not his to give.

The cosmic personalism of the Bible's universe is obviously in total opposition to the autonomous multiverse of modern man. This is God's universe. He brings blessings and curses as he sees fit (*Job 38-41*), but he has covenanted himself to bring earthly blessings and troubles to communities (though not necessarily to individuals) in terms of their covenantal responses to him. Deuteronomy 8 and 28 outline this relationship: blessings for obedience; curses for rebellion. All human sovereignties are derivative. All attempts to escape the limitations set by God on the exercise of property rights are therefore self-defeating.

The Good Creation

"And God saw every thing that he had made, and, behold, it was very good. And the evening and the morning were the sixth day" (*Gen. 1:31*). The creation was originally good. This included even Satan himself. At a point in time (presumably after the seventh day of creation-rest), he rebelled. His own pride was his downfall (*Is. 14:12-15*). He then led Adam and Eve into this same path of destruction (*Gen. 3*). As Van Til has pointed out so well, our parents in Eden were tempted to think of themselves as determiners of reality. They would test God's word to see if it would hold true. They placed their own logic and interpretation of the universe on a level with God's interpretation. Thus, they viewed the universe as problematical, and therefore God's word as problematical. They denied the absolute sovereignty of God's word over history and nature. It was this that constituted the fall—knowing (determining) not only good and evil, but also knowing (determining) possible and impossible.[18]

Through Adam, sin entered the world (*Rom. 5:12*). Man's rebellion, like Satan's, was therefore *ethical*, not metaphysical. It was not some flaw in man's being, but a willful rejection of God's sovereignty. It was an attempt to play God. It was a matter of purpose and will, not a defect in creation. Man did not slide into a lower realm of "Being in general"; he simply rebelled. Sin, therefore, is not a built-in eternal aspect of the creation. The fault was in the will of Satan and man: "Let no man say when he is tempted, I am tempted of God: for God cannot be tempted with evil, neither tempteth he any man: But every man is tempted, when he is drawn away of his own lust, and enticed. Then when lust hath conceived, it bringeth forth sin; and sin, when it is finished, bringeth forth death" (*Jas. 1:13-15*).

Ethical rebellion led God to curse the world (*Gen. 3:17-18*). Men are now ethically blind and willfully rebellious (*Rom. 1*). But this evil is restrained, as in the case of the Tower of Babel (*Gen. 11:6*). It must not be regarded as a permanent phenomenon. The final end of rebellion is the lake of fire, into which hell, death, Satan, and all his followers shall be dumped on the day of judgment (*Mt. 25:41; Rev. 20:13-14*). It is a place of true existence—the eternal reminder of the results of ethical rebellion, eternally glorifying God and his justice—but a place of utter impotence. But even as hell is only a temporary dwelling place of disembodied rebellious souls, so is heaven an equally temporary dwelling place for disembodied regenerate souls. Heaven is not a place of total bliss and perfection, just as hell is not a place of total desolation, for final bliss and final desolation come only after souls and bodies are reunited on the day of judgment (*1 Cor. 15:39-57*). The souls of the slain saints of God are in heaven, John informs us, crying, "How long, O Lord, holy and true, dost thou not judge and avenge our blood on them that dwell on the earth?" (*Rev. 6:10*). Yet even this scene is temporary, for evil is limited in time, however strong it may appear prior to the final judgment.

God has promised a final restoration of edenic bliss for his elect (*Rev. 21, 22*). Yet he graciously gives us a foretaste of this ultimate internal and external victory as an "earnest"—down payment—on our blessed hope. Isaiah 65 and 66 tell of a preliminary manifestation of the new heavens and new earth, prior to the day of judgment, for in these promised days of earthly peace, there shall be sinners still alive (*Is. 65:20*). Similarly, Ezekiel 37 presents us with the famous vision of the valley of dry bones. The dead shall be resurrected. But this passage can be interpreted in terms of spiritual death as well as physical death. In fact, it must be seen as applying to both forms of death and both forms of resurrection. Ezekiel was called to "Prophesy upon these bones"; it was a preaching ministry to the spiritually dead people of Israel. Men are spiritually dead (*Lk. 9:60*); he who believes in Christ "is passed from death unto life" (*Jn. 5:24*). Ezekiel 37 therefore promises an age of spiritual rebirth as well as a day of judgment and resurrection. "For for this cause was the gospel preached also to them that are dead, that they might be judged according to men in the flesh, but live according to God in the spirit" (*1 Pet. 4:6*). Spiritual death is the foretaste of physical and eternal death; spiritual life is the foretaste of physical and eternal life. God promises to raise up the dead bones of the valley, spiritually and physically. The image loses its impact if either aspect is ignored.

Chapters 8-10 and 12-14 of the book of Zechariah are deeply imbued with the spirit and language of external victory over evil. The restoration of godly rule is prophesied in all of its force and clarity. Restoration shall be in time and on earth; the rule of the saints on earth is a preliminary of the day on which men shall judge the angels (*1 Cor. 6:3*). The nations and their false gods shall be utterly defeated, writes Jeremiah (*Jer. 10:10-11*). These false gods "shall perish from the earth, and from under these heavens" (*v. 11*). In Daniel's explanation of King Nebuchadnezzar's dream, we learn of the great kingdom stone of God: "the stone that smote the image became a great mountain, and filled the whole earth" (*Dan. 2:35b*). Restoration is the premise of the prophetic vision.

How does God intend to bring this about? Not by some discontinuous political event, or some miraculous intervention into the daily processes of the world, but by steady spiritual progress. "For whatsoever is born of God overcometh the world: and this is the victory that overcometh the world, even your faith. Who is he that overcometh the world, but he that believeth that Jesus is the Son of God?" (*1 Jn. 5:4-5*). The day of judgment itself is not a discontinuous event in the midst of some steady, relentless spiritual decline, but rather a discontinuous event which will have been preceded by long ages of spiritual and social sanctification (*1 Cor. 15:25-28*), and which will have been briefly interrupted at the end by a rebellion of a tiny minority ("remnant") of Satan's host (*Rev. 19:19-21*). Then the whole creation will be restored:

> For I reckon that the sufferings of this present time are not worthy to be compared with the glory which shall be revealed to us. For the earnest expectation of the creature waiteth for the manifestation of the sons of God. For the creature was made subject to vanity, not willingly, but by reason of him who hath subjected the same in hope: Because the creature itself also shall be delivered from the bondage of corruption into the glorious liberty of the children of God. For we know that the whole creation groaneth and travaileth in pain together until now. And not only they, but ourselves also, which have the firstfruits of the Spirit, even we ourselves groan within ourselves, waiting for the adoption, to wit, the redemption of our body. (*Rom. 8:18-23*)

Ethical response outwardly to the law of God brings God's covenantal blessings. The very blessings will tempt those who are only outwardly obedient to forget God and violate his statutes. But the regenerate community will use his blessings to further his glory and expand his kingdom into all areas of life. Thus, special grace is necessary to maintain common grace's blessings. (By common grace, theologians mean—or should mean—the *unearned* gifts of God to all men, including the unregenerate. All men deserve death as a result of Adam's sin [*Rom. 5*]; life itself is a sign of common grace, that is, an unearned gift.) What we learn in Deuteronomy 8 and 28 is that the external world of nature responds in terms of a community's outward conformity to or rejection of God's law. Thus, as always, ethical questions are primary, not metaphysical questions of being. The creation itself is closely linked to man's ethical response to God; it was cursed when man sinned, and it shall be restored progressively as men are conformed once again to God's legal requirements.

God makes it plain that his requirements are ethical rather than metaphysical. Magic is therefore rejected as a means of pleasing God. Men do not manipulate God by manipulating some aspect of the creation. The magical formula, "as above, so below," which undergirds astrology, divination, and other forms of ritualistic manipulation, is a false formula. Man is only analogical to God, not a participant with God in some universal "being." God requires ritual, but not ritual devoid of spiritual content. "Will the LORD be pleased with thousands of rams, or with ten thousands of rivers of oil? shall I give my firstborn for my transgression, the fruit of my body for the sin of my soul? He hath showed thee, O man, what is good; and what doth the LORD require of thee, but to do justly, and to love mercy, and to walk humbly with thy God?" (*Mic. 6:7-8*). This is why God can promise external restoration; it will have been preceded by personal regeneration in the elect and by outward conformity to the law of God by both the regenerate and the unregenerate.

Fatherhood and Adoption

As far as man is concerned, no more crucial distinction in the Bible exists: created sonship and adopted sonship. Men's eternal destinies rest upon this distinction. God has created all men. Paul, preaching to the Athenians, announced that God "hath made of one blood all nations of men for to dwell on all the face of the earth" (*Ac. 17:26a*), and therefore all men are brothers in the flesh. This constitutes the *equality* of all men in Adam—absolute total depravity, regardless of race or color—and it serves as the sole *point of contact* in all men for the message of the gospel, since all men are

created in God's image. There can be no other point of contact,
certainly not in hypothetically "neutral" logical proofs of God.[19]
Paul preached to the pagans of Athens, not using logical proofs of
God, but using an appeal to their common, but sinful, humanity.

The Christian goal is not the universal brotherhood of man
on earth and in time. We already have the brotherhood of man; we
have had it since Cain and Abel walked on earth. What the Bible
calls for is the adoption of the elect into the family of God. It is no
accident that the Gospel of John begins with a call to adopted
sonship: "He came unto his own, and his own received him not.
But as many as received him, to them gave he power to become
the sons of God, even to them that believe on his name: Which
were born, not of blood, nor of the will of the flesh, nor of the will
of man, but of God" (*Jn. 1:11-13*). The regenerate "have received
the Spirit of adoption" (*Rom. 8:15*). This is God's greatest gift to
individual men: ethical adoption by the imputation of Christ's
righteousness into God's holy (set apart) family. "Even so we, when
we were children, were in bondage under the elements of the world:
But when the fulness of the time was come, God sent forth his
Son, made of a woman, made under the law, To redeem them that
were under the law, that we might receive the adoption of sons"
(*Gal. 4:3-5*).

Adoption is exclusively in terms of God's total sovereignty and
total predestination. "According as he hath chosen us in him before
the foundation of the world, that we should be holy and without
blame before him in love: Having predestinated us unto the
adoption of children by Jesus Christ to himself, according to the
good pleasure of his will" (*Eph. 1:4-5*). It could not be made any
plainer than this. The children of God by adoption were chosen
before the foundation of the world, even as God chose Jacob and
hated Esau, before either was born or could do evil (*Rom. 9:10-
13*). (The amazing fact, it should be noted, is that God loved Jacob,
not that he hated the unregenerate, though unborn, Esau.
Secularists and Arminians would paint the picture as a mirror image
to the Bible's: it seems astounding to them that God could hate
Esau.) In short, writes Paul, "They which are the children of the
flesh, these are not the children of God: but the children of the
promise are counted for the seed" (*Rom. 9:8*).

God imposes a basic division between men. There is no universal gift of peace on earth, good will toward men. This extremely unfortunate mistranslation of the Authorized (King James) Version of the Bible—loved by all secularists because of its implication of universal salvation—says in the original Greek, "peace on earth toward men of good will" (*Lk. 2:14*). Jesus' own account of his ministry could not be any plainer: "Think not that I am come to send peace on earth: I came not to send peace, but a sword. For I am come to set a man at variance against his father, and the daughter against her mother, and the daughter in law against her mother in law. And a man's foes shall be they of his own household" (*Mt. 10:34-36*).

There are therefore two distinct brotherhoods, for there are two fatherhoods: God the Father-Creator of *all* men and God the Father-Redeemer of *some* men. God disinherited the sons of the first Adam; he adopts sinners because of the work on the cross of his own Son, the second Adam (*1 Cor. 15:45*). All men are *brothers metaphysically*, a fact which, were it not for God's saving grace (*Eph. 2:8-9*), would unite all men in destruction. Not all men are *brothers ethically*; the brotherhood of the promise of grace is limited to God's predestined elect.

Creation and Covenant

The fall of man was ethical, not metaphysical (that is, having to do with some abstract "being" or essential reality). The creation therefore was originally good. The concern of the gospel of God's grace through Jesus Christ is with adoption. This means that God's concern is exclusively covenantal. God covenants himself with a chosen and exclusive people. He will be their God; they will be his people. He acts on their behalf as their sovereign monarch. He delivers them from evil. He intervenes in a special way in the history of his people. The so-called "two tables of the law" given by God to Moses were not separated in terms of two sets of five commandments each (with the second half—social laws— somehow less crucial than the first half, or spiritual commandments). The two tables were almost certainly two sets of the same ten laws, one serving as a copy for God the King, and the other serving as a copy for his covenanted people. This was the

standard practice of kings in the second century, B. C.[20] God the
sovereign monarch sets forth the terms of his treaty with his people;
his people must respond in obedience, or else suffer the wrath of
the monarch's hand upon them. (This is the meaning of both
circumcision and baptism: an oath sign promising blessings to the
faithful or wrath to the unfaithful.[21])

The prophets, time and again, confronted the people of Israel
with the claims of God. They recapitulated his dealings with them.
The God of Abraham, Isaac, and Jacob, who delivered the captive
people out of the bondage of Egypt, who led them into a promised
land, now calls his people to repentance. The focus is on the history
and provisions of the covenant. Stephen, in his testimony before
his accusers, begins with God's call to Abraham to leave pagan
Mesopotamia (*Ac. 7:2*). In terms of the rituals of the chosen people,
God is primarily the God of the covenant. Ritually, he is only
marginally the God of Creation. In only one Biblical passage, Psalm
136, is the creation mentioned in the otherwise familiar
recapitulation of God's covenant history.

The fact that must be grasped is that this aspect of Bible history
is in absolute contrast to virtually all pagan and "primitive" (that is,
degenerate) cultures. The pagans pay exclusive attention to the
creation in their accounts of God's activities. The primary Christian
and Hebrew festivals are associated with the Passover, that is, the
exodus from Egypt. The first communion service held by the
Christians was during the Passover (*Mt. 26:17-35*). Paul writes,
"Purge out therefore the old leaven, that ye may be a new lump, as
ye are unleavened. For even Christ our passover is sacrificed for us:
Therefore let us keep the feast, not with old leaven, neither with
the leaven of malice and wickedness; but with the unleavened bread
of sincerity and truth" (*1 Cor. 5:7-8*). The Passover feast was
covenantal and ethical. The pagan creation festivals are exclusively
metaphysical. They assume a common bond between God and
man—a common bond of pure being. The Passover assumed a
covenantal and ethical bond between God and his people; in the
communion service, this is symbolized by the eating of bread and
the drinking of wine. Christ's body and blood are symbolized, and
men participate in his *perfect humanity*. They hope for the day when
they shall be recreated and dressed in perfection like his body (*Phil.*

3:21). But we can never participate in Christ's *divinity.* God is fundamentally different from man.

The pagan festivals have basic similarities. They all are based on the idea that the world was created by God in a massive struggle with chaos. Creation was not out of nothing; it was the triumph of order over chaos. God therefore is said to confront chaos. The implication is that God, no less than men, faces zones of pure chance and unpredictability. He faces a world which is only partially known to him. In other words, we are like God, only less powerful and less knowledgeable, relatively speaking. By reenacting the original creation, men believe that they can participate in the original pre-time event. Men can share the act of creation, thereby escaping ritually (and, in some cultures, actually) the bondage of time. Saturnalia, Mardi Gras, and Carnival are all chaos festivals. Laws are broken, mores are violated, masks are worn, and men are revitalized from below. They become co-creators, co-participants with God in the act of original creation.[22] The creation, since it was not an absolute creation out of nothing by the fiat word of a sovereign God, can therefore be thought of as just one more finite event, however important. Paradise is to be reestablished through ritual chaos—total moral discontinuity brings back the age of gold.

The Biblical promise of the new creation is based upon the grace of a totally sovereign Creator. He restores men ethically. He puts his law in their hearts. This was the promise in Jeremiah 31:31-34; it was fulfilled by Christ (*Heb. 8:9-13; 10:16-17*). God's promises and his prophecies are being fulfilled or have been fulfilled in this age, the age of the Church, the body of Christ. We can thus celebrate the covenant of God with the people of Israel, for we are called "the Israel of God" (*Gal. 6:16*).[23] Our celebrations are not disorderly, for they deny the existence of some metaphysical chaos confronting a limited God. Our rule is simple: "Let all things be done decently and in order" (*1 Cor. 14:40*).

The celebrations of the church call us to acknowledge our total dependence, metaphysically and ethically, on the Creator God. He has covenanted with us out of mercy. We therefore do not celebrate the creation, for that act was exclusively God's as sovereign Creator. We had no part in it, due to the fact that we are the work of his hands. We do not participate in the acts of divinity, for there is an unbridgeable gulf between our being and God's being. The Son of God, through the incarnation, once walked on earth, perfectly human and perfectly divine, two natures in union but without intermixture. This is the foundation of our faith. Only through the greatest discontinuous event of all history—the incarnation of the Son of God—is man restored to wholeness. Christians therefore neglect the celebration of the creation, not because our God is not the Creator, but because he, and he alone, is the Creator. We do not attempt through ritual to participate in his divine acts or his divine being. We acknowledge the greatest of all distinctions, the Creator-creature distinction. And we announce, in confidence: "My help cometh from the LORD, which made heaven and earth" (*Ps. 121:2*).

---

[1] *The Torah* (Philadelphia, 1962). For a scholarly refutation of this approach to Genesis 1:1, see Edward J. Young, *Studies in Genesis One* (Philadelphia: Presbyterian and Reformed, 1964), 1-7. Young's study also offers refutations of the so-called "gap theory"—eons of time between Genesis 1:1 and 1:2—and the literary or framework hypothesis, which argues against the chronological succession of the seven days of creation.

[2] On Plato's position, see Cornelius Van Til, *A Survey of Christian Epistemology*, vol. II of *In Defense of the Faith* (den Dulk Foundation, 1969), ch. 3. (This was published originally in 1932 as *The Metaphysics of Apologetics*.) On Barth's dualism between God as wholly revealed, yet wholly hidden, see Van Til, *Christianity and Barthianism* (Philadelphia, 1962), ch. 6.

[3] Van Til, *Survey of Christian Epistemology*, 16.

[4] Van Til, *A Letter on Common Grace* (Philadelphia, 1955), 40-41.

[5] Van Til, *Common Grace* (Philadelphia, 1954), 54.

[6] Arminians will, in rare instances, affirm the doctrine of predestination. The most common example is the promise given to unattractive daughters by their mothers that God has a special man all picked out for them. In times of desperation, even the most hardened opponent of predestination will appeal to the sovereignty of God.

[7] Gilkey, *Maker of Heaven and Earth: The Christian Doctrine of Creation in the Light of Modern Knowledge* (Garden City, NY, [1959] 1965), 203-04.

[8] Cf. Eugene Wigner, "The Unreasonable Effectiveness of Mathematics

in the Natural Sciences, *Communications on Pure and Applied Mathematics*, XIII (1960), 1-14. Cf. Van Til, *Christian Theistic Evidences* (Syllabus, Westminster Theological Seminary, 1961), chs. 6, 7.

[9] A classic example of liberal religion's opposition to the concept of the fall of man is found in the Rev. James Maurice Wilson's essay, "The Religious Effect of the Idea of Evolution," in *Evolution in the Light of Modern Knowledge* (London, 1925). He was a contemporary of Darwin's, and he recalled the effect of Darwin's teachings on his generation and the one following: "The evolution of man from lower forms of life was in itself a new and startling fact, and one that broke up the old theology. I and my contemporaries, however, accepted it as fact. The first and obvious result of this acceptance was that we were compelled to regard the Biblical story of the Fall as not historic, as it had long been believed to be. We were compelled to regard that story as a primitive attempt to account for the presence of sin and evil in the world. It might have been easy for us in the light of science to treat that story, like those of the Flood or of Babel, as imaginative, if it had not been for the close connection, which has characterized Christian theology, between the doctrine of the Fall and the doctrine of the 'Atonement' through Christ's self-sacrifice . . . .But now, in the light of the fact of evolution, the Fall, as a historic event, already questioned on other grounds, was excluded and denied by science. . . . How does Jesus save His people from their sins? *He makes men better*" (497-99). "Salvation is not then thought of as an escape from hell; but as a lifting us all out from living lives unworthy of us. Religion so conceived is not the art of winning heaven, but the effort to become better and to work with God" (501). Man is to work his way up the scale of being. Wilson is far more aware of the implications of evolution than most of our contemporary evangelical Christians are. "Evolution is now approaching the citadel of our Christian faith. It is affecting Soteriology and Christology. The fact must be faced" (499). "The idea of evolution affects Christology because it assumes and implies *continuity* along with advance in creation. And it is this idea and fact of continuity, impressed on us from all quarters, that is now determining what men are able to believe concerning Divine action in every sphere. The evidence for continuity everywhere is overwhelming. The implicit or explicit recognition of it among educated people, and a general sense of it, are becoming universal and axiomatic" (501). There is, for example, continuity in intelligence. "What a chain it is!" From plants to animals to man to . . . He does not say God, but it is implied: "You cannot find the end of the chain." This, contrary to Wilson's explicit denial, is the theology of pagan antiquity. Cf. Arthur O. Lovejoy, *The Great Chain of Being* (New York, [1936] 1965).

[10] Gilkey, *Maker of Heaven and Earth*, 188-89.

[11] *ibid.*, 65-66.

[12] Cf. Gunther Stent, *The Coming of the Golden Age: A View of the End of Progress* (Garden City, NY, 1969).

[13] For various examples of this attempted "escape from time," see the works of the comparative anthropologist, Mircea Eliade, such as *Patterns in Comparative Religion* (New York, 1958), 399-407; *Myth and Reality* (New York, [1963] 1968), chs. 3, 5; *Cosmos and History: The Myth of the Eternal Return* (New York, [1954] 1959).

[14] See my study on Marxism, *Marx's Religion of Revolution: The Doctrine of Creative Destruction* (Nutley, NJ, 1968).

[15] Van Til, *Common Grace*, 62.

[16] Gary North, "Stewardship, Investment, and Usury: Financing the Kingdom of God," in R. J. Rushdoony, *The Institutes of Biblical Law* (Nutley, NJ, 1973), Appendix 3. This is also reprinted in my book, *An Introduction to Christian Economics* (Nutley, NJ, 1973), ch. 31.

[17] For an analysis of the Hebrew restrictions on the sale of land, see Rushdoony, *The Institutes of Biblical Law*, 488-93.

[18] Van Til, *Survey of Christian Epistemology*, 19-20.

[19] For a Christian refutation of the so-called "proofs of God," see Van Til, *The Defense of the Faith* (2nd ed.; Philadelphia, 1963), 248-59; *Christian-Theistic Evidences* (Syllabus, Westminster Theological Seminary, 1961). Van Til asserts that the premise of all human thought must be the sovereign, trinitarian, Creator God of the Bible. Anything other than this as an operating presupposition is simply argumentation from a void to a void.

[20] Meredith G. Kline, *Treaty of the Great King* (Grand Rapids, 1963), ch. 1.

[21] Meredith G. Kline, *By Oath Consigned* (Grand Rapids, 1969). Kline is as superb in his studies of the meaning of covenant as he is appalling in his "framework hypothesis" concerning the creation. Fortunately, he is better known for his covenant studies.

[22] See the references to the world of Mircea Eliade, footnote no. 13.

[23] Roderick Campbell, *Israel and the New Covenant* (Philadelphia, 1954).

Vol. 5, No. 2, 1978-79

Calvinism and "The Judicial Law of Moses": An Historical Survey

by James B. Jordan

The problem of relating the Christian faith to vital social and political issues is very much before the evangelical and Reformed communities today. The Christian capital laid up by former generations has just about been used up as the 1980s draw near. The left wing, with its optimistic view of human nature, offers little to the Christian thinker, while the negativism and rootlessness of the American right wing prevent it from articulating a clear-cut alternative.

Into this milieu has come the suggestion that the Christian finds a political philosophy laid out in the specific social laws of Scripture. These laws, it is contended, exemplify Christian principles in socio-political affairs, for they express God's unchanging standard of justice. Thus, they should be studied as guidelines for Christian thought today. To the extent that these laws, given comprehensively through Moses, address abiding social problems, such as adultery or theft, their dictates are binding. The remaining laws should still be consulted, and the wisdom gained from meditating upon them should be applied to latter-day affairs.

Recent writers defending this basic view include most prominently R. J. Rushdoony and Greg L. Bahnsen.[1] Others have proven sympathetic to this thesis, and the reasons are not far to seek. As John Frame has noted in his review of Bahnsen's book, "It might turn out that our search will lead us after all to a closer imitation of the old covenant order, not out of Biblico-theological necessity, but out of a general Christian political wisdom; for 'what nation is there so great, that hath statutes and judgments so righteous as all this law, which I set before you [Israel] this day?' (*Dt. 4:8*)."[2]

The thesis that the whole law of God—including details addressing social and political morality—is valid today must, of course, be attacked or defended on the basis of Scripture alone. As of the date of this essay, no scriptural argument against the whole-law position has been issued, either into print or into the many discussions the present writer has engaged in. A variety of questionable arguments have been presented at various times to the present writer, and since these arguments apparently do circulate in conversations regarding the whole-law position, it may be well to deal with them at this point as a debris-clearing operation before moving to the matter at hand.

Criticisms of Theonomic Ethics

1. It has been contended that the laws of the Bible are *harsh and unreasonable*. Indeed, some have engaged in ridicule of them.[3] What are we to make of this argument? Marcion, the early church heretic, argued the same way, maintaining that the God of the Older Testament was harsh and cruel, but that the God of the New Testament is kind and loving. This is an ancient heresy. Christianity has always maintained that when men accuse God of being "harsh," it is only because they want an excuse for sin. Is God's law really harsh, however? The law states, for instance, that homosexual acts should be punished by death, on the testimony of two or three eyewitnesses. What is the effect of this law? It can be seen right away that few if any homosexuals would ever be executed under this law, since it would be very difficult to procure two eyewitnesses to such an act. The effect of this law would be to drive homosexuality far, far underground. It would help to protect young persons from homosexual solicitation. It would be an incentive to those of homosexual tendencies to prevent them from turning to a life of depravity. It would help to protect society at large from the judgment God visited on Sodom and Gomorrah. It would help to protect society from the rampant moral decay seen in the history of the Roman Empire. Is this "harsh"?

2. It has been contended that we today are not living in a "theocracy," but are living under "*pluralism*." What does this mean? Surely every Christian desires Christ to be King in some sense, and thus in some sense desires a "theocracy." Moreover, even if we are not living today in a theocracy, is this not just the issue at stake? To argue that our present government is pagan is simply to admit the need for a Christian theocracy. *Theocracy*, after all, means "the

rule of God" or "the authority of God." Common use of the term has equated it with "the rule of churchmen," but *ecclesiocracy* has always been denied by Reformed Protestants, especially those in the Puritan tradition.

The modern concept of "pluralism" is to the political order what polytheism is to the religious order. Surely "pluralism" is the devil's own lie, that society can be neutral, neither for nor against God. In reality, no zone of life is neutral, and "pluralism" is heresy. That some modern Calvinists believe that total religious pluralism is the proper goal of Christian politics simply illustrates the poverty into which such "Calvinism" has sunk.

3. It has been contended that *the Older Testament does not actually set forth a series of judicial or civil laws.* With this criticism we may agree. A simple reading of Exodus or Deuteronomy will show that there is no place where a set of laws constituting a legal civil code is to be found. Rather, social, personal, civil, familial, and "ceremonial" laws are found all mixed up together. This shows that the law of God all stands or falls together. It would be improper to maintain, as some of the Fifth Monarchy Men did, that we find in the Bible a full-blown legal system. Rather, what we find is the *basis* for a Christian legal system. The laws of the Bible are *case laws*, and it is the duty of the Christian ruler to extend the *equity* of these cases to cover the details he finds in his own society.

To return to the case we discussed above, the Bible prescribes death for a man who lies with another man in the way a man lies with a woman (*i.e.,* for homosexual acts). This case does not explicitly condemn lesbian acts, and we do not find a parallel case law forbidding a woman to lie with a woman. If the Bible intended to set forth a comprehensive legal code, we should expect to find such an anti-lesbian law. It is rather the case that the Bible expects us *to extend the equity* of the anti-homosexual law so as to cover lesbian activities, pornography, solicitation, and so forth. We are not free, however, to *change* the case law so as, for instance, to punish homosexuality with prison rather than with death.[4]

This criticism does, however, raise a difficult point. In the literature of Protestantism, it is *assumed* that the law of God comes in three categories: moral, judicial, and ceremonial. The criticism rightly shows that *this category scheme is erroneous*. What has been termed "judicial law" is not in fact a legal code, but rather is a *set of explanations of the moral law*. These explanations have judicial aspects and judicial implications, but are not a judicial code.

What this means is that it cannot be argued that "the judicial law of Moses" has been dropped out in the New Testament era, because *there is no such thing in Scripture as "the judicial law of Moses."* What the opponent of theocracy must argue is this: that the *judicial implications* of the moral law have dropped out in the New Covenant era. This argument, however, proves too much, for virtually nobody wants to maintain that our legal code should be *totally* divorced from moral considerations.

It would seem that there is greater wisdom in humbly and gratefully receiving from the hand of God whatever explanation of the moral law he sees fit to reveal, whether such explanations be personal, familial, or civil.

4. It has been contended that this position does not do justice to *"common grace"*—whatever that extraordinarily ambiguous term means. However the term is used, it is not apparent how "common grace" removes the revealed laws of God from operation. Did not "common grace" operate in ancient Israel? Did God not give sunshine and rain to the reprobate in Israel? Did God not restrain the sin of reprobates in the Older Testament era? If it is contended that "common grace" has been increased in the New Covenant, so that the Older Testament laws have dropped away, where is the textual, scriptural evidence for this? Moreover, such a contention assumes a "law versus grace antagonism," which is anathema to the Reformed faith.[5]

5. It has been contended that this position does not do justice to the *"flow of redemptive history."* This contention, however, is not an argument, but only the *form* of an argument. It is necessary for the opponent to come forth with texts which *demonstrate* that the "flow of redemptive history" has removed from operation God's own explanations of his moral law. Bahnsen's book has shown at great length that, despite very real and great changes in economy from the Older to the New Covenant, the laws of God are not among the changes.[6]

6. A similar contention has been that the theonomic-theocratic position is against the *"tenor"* of the New Testament.[7] Like the

preceding argument, this is only the form of an argument, not the substance of one. If there be such a thing as a "tenor" of a book,[8] such a "tenor" or "feel" would have to be built up from the *text* of the book.

7. It has been contended that *whatever is not repeated in the New Testament has been dropped from the Older.* No argument is offered in defense of this slogan, except the *assertion* that the Older and New Covenants are wholly disparate. Against this dispensationalistic argument is (a) the fact that Matthew 5:17-19 asserts that nothing of the Older Testament has been dropped, and (b) the fact that the weekly Sabbath is usually admitted to be nowhere explicitly repeated in the New Testament, yet Calvinists continue to observe it.

8. It has been contended that the theocratic position fails to *interpret the Older Testament in the light of the New,* but reverses the order. Those arguing in this fashion reveal that they have read neither Rushdoony nor Bahnsen, both of whom rigorously argue from the New to the Older.

The fact that such arbitrary, sloganizing, and prejudicial arguments are seriously advanced calls into question the theological competency of those advancing them. These "arguments" have weight only for those who already agree with them. They are embarrassingly light-weight arguments.

9. An emotionally more cogent and persuasive argument has been that *the Reformed tradition has always maintained that "the judicial laws of Moses" no longer bind the New Covenant community,* and that the Westminster Confession of Faith, at section 19:4, stands against theonomy. If this were truly the case, it would not settle the matter once and for all, since creeds and councils can err. Moreover, the Protestant principle is not to test new ideas by tradition, but by Scripture.

Traditionalism, however, does hold sway unofficially in modern Reformed circles. Thus, it is the purpose of this essay to take up this argument from history. Our purpose is *not* to try to prove that historic Calvinism has always held to the whole-law position, or even that a majority of Calvinists have held to it. Rather, our purpose is to demonstrate that *many* within the Reformed fold, especially during the first one hundred years of its existence, highly

favored "the judicial laws of Moses" as a model for the civil
magistrate, and thus that there is no valid *historical* argument against
the position advanced by Rushdoony and Bahnsen.

At the outset, however, it should be noted that the phrase "the
judicial law of Moses" is problematic. We saw above, under
argument 3, that the Mosaic law does not set forth a civil code,
and thus that the phrase "judicial law of Moses" is theologically
erroneous. Moreover, the phrase is *ambiguous*, in that the social or
case laws in the Older Testament address much more than only
judicial or civil penalties. There are laws for the family, for the
individual, for ecology, and for many other areas of life. The only
"civil laws," properly speaking, are those which have *civil penalties*
attached to them. Thus, even if we were to try to break down the
law of God into categories—and it would be a reductionistic error
to attempt it—we would find far more than the three categories of
moral, civil, and ceremonial. We would also find ecological, familial,
marital, and other kinds of laws as well. Because of this, we can
expect to find much confusion and ambiguity in any discussion of
"the judicial laws of Moses." And this is what we do in fact find.
Many writers state that "the judicial laws of Moses" no longer bind
Christians, and then turn around and cite the Mosaic prescriptions
as if they were binding. Martin Bucer is a perfect example of this.[9]
One is left wondering precisely what the author had in mind when
he used the term "judicial law," and it is usually impossible to find
out, since few writers actually discussed the matter at any length.

John Calvin and Martin Bucer

In researching historical documents, the student can easily be
fooled if he fails to take into account historical context. John Calvin
can serve as a case in point. At *first* glance, Calvin's hostility to the
modern use of the Mosaic judicials could hardly be more marked:

> For there are some who deny that a commonwealth is duly framed
> which neglects the political system of Moses, and is ruled by the
> common law of nations. Let other men consider how perilous
> and seditious this notion is; it will be enough for me to have
> proved it false and foolish.[10]

What could be clearer? Yet in fact what Calvin calls the

"common law of nations" included much that was derived from Moses, via Justinian and other sources. This "common law of nations" is no longer available, in our era of relativism on the one hand and Communist totalitarianism on the other, for twentieth-century Calvinists to appeal to. What would Calvin have written had he faced today's naked choices?

Although the quotation cited above seems completely clear in indicating a radical hostility toward the Mosaic judicials on Calvin's part, there are several reasons against taking it as such. Firstly, Calvin uses the Mosaic judicials in arguing for the death penalty for adultery. Commenting on Deuteronomy 22:22, he writes:

> Nay, by the universal law of the Gentiles, the punishment of death is always awarded to adultery; wherefore it is all the baser and more shameful in Christians not to imitate at least the heathen. Adultery is punished no less severely by the Julian law than by that of God; whilst those who boast themselves of the Christian name are so tender and remiss, that they visit this execrable offence with a very light reproof.[11]

Note that the punishment is said to be that of the law "of God," not more restrictedly the law of Moses. It is clear that Calvin is commending the Mosaic penalty here, yet an element of confusion still remains in the text. Whatever this "universal law of the Gentiles" may have been, it operates no longer in the twentieth century.

Secondly, Calvin writes in his defense of the execution of Servetus:

> Whoever shall now contend that it is unjust to put heretics and blasphemers to death will knowingly and willingly incur their very guilt. *This is not laid down on human authority; it is God who speaks and prescribes a perpetual rule for his Church.* It is not in vain that he banishes all those human affectations which soften our hearts; that he commands paternal love and all the benevolent feelings between brothers, relations, and friends to cease; in a word, that he almost deprives men of their nature in order that nothing may hinder their holy zeal. Why is so implacable a severity exacted but that we may know that God is defrauded of his honor, unless the piety that is due to him be preferred to all

human duties, and that when his glory is to be asserted, humanity must be almost obliterated from our memories.[12]

Philip Schaff's comment is important:

Calvin's plea for the right and duty of the Christian magistrate to punish heresy by death, stands or falls with his theocratic theory and the binding authority of the Mosaic code. His arguments are chiefly drawn from the Jewish laws against idolatry and blasphemy, and from the examples of the pious kings of Israel.[13]

Thus, Schaff considers that Calvin held a high respect for the Mosaic judicials.

Thirdly, Calvin was a close friend and, in his earlier years, a disciple of the first-generation Reformer Martin Bucer. Bucer plainly held that the penal sanctions of the Older Testament were the best ever devised, being authored by God himself, and thus should be enacted in all Christian states.[14] Calvin's high regard for Bucer may be seen in the following statement by Calvin:

Martin Bucer, a most faithful doctor of the Church of Christ, besides his rare learning and copious knowledge of many things, besides his clearness of wit, much reading and other many and various virtues (wherein he is almost by none now living excelled, has few equals, and excels most), has this praise peculiar to himself, that *none in this age has used exacter diligence in the exposition of the Scripture.*[15]

This statement is important in two respects. First, it shows the very great respect Calvin had for Bucer. Second, it shows in particular that Calvin regarded Bucer as a master exegete. It must be remembered that even today Calvin himself is regarded as the greatest expositor of Scripture of the Reformation era, and his works are still cited in Bible commentaries written today. Thus, if Calvin held Bucer's use and exegesis of Scripture in high regard, this is no faint praise.

Also, Bucer's personal friendship and influence on Calvin must be considered. Pauck notes:

> There was a deep affinity between Bucer and Calvin, not only because their outlook, especially on the needs of the Church, was similar ... , but chiefly because *Calvin's mind was profoundly shaped by what he learned and took over from Bucer*, particularly during the years (1538-1541) when they were associated in common work in Strassburg.[16]

When Bucer died, Calvin told a friend he felt as lonesome as an orphan, so close and personal was the relationship between the two men.[17]

Bucer placed a tremendous emphasis on the love of the brethren and the communion of the saints. Thus, he ever worked for the uniting of the Lutheran, Reformed, and Roman churches. When Bullinger attacked Bucer for compromising too much in this direction, Calvin, though sometimes having sentiments similar to Bullinger's, nevertheless defended Bucer. Because of his emphasis on love and community, Bucer stressed church discipline and the rule of discipline, the law of God.[18] As a result, Bucer readily turned to the social legislation recorded in the books of Moses, and held that modern Christian states should conform to them.

Bucer distinguished between the state "sanctified to God"[19] and the non-Christian civil order. With respect to the latter, he was anti-revolutionary.

> It is agreed by all who determine the Kingdom, and offices of Christ by the Holy Scriptures, as all godly men ought to do, that our Saviour upon the earth took not on him either to give new laws in civil affairs, or to change the old, but [commanded] his own, in respect to civil life, to be subject themselves to the laws of the commonwealth in which they might live.[20]

The Christian civil order was different. While Christians are not bound to the Mosaic legislation in terms of circumstances peculiar to the Older Testament era, yet,

> Whoever does not reckon that such commandments are to be conscientiously observed is certainly not attributing to God either supreme wisdom or a righteous care for our salvation.[21]

Bucer's position thus is this: In a Christian state, the Mosaic legislation has a binding force; but Christians in a pagan state should submit to the powers that be, until a time of reformation.

Now, the issue at hand is whether or not it is reasonable to think that Calvin's attack on those advocating the Mosaic judicials has application to his close friend Martin Bucer. Is it likely that Calvin would term Bucer's position "perilous, seditious, false, and foolish"? Moreover, is it in fact the case that Bucer's position is seditious? The answer to these questions is clearly "no." Bucer is not advocating sedition.

Is there, then, some other person or group to whom Calvin might be referring? There is indeed: the Anabaptists. Calvin's hostility to the Anabaptists is well known. That he regarded them as seditious is clear from many parts of the *Institutes.* Some of the Anabaptists did advocate the Mosaic judicials, and did so in a revolutionary manner.

> In 1534 the Anabaptists of Münster drew up a legal code which restored the capital offences of the Bible, such as blasphemy, adultery and disobedience to parents, as well as imposing death for theft, begging, and even greed. The radical German reformers Müntzer and Carlstadt were in favor of restoring the judicial laws.[22]

The Anabaptists did indeed recommend the Mosaic judicials, but they also recommended civil disobedience and revolution. Calvin is attacking a position that is "perilous and seditious." There can be no question but that he has in mind not Bucer but the Anabaptists.

The final question, then, is this: does the modern theonomic-theocratic position advocated by Rushdoony, Bahnsen, *et al.*, stand in line with Bucer or with the Anabaptists? Rushdoony's and Bahnsen's writings make it more than plain that they are not sympathetic to the use of violence as a means to institute the Mosaic judicials. Thus, *the modern theonomic position is a descendent of Bucer, and is not condemned by Calvin.*

While Calvin did not himself advocate the Mosaic judicials, he regarded some of them at least as permanently binding, and did not condemn those such as Bucer (and Rushdoony and Bahnsen) who sought their implementation in a peaceful manner.

The Sixteenth Century

The Belgic Confession of 1561 actually makes no remarks on our subject one way or another. Of interest, however, is the fact that one entire chapter (Article 25) is given over to "Of the Abolishing of the Ceremonial Law," while there is no equivalent statement regarding the judicial laws. Also, Article 36 states that it is the duty of the civil magistrate to "remove and prevent all idolatry and false worship," indicating a rather more favorable view of the Older Testament "legislation" than we meet with in some today.[23]

The Second Helvetic Confession, of 1566, was almost entirely the work of Heinrich Bullinger of Zurich, one of the great second-generation Reformers, who lived from 1504 to 1575. In an earlier work, *Antiquissima Fides et vera Religio*, translated by Miles Coverdale (1488-1568) as *The Old Faith*, Bullinger had written regarding the judicial law:

> Whereas, besides the ceremonies, there is much written also in the law concerning civil polity, ordinance, judgment, to live peaceable and well in city and land; of buying and selling, of war and peace, of inheritance and properties, of laws matrimonial, of the punishment of the wicked, of the judgment and council, of lending and borrowing, etc.; it is no news at all, and serveth altogether for the declaration of the six commandments of the second table....

> Such laws and rules to live in peace, in a civil order and virtue, have also the holy fathers had from the beginning of the world written in their hearts by God himself. Now hath God also caused all to be comprehended in writing by Moses, to the intent that the world might have all more clearly and perfectly, and that no man might excuse himself of ignorance.[24]

Bullinger's Second Helvetic Confession does not, any more than the Belgic Confession, state that the judicial law of Moses has expired. Chapter 27 clearly states that the ceremonial was abolished. In chapter 12, "Of the Law of God," we read:

> For plainness' sake we divide it into the moral law, which is

contained in the commandments, or the two tables expounded in the books of Moses; into the ceremonial, which does appoint ceremonies and the worship of God; and into the judicial, which is occupied about political and domestic affairs.

We believe that the whole will of God, and all necessary precepts, for every part of this life, are fully delivered in this law. For otherwise the Lord would not have forbidden that "anything should be either added or taken away from this law" (*Dt. 4:2; 12:32*); neither would he have commanded us to go straight forward in this, and "not to decline out of the way, either to the right hand or to the left" (*Jos. 1:7*).[25]

The second paragraph cited above certainly reads as if Bullinger intended us to keep all of the Mosaic law. The same is the case in chapter 30, "Of the Magistracy":

In like manner, let him govern the people, committed to him of God, with good laws, made according to the Word of God in his hands, and look that nothing be taught contrary thereto.

Therefore let him draw forth this sword of God against all malefactors, seditious persons, thieves, murderers, oppressors, blasphemers, perjured persons, and all those whom God has commanded him to punish or even to execute. Let him suppress stubborn heretics (who are heretics indeed), who cease not to blaspheme the majesty of God, and to trouble the Church, yea, and finally to destroy it.[26]

Noteworthy is the statement that the laws of nations are framed according to the word of God, and that additionally the state is to ensure that nothing be taught contrary to the Bible. Of further note is the phrase "and all those whom God has commanded him to punish or even to execute." Apparently God has *commanded* the magistrate to execute some criminals. These commands are found nowhere but in Scripture, so that penal sanctions of Scripture must of necessity be what is referred to here. This statement, as it stands in and of itself, can only mean that those things which were civil offenses in the Older Testament economy continue to be civil offenses in the New Testament era (these offenses are listed), and also that the specific punishment ordered by God for some crimes (execution) is still mandated.

In the *Decades*, however, Bullinger firmly insists upon the abrogation of the Mosaic judicials.[27] No nation is bound to receive them as its laws. Nonetheless, "the substance of God's judicial laws is not taken away or abolished, but ... the ordering and limitation of them is placed in them is placed in the arbitrement of good Christian princes. . . ."[28] Bullinger also argues that the good laws of the ancient world (Calvin's "common law of nations") trace back to Moses,[29] so that one reason Moses' specifics are no longer binding is that the laws of the nations so closely approximate them.[30] Thus, in a concrete sense, Bullinger's rejection of the *letter* of the Mosaic judicials is related to the fact that he saw their continuation in *spirit* in his own culture.

Bucer and Bullinger have a number of things in common. It would be well to summarize these, for we shall find them commonly occurring in Calvinistic writings of this century and the next.

1.   Both state categorically that the Mosaic judicial laws were designed for ancient Israel and no longer bind the modern Christian nations.

2.   Both turn around and invoke the penal sanctions of the Mosaic laws as if they were fully binding on modern magistrates.

3.   Both hold that even though the Mosaic judicials are not binding, yet they are also not abolished or removed.

4.   Both hold that the Mosaic judicials must inform the thinking of good Christian princes, who nonetheless have the right to alter them somewhat.

5.   Both seem to believe that the Mosaic judicials cannot be improved upon.

How are we to understand this? We should like to suggest that the following is what is meant by these men. The civil aspects of the unchanging moral law of God were phrased in case law, dealing with cases common and sometimes peculiar to the ancient, agrarian Israelite economy. Some, perhaps many, of these cases no longer exist in the modern world. Nonetheless, the basic principles contained in the case laws can be and must be applied to the modern civil order. Some cases, such as murder, adultery, blasphemy, and

Sabbath breaking, remain the same; and thus the civil laws regarding these also remain the same from age to age. As will appear later on, the English Puritans used the term "equity" to denote this phenomenon of basic principles and common cases still being binding in the New Testament era.

Turning, then, to the English Reformers, we must examine the views of Hooper, Latimer, and Becon. Bishop John Hooper died a martyr of the Reform in 1555. His work is useful in showing that the Biblical death penalty was *commonly* received in his day. "It sufficeth us loyallement and with good faith to hear this commandment, 'Commit no adultery'; which forbiddeth not only to abstain from another man's wife, the which both God's laws and man's laws, Christians' and gentiles', punisheth with death, Dt. 22, Lev. 24...."[31]

Hugh Latimer (1485-1555) was also a bishop and martyr. The following quotation demonstrates a high regard for the civil use of the law of Moses:

> There is no king, emperor, magistrate, and ruler, of what state soever they be, but are bound to obey this God, and to give credence unto his holy word, in directing their steps ordinately according to the same word. Yea, truly, they are not only bound to obey God's book, but also the minister of the same, "for the word's sake," so far as he speaketh "sitting in Moses' chair": that is, if his [the preachers' – J. B. J.] doctrine be taken out of Moses' law. For in this world God hath two swords, the one is a temporal sword, the other a spiritual. The temporal sword resteth in the hands of kings, magistrates, and rulers, under him; whereunto all subjects, as well the clergy as the laity, be subject, and punishable for any offence contrary to the same book.[32]

In short, the preacher explains the law of Moses to the civil magistrate, who then enforces the relevant sections of it with the sword. Latimer also declared, "I would wish that Moses's law were restored for punishment of lechery."[33]

Thomas Becon (1512-1567) studied under Latimer. He was a chaplain to Archbishop Cranmer, and his *Catechism* was written during the reign of Edward the Sixth, during the period of Bucer's influence in England. Becon cites the penal laws of Moses as examples to civil magistrates of every age.[34] He emphasizes that if wrongs against man are to be punished—the second table of the law—how much more should wrongs against God be punished.[35] He adds: "But we have . . . an expressed commandment to kill and put out of the way all idolaters and false prophets. . . ."[36]

This evidence from the mid-sixteenth century, while not always evidence of a rigorously consistent approach to the matter, surely does serve to indicate a deep respect for the civil implications of the law of Moses.

The Rise of Puritanism

The term "Puritan" is very difficult to define closely, and we need not enter the controversy over exactly what it denotes. For our purposes, Puritanism reflected an attitude regarding God and man which stressed the sinfulness and the duty of man, and the sovereignty and law of God. As to doctrine, the Puritans were strongly predestinarian. As to law, they believed that the Bible sets forth the specific pattern for church government, though they were not all in agreement regarding exactly what that pattern is. With regard to society, they were not retreatist, but maintained the old Christian and medieval notion of a Christian social order, of "Christendom." In terms of this, they had a high regard for the judicial laws of Moses.[37]

There was a long legal tradition favoring the Mosaic judicials, which fed into Puritanism. B. S. Capp has noted that the Lollards were strongly influenced in their social programs by the laws of Moses.

> Wyclif attacked the profiteering lawyers and argued that men were not bound to obey laws not based on scripture. He condemned the view that "sinful men's laws, full of error, be more needful than the gospel." William Swynderby condemned the imprisonment of debtors. Walter Brute, preaching in 1392, declared it was "to be wondered at, why thieves are, among Christians, for theft put to death, when after the law of Moses they were not put to death. Christians suffer adulterers to live, Sodomites, and they who curse father and mother, and many other horrible sinners; ... So we neither keep the law of righteousness given by God, nor the law of mercy taught by

Christ." This sermon was printed by Foxe, and was thus readily available in the seventeenth century. The chronicler, Henry of Knighton, claimed that the cry "Legem dei, Goddis law," was the watchword of the Lollard movement.[38]

Another source of Puritanism was John Knox. Thomas M'Crie comments on Knox's view in a passing remark while discussing Knox's debate with Maitland: "... both parties held that idolatry might justly be punished by death. Into this sentiment they were led in consequence of their having adopted the untenable opinion, that the judicial laws given to the Jewish nation were binding upon Christian nations, as to all offenses against the moral law."[39]

Thomas Cartwright was among the most highly respected Puritan leaders of English Presbyterianism. He lived from 1535 to 1603. In a lengthy interchange with Archbishop Whitgift, his *Second Reply* included the following remarkable statement:

> And, as for the judicial law, forasmuch as there are some of them made in regard of the region where they were given, and of the people to whom they were given, the prince and magistrate, keeping the substance and *equity* of them (as it were the *marrow*), may change the circumstance of them, as the times and places and manners of the people shall require. But to say that any magistrate can save the life of blasphemers, contemptuous and stubborn idolaters, murderers, adulterers, incestuous persons, and such like, which God by his judicial law hath commanded to be put to death, I do utterly deny, *and am ready to prove*, if that pertained to this question.[40]

Archbishop Whitgift complained in 1574 that "it is now disputed at every table, whether the magistrate be of necessity bound to the judicials of Moses, so that he may not punish otherwise than is there prescribed . . .; which is most absurd, . . . and . . . seditious."[41] Whitgift, ever a determined foe of Puritanism, was happy to be able to apply Calvin's adjective "seditious" to them, for it was the Puritans who advocated the Mosaic judicials.

William Perkins (1558-1602) argued in the same vein. Perkins was one of the formative thinkers of the Puritan movement. Perkins' discussion of witchcraft brings out his view of the Mosaic judicials. Thomas Pickering, a contemporary of Perkins, summarized his view thusly: "That the witch truly convicted is to be punished with death, the highest degree of punishment, and that by the law of Moses, the *equity* whereof is perpetual."[42] Perkins specifically noted that not only evil witches but also good witches were to be executed under Moses' law, because the essence of the anti-sorcery law was not directed against those who harm others but against those in pact with Satan.[43]

It should not escape notice that Cartwright and Perkins were two of the greatest and most influential of the early Puritans. Note that both use the term *equity*, which is used in the Westminster Confession of Faith, chapter 19:4. This will be explained further below. Note also that Cartwright is "ready to prove" the continuing validity of the Mosaic judicials. This is no mild view, but a very confident and assured one. Note finally that, according to Whitgift, the subject was under constant discussion at the end of the sixteenth century. It was a live issue in British Calvinism.

On the separatist side of Puritanism, Henry Barrow (d. 1593) was one of the principal leaders. His *Discovery of the False Church* (1590) included the following:

> But the statutes and judgments of God which are delivered and expounded unto us by his holy prophets, endure for ever; the pure wisdom, the upright justice, the true exposition and faithful execution of his moral law: which laws were not made for the Jews' state only (as Mr. Calvin hath taught) but for all mankind, especially for all the Israel of God, from which laws it is not lawful in judgment to vary or decline either to the one hand or to the other.[44]

Barrow is quite straightforward: the judicial law ("statutes and judgments") is "the true exposition and faithful execution of God's moral law."

Philip Stubbs (c. 1555-1610?), a Puritan pamphleteer, composed *An Anatomie of Abuses* in 1583. Very popular, it ran through three editions in two years, and was reprinted a fourth time in 1595.[45] His view was as follows:

> S. What kind of punishment would you have appointed for these notorious bloody swearers? P. I would wish (if it pleased God)

that it were made death: For we read in the law of God, that
whosoever blasphemeth the Lord, was presently stoned to death
without all remorce. Which law *judicial* standeth in force to the
world's end.[46]

We have seen that the early leaders of Puritanism in England
frequently espoused the normativity of the judicial law of Moses,
insofar as that law addressed abiding circumstances. This is
important as background to the Westminster Assembly, especially
the use of the term *equity*. The question may well be asked, however:
Did the Puritan movement retain this emphasis in its full bloom?
The answer has to be an unequivocal "yes," for precisely when the
Puritans had opportunity to begin *de novo* with a new society, in
New England, they turned to Moses' law as their own social code.

The Era of the Westminster Assembly

Chapter 19:4 of the Westminster Confession of Faith reads as
follows:

To them [Israel] also, as a body politic, He gave sundry judicial
laws, which expired together with the State of that people; not
obliging any other now, further than the general equity thereof
may require.

What precisely does this mean? How are we to understand
the phrase "general equity"? This will be the substance of our
discussion in this section. In order to discover what this statement
intends to set forth, we shall examine opinions from several
contemporary quarters: the Continent, the Scottish Presbyterians,
the English Congregationalists, and the New World colonists.
Representatives from each of these groups will prove to have taken
a very high view of the Mosaic judicials, and this will demonstrate
that the Westminster Confession does not militate against such a
view, but may well assume it.

A. *The Continent*

Johannes Wollebius (1586-1629), a theologian at Basel,
published in 1626 a *Compendium Theologia Christianae*. According
to Beardslee, Wollebius provides us here with "the best brief
summary of Reformed dogmatics available from the period" – the

period being the first third of the seventeenth century.[47] Beardslee further informs us that Wollebius' work was very popular on the Continent, and circulated widely. In chapter 14, "The Ceremonial and Political Law," section 6 reads as follows:

So much for the ceremonial law. The political law dealt with the civil constitution of the Jews.

Propositions

I. As the ceremonial law was concerned with God, the political was concerned with the neighbor.

II. In these matters on which it is in harmony with the moral law and with ordinary justice, it is binding on us.

III. In those matters which were peculiar to that law and were prescribed for the promised land or the situation of the Jewish state, it has no more force for us than the law of foreign commonwealths.[48]

Notice that according to Wollebius *all* of the judicial law is permanently binding except what is unique to the geography of Palestine or deals with the formal construction of the state. As will be seen in the sequel, these same provisions were made by the New England Puritans.

B. *Scotland*

Turning to Scotland, we have an interesting and detailed series of remarks on this subject by George Gillespie, one of the Scottish commissioners to the Westminster Assembly. Gillespie's full remarks on the relation between church and state consume a very large volume and cannot be treated of here. He does, however, identify his sympathies immediately in *Aaron's Rod Blossoming* (1646), where in I:1 he writes:

I know some divines hold that the judicial law of Moses, so far as concerneth the punishments of sins against the moral law, idolatry, blasphemy, Sabbath-breaking, adultery, theft, etc., ought to be a rule to the Christian magistrate; and, for my part, I wish more respect were had to it, and that it were more consulted with.

Gillespie goes on to distinguish between the roles of state and church in civil matters. A clearer statement is found in his *CXI Propositions Concerning the Ministry and Government of the Church* (1644), where he states:

> 47. ... It is one thing to govern the commonwealth, and to make political and civil laws; another thing to interpret the word of God, and out of it to show the magistrate his duty, to wit, how he ought to govern the commonwealth, and in what manner he ought to use the sword. The former is proper and peculiar to the magistrate (neither doth the ministry intermeddle or entangle itself into such businesses), but the latter is contained within the office of the ministers.

> 48. For to that end also is the holy Scripture profitable, to show which is the best manner of governing a commonwealth, and that the magistrate, as being God's minister, may by this guiding star be so directed, as that he may execute the parts of his office according to the will of God, and may perfectly be instructed in every good work. . . .

Note that Gillespie states that the Bible instructs the magistrate on how to use the sword, *i.e.*, on penal sanctions. Gillespie saw the magistrate bound to rule according to the Scriptures, and especially according to the judicial laws of Moses. Gillespie's testimony is highly significant, since it addresses the issue directly, and in that Gillespie was very influential at the Westminster Assembly.[49]

C. *England*

John Owen (1616-1683) wanted Oliver Cromwell to rule by the Mosaic judicials. In a sermon, "Christ's Kingdom and the Magistrate's Power," preached before Parliament on October 13, 1652, the great congregationalist leader said:

> Although the institutions and examples of the Old Testament, of the duty of magistrates in the things and about the worship of God, are not, in their whole latitude and extent, to be drawn into rules that should be obligatory to all magistrates now, under the administration of the gospel,—and that because the magistrate was "custos, vindex, et administrator legis judicialis, et politiae Mosaicae," from which, as most think, we are freed;— yet, doubtless, there is something moral in those institutions,

which, being unclothed of their Judaical form, is still *binding to all* in the like kind, as to some analogy and proportion. Subduct from those administrations what was proper to, and lies upon the account of, the church and nation of the Jews, and *what remains upon the general notion of a church and nation must be everlastingly binding.*[50]

We must not miss the force of the last sentence. What Owen is saying is that whatever *can* be applied *must* be applied. Notice the parallel with the Westminster Confession statement: some laws applied to the Jews as a national entity, and had to do with their structures and institutions. These have passed away. Other laws, however, are *equally* applicable to all nations, and these are *binding.* In the language of Westminster, "further than the general *equity* thereof may *require.*"

Thomas Gilbert was chaplain of Magdalen College, Oxford, from 1656 to 1660. In the Whitehall debates of December, 1648, he argued that insofar as the judicial law "was a fence and outwork to the Moral law, it stands with the Moral law, and that still binds upon men. . . . So . . . the Judicial law . . . is still the duty of Magistrates."[51]

D. *New England*

The Puritan experiments in the New World clearly reveal what their conceptions were. Whatever ambiguity may have afflicted them in England, given the opportunity to start from scratch they turned unanimously to the judicials of Moses for their civil order. We shall look briefly at three of their leaders, and then examine the laws of three colonies, in order to confirm this point.

John Cotton (1584-1652) was one of the most prominent of the Puritan pastors in Massachusetts Bay. He was an unabashed theocrat. Like all Puritan thinkers, he did not interpret theocracy to entail the unification of church and state, but rather saw both institutions as under the one rule of Christ. Greg L. Bahnsen has reprinted Cotton's most succinct theocratic work, *An Abstract of the Laws of New England, as They are Now Established* (1641), which is (apparently) the same work as Cotton's *Moses His Judicials* (1636).[52] This work consists largely of verbatim quotations from the law of Moses. Although it was not adopted by Massachusetts, it greatly influenced the Bible-based code which was adopted,

Nathaniel Ward's *Body of Liberties* (1641). The *Body of Liberties* influenced the *Massachusetts Code* (1648), and this in turn influenced the constitutions of all the colonial states.

Cotton distinguished between the permanent judicials, which were appendages to the moral law, and temporary judicials, which were appendages to the ceremonial law. Some examples of temporary laws, peculiar to the Israelite state, were:

1. the Levirate,
2. some aspects of the Jubilee,
3. Spirit-inspired Judges and the hereditary monarchy,
4. putting away heathen wives,
5. the inalienability of family property,
6. prohibition on mixed cloth,
7. prohibition on yoking ox and ass,
8. prohibition on rounding beard,
9. the Levitical requirement to drain blood from meat (though the prohibition on drinking fresh blood is permanent).[53]

Another prominent pastor was Thomas Shepard (1605-1649), who ministered at Newtown, Massachusetts, from 1636 until 1649. Shepard provides us with an extended comment on the permanent aspects of the Mosaic judicials:

> Thesis 41: The judicial laws, some of them being hedges and fences to safeguard both moral and ceremonial precepts, their binding power was therefore mixed and various, for those which did safeguard any moral law, (which is perpetual,) whether by just punishments or otherwise, do still morally bind all nations; … and hence God would have all nations preserve their fences forever, as he would have that law preserved forever which these safeguard…. As, on the contrary, the morals abiding, why should not their judicials and fences remain? The learned generally doubt not to affirm that Moses' judicials bind all nations, so far forth as they contain any moral equity in them, which moral equity doth appear not only in respect of the end of the law, when it is ordered for common and universal good, but chiefly in respect of the law which they safeguard and fence, which if it be moral, it is most just and equal, that either the same or like judicial fence (according to some fit proportion) should preserve it still, because it is but just and equal that a moral and universal law should be universally preserved….[54]

Several aspects of this quotation are noteworthy. First is Shepard's assertion that the "just punishments" or something proportionately like them are included in the permanently binding aspects of the Mosaic judicials. Second is his statement that the educated thinkers of his day were in agreement that insofar as the Mosaic judicials contained *equity*, they were *binding* on all nations.

Third, Shepard contends that the equity is not contained in the *purpose* of the moral law, but in the moral law *itself*. According to the *Oxford English Dictionary*, "equity" is here used in the sense of a recourse to a general principle of justice. To be precise, "Equity of a statute according to its reason and spirit so as to make it apply to cases for which it does not expressly provide."[55] Thus, what Shepard is saying is that the case laws of the Mosaic system reflect perfectly, in their particular applications, the universal justice of the moral law. Though some of these cases do not apply directly today, they do show concretely how the general principles are to be worked out in particular situations.

Some cases apply directly to all times, such as death for adultery, since adultery is the same in all times and places. Other cases, such as the requirement that a fence be put on the roofs of newly constructed houses, have little relevance to us today as they stand, since our roofs are not flat and we do not use them for social gatherings. There are, however, similar situations and equivalent circumstances in the modern world (such as high porches), and by studying the Mosaic legislation, we can discern how properly to apply the moral law equitably to our modern situation.

It is very important that this concept of equity be understood, for it is this very concept which is employed by the Westminster Confession of Faith in section 19:4. The equity of the Mosaic judicials is permanently binding, even though some of the cases or particular illustrations in the Mosaic law do not appear today.

Shepard also is helpful in delimiting the use of the law of the Older Testament in another way. In *A Wholesome Caveat* (1648), he notes that there were various forms of government authorized by God in the Older Testament.[56] Thus, as regards the precise *form* of government, as distinct from its legal *matter*, none is legislated by Scripture. The other work cited above was published in 1649. These works, written and issued in the same decade as the Westminster Assembly, give us a good idea of what the consensus must have been among the stricter Calvinists at that august assemblage.

More rigorous in his views was John Eliot, the apostle to the Indians. Eliot was one of the most remarkable missionaries of all time, in that he not only brought the good news of personal salvation to his Indian hearers, but also sought to reorganize completely their societies in order to make them prosperous, productive, and happy. His labors, which were ceaseless, ran until his death in 1690 at the age of 86. In a remarkable book, *The Christian Commonwealth* (1659), he argued from Exodus chapter 18 that society should be organized by households, with elders over groups of ten, of 50, of 100, and so forth. He noted that Jesus operated on this principle in the New Testament (*Mk. 6:40*). Eliot worked out this surprising scheme in great detail, going into relatively fine points regarding at which level in the pyramid capital crimes should be tried, and so forth.[57] If this seems innocuous to us today, it was regarded as "full of seditious principles and notions" by the Governor and Council of Massachusetts when they took it up on March 18, 1660. This extreme denunciation reflects the fact that Charles II had ascended the throne in Britain, and all Puritan thought was suspect.[58] Eliot was required to renounce it, and with wise discretion (*Mt. 5:41*) he did so.[59] Still in all, his little work shows us to what lengths the careful Puritans were ready to go to in order to follow the dictates of God. We must note, then, that if Eliot was to the right of the consensus of his times, that consensus must have been well to the right of what is popular in Reformed circles today.

We turn now to consider the legislation of three of the New England settlements. Revisions were made in English law under the Cromwellian administration, as might be expected. Capp notes that "The Rump [Parliament] actually passed measures establishing the death penalty for adultery, incest, and blasphemy, and severe penalties for swearing and for profanation of the Sabbath."[60] Despite this, the Calvinistic experiment did not have full opportunity to do things its own way except in the New World, where there were no traditions to overcome, no unbelieving power bloc to contend with, and little social inertia from within the ranks, the New England breed being by and large the stricter sort. In America they had a chance to start from scratch, and it is surely significant that they turned directly to the Mosaic judicials in doing so. We have noted already John Cotton's input in this, but let us now briefly examine the legal records themselves.

The *Records* of the New Haven Colony include the following entry, which speaks for itself.

> March 2, 1641/2: And according to the fundamental agreement, made, and published by full and general consent, when the plantation began and government was settled, that the judicial law of God given by Moses and expounded in other parts of scripture, so far as it is a hedge and a fence to the moral law, and neither ceremonial nor typical nor had any reference to Canaan, hath an everlasting equity in it, and should be the rule of their proceedings.[61]

Note that the judicial law is that of God, not that of Moses. Note also the recurrence of "equity," which is here said to be "everlasting."

Thomas Hutchinson summarizes the laws of The Massachusetts Bay Colony. As regards the 1648 Code, referred to above in our discussion of John Cotton, Hutchinson notes that, in common with English law, it penalized with death: murder, sodomy, witchcraft, arson, and the rape of a child under ten years of age. Added to these were: idolatry, blasphemy, kidnapping, adultery (several were executed under this law), willful perjury designed to do another to death, unprovoked cursing or striking of parents by children over 16 years of age. Additionally, many lesser crimes were capital if repeated twice or thrice. Since high treason against the king and rape of an unengaged girl were not capital crimes in the Biblical system, neither were they capital in Massachusetts.[62] Hutchinson also gives an interesting case of the application of Biblical restitution laws: "Josias Plaistowe, for stealing four baskets of corn from the Indians, was ordered to return them eight baskets. . . ."[63] Wertenbaker adds that, according to an order of the General Court on November 4, 1646, incorrigibly delinquent teenagers were to be put to death. This also was according to the Biblical judicials. No Massachusetts teenager was ever actually executed under this law — It seems to have had its intended sobering influence.[64]

At Plymouth Colony the same situation prevailed. Hutchinson remarks, "Cartwright, who had a chief hand in reducing puritanism to a system, held, that the magistrate was bound to adhere to the judicial law of Moses, and might not punish or pardon otherwise than they prescribed, and him the Massachusetts people followed."[65] Hutchinson here is speaking specifically of the Plymouth settlement, which was of a slightly different theological stripe than the Massachusetts Bay settlement, but was Puritan all the same.

E. *The Westminster Standards*

We have now spiraled in upon the actual Westminster Assembly and Standards themselves. In that influential Continental, Scottish, Congregational, Puritan, and colonial divines of the period highly favored the civil use of the Mosaic judicials, and many maintained that their use was not optional for a Christian state, *we may be certain that the Westminster Standards were not intended to exclude their views.* Summarizing our case to this point, we have found in the background and milieu of the Westminster Assembly the following factors:

1. The Wycliffite background of the English Reformation favored the continued use of the Mosaic judicials.

2. The influential Bucer insisted that the Mosaic judicials could not be improved upon.

3. The influential Bullinger was more ambiguous, but generally favored the Mosaic judicials.

4. The English Reformers, Hooper, Latimer, and Becon, were favorable to the Mosaic judicials.

5. John Knox held to the binding nature of the Mosaic judicials.

6. Thomas Cartwright, the father of Puritanism, held rigorously to the Mosaic judicials, and was ready to debate the point.

7. Archbishop Whitgift, the opponent of Puritanism, complained that the Mosaic judicials were being advocated and debated everywhere.

8.   Wollebius held that the Mosaic judicials were still binding.

9.   Gillespie noted that many were advocating the Mosaic judicials at the time of the Westminster Assembly, and expressed his partiality to their view.

10. John Owen advocated the Mosaic judicials.

11. The New England colonies implemented the Mosaic judicials. It is important to note that many books written in New England were printed and distributed in England, at precisely the time during which the Westminster Assembly was meeting. It is also important to remember that the most brilliant and influential theologians of Puritanism were among those who migrated to New England. Their opinions were highly respected by their contemporaries. (For instance, John Owen was converted to Congregationalism by John Cotton.)

If the Westminster Standards do not contradict the whole-law position, how favorable are they to it? Or are the Standards ambiguous? An examination of the evidence will show that *the Standards are ambiguous regarding the Mosaic judicials, but mildly favorable to them.* Given the consensus of the time, this is what we should expect to find.

The ambiguity is clear in Confession section 19:4, which reads in such a way as almost to contradict itself.

> To them also, as a body politic, He gave sundry judicial laws, which expired together with the State of that people....

We have noted that the Confession is in error at this point in assuming that the Mosaic case laws were designed as a civil code for any nation. Rather were they *explanations* of the moral law, and thus form a foundation for civil codes. Howbeit, this statement of the Confession *seems* clearly to state that the Mosaic case laws no longer bind the Christian community. The second half of the statement, however, gives back with the right hand what was removed with the left:

> ... not obliging any other now, further than the general *equity* may *require* (emphasis added).

Modern readers will interpret this statement to mean that there is a "spirit of fairness" in the laws which ought to be emulated by modern states. This, however, is not the meaning of the term "equity" in its historical context. As noted above, the *Oxford English Dictionary* gives the meaning of "equity" as follows: "Equity of a statute according to its reason and spirit so as to make it apply to cases for which it does not expressly provide." In other words, the Confession is saying that though the precise cases addressed by the case law may no longer be found in modern society, there are *parallel cases* to which they *do* apply, and where these parallel cases are found, the case laws are *binding* ("require").

The prooftexts of this paragraph reveal some of the same ambiguity. The pattern of the proofs in the Standards is that each phrase or term is footnoted with texts. Thus, we should expect that prooftexts would be given at three points in this paragraph: after "sundry judicial laws," after "of that people," and after "equity thereof may require." This, however, is not the case. Rather, the whole paragraph is given one footnote. The texts given do not point to the various phrases of the paragraph, however. Exodus 21 and 22 are cited as being the laws in question. Genesis 49:10, 1 Peter 2:13f., and Matthew 5:17+38f. are cited apparently to show changes or expirations in the law. Finally, 1 Corinthians 9:8ff. is cited to show the permanent equity of the law. What are we to make of this? It is clear that the framers of the Standards felt that there was both *continuity and discontinuity in the law of God.* God had given to ancient Israel a civil code, which was designed for that people at that time. This code, in the strict sense, was not designed for other nations particularly, and thus expired. Jesus was free to make some changes in this law. At the same time, this civil code was based on eternal moral principles, and these moral principles could clearly be seen in the laws themselves, so that these laws should form the basis of all Christian civil codes, according as the "general equity thereof may require." Thus, these laws could not be ignored or overlooked. Christians are not free to take them or leave them. They *must* be consulted for their "equity."

What the Standards do *not* do is spell out to what extent and how these laws are binding and to what extent and how they have been loosed. This is doubtless because this was an open question, much debated at the time. Some held, as we have seen, that whatever could be applied from these laws had to be applied, without any alteration. Others held more lax views regarding their binding nature. The Standards do not settle this issue in full. If, however, we make a careful examination of the Standards, we will be able to see at some points how the framers regarded the binding nature of the judicial aspects of the law of God, and to this we now turn.

In Confession 1:2, the Confession affirms that *all* of the books of Scripture, not just the New Testament, are given by God "to be the rule of faith *and life*." In 1:6 we are told that everything man needs for his life is "either expressly set down in Scripture, or by good and necessary consequence may be derived from Scripture." Since civil life is not optional but needful for man, the Confession implies that to some degree, at least, the ordering of civil life is found in Scripture. This is an implicitly *anti-pluralistic* declaration.

In 20:1, discussing liberty of conscience, the Confession states:

> But, under the new testament, the liberty of Christians is further enlarged, in their freedom from the yoke of the *ceremonial law*, to which the Jewish Church was subjected, and in greater boldness of access to the throne of grace, and in fuller communications of the free Spirit of God, than believers under the law did ordinarily partake of (emphasis added).

Mark that in noting the New Testament's improvements over the Older Covenant, nothing whatever is mentioned by the Confession regarding the abrogation of the judicial laws. This is, granted, an argument from silence, but it is a significant silence in context. Most modern writers would surely have added the judicial laws' abrogation as an enlargement of Christian liberty. That the Standards do not do so indicates that at the very least the framers as a group had no settled opinions on the matter.

In 20:4, the Confession affirms that *the magistrate must punish those who teach against Christianity or against the church*. The prooftexts begin with Deuteronomy 13:6-12, which requires death for those who advocate false religions. Also cited are Nehemiah 13:15-25 on the enforcement of the Sabbath, 2 Kings 23:5-21 and several other passages in Kings and Chronicles wherein a godly ruler executed the priests of false religions, and Zechariah 13:2-3, which makes the same point as Deuteronomy 13.

In 22:3, the case law of Numbers 5:19ff. is cited as still binding with respect to *oaths and vows*, as is Exodus 22:7-11. In 22:7, the case law provisions of Numbers 30:5-13 are invoked as still regulative with respect to oaths and vows.

In 23:3, the civil ruler is directed to suppress all "blasphemies and heresies." The prooftexts include Leviticus 24:16 and Deuteronomy 13:5, which order *death for blasphemers and heretics* respectively.

In 24:4, the Older Testament laws regarding *degrees of consanguinity and affinity* in marriage are cited as binding (*Lev. 18; 20*). In 24:6, the case law of Deuteronomy 24:1-4 is cited as procedurally binding in cases of *divorce*.

Larger Catechism question 28 tells us that the *blessings and curses* of the Covenant operate under the New Covenant in the same way as under the Older Covenant, citing Deuteronomy 28:15ff.

In Q. 99:7 the Catechism directs "that what is forbidden or commanded to ourselves, we are bound, according to our places, to endeavor that it may be avoided or performed by others, according to the duty of their places." This statement is wholly anti-pluralistic, in that it requires those in positions of authority to *enforce the law of God on unbelievers*. Cited is Exodus 20:10, the *law of the Sabbath*.

In Q. 108 we are directed to *remove false religions*, according to our position in life (*Dt. 7:5*), and in Q. 109 we are told that "tolerating a false religion" is a sin (*Dt. 13:6-12; Zech. 13:1-3*). According to the Catechism, thus, pluralism is wicked and evil.

In Q. 128, Exodus 21:15 and Deuteronomy 21:18ff. are cited, which require the *death penalty for striking parents and for rebellion*.

In Q. 136, Numbers 35:31 is cited in defense of *capital punishment*, and Numbers 35:16-21 and Exodus 21:18ff. are cited "concerning the laws for smiters, for an hurt by chance, for an ox that goreth, and for him that is an occasion of harm."

Apparently the permanent equity of these laws was regarded as binding by the Assembly. These laws, it would seem, are not among those that "expired together with the State of that people."

In Q. 139 the Catechism cites Leviticus 20:15f., which requires *death for bestiality*.

In Q. 141 *restitution* is required for theft. Leviticus 6:2-5 is cited, and the command to add a fifth part in making voluntary restitution is italicized, showing that the concept of 120 percent restitution was embraced by the Assembly. Also cited are the case laws concerning *helpfulness*: Leviticus 25:35, Deuteronomy 21:1-4, and Exodus 23:4f.

In Q. 142 the sins forbidden include the *removing of landmarks*, citing Deuteronomy 19:4.

In Q. 145 the sins include *concealing the truth* (*Lev. 5:1; Dt. 13:8*), *failure to reprove sin* (*Lev. 19:17*), *lying* (*Lev. 19:11*), *talebearing* (*Lev. 19:16*), and *raising false rumors* (*Ex. 23:1*).

Finally, in Q. 151:3, Deuteronomy 22:22, 28f. are cited as binding exemplars of *differing degrees of sin*.

Much of the preceding argument has been taken from the prooftexts appended to the Confession and Catechisms, and of course these original prooftexts are not considered as having creedal status. Modern Presbyterian denominations have often replaced these prooftexts with new sets of texts. Our concern, however, is to locate the thinking of the framers of the Standards, and for this purpose a consultation of their original prooftexts is helpful.

It is also often noted that the Assembly did not originally attach prooftexts, and was reluctant to do so when so ordered by Parliament. This reluctance is probably overdrawn by modern observers, in that the delegates to the Assembly had been removed from their families for several years already by this time. Even if they did have principled objections to prooftexting, and were reluctant for this reason, the fact remains that *their thinking had been so shaped by Older Testament laws that they instinctively wrote the content of these into the Standards*, and thus had to cite the Mosaic judicials when they added in the prooftexts. Thus, the prooftexts are indeed of value in indicating the thinking of the delegates to the Westminster Assembly.

In summary, then, these citations serve to highlight the ambiguity of the Standards' position, and demonstrate that modern opponents of the whole-law theonomic-theocratic position cannot appeal to the Westminster Standards to back up their views.

Particularly as regards the suppression of heresy and idolatry, the Standards are thoroughly theocratic and wholly anti-pluralistic.

The Later Colonial Period in America

Samuel Willard (1640-1707) was for many years the pastor at Boston's Old South Church. His *Compleat Body of Divinity*, when published after his death in 1726, was at that time the largest volume ever issued from the presses in America. It was close to 1,000 folio pages. Because several printing presses were used, some page numbers were repeated. The second time page 622 is encountered, we read:

> With respect to the *Judicial Laws*, we must observe, that these were Appendices, partly of the Moral, partly of the Ceremonial Law: Now such as, or so far as they are related to the *Ceremonial*, they are doubtless Abolished with it. As, and as far as they bear respect to the *Moral* Law, they do, *eo Nomine*, require Obedience perpetual, and are therefore reducible to Moral Precepts....[66]

Willard goes on to distinguish, within the penal laws, those which are permanent and those which are not:

> Some indeed were Moral, as the Death of a Murderer, and without any Ransom; and some also suppose that the making Adultery a Capital Crime belongs hither: But others were proper only to the Time and State of that People, as the Law about Profaning the Sabbath, Numb. 15:33, etc.[67]

Unfortunately, that is as far as Willard takes us. We do not discover precisely where he draws the line because his principle of differentiating the moral judicials from the ceremonial judicials is not made explicit. His view does, however, place him squarely in the Puritan tradition.

Samuel Sewell in his famous diary gives the best picture of New England life at the time of Willard's pastorate. The two men were close friends. In his entry for April 2, 1674, Sewell records that "Benjamin Gourd of Roxbury (being about 17 years of age) was executed for committing Bestiality with a Mare. . . ."[68] The recent editor of Sewell's diary, M. Halsey Thomas, notes that by the Province Laws of 1697, 23 years after this incident, the death penalty was still on the books for rape and bestiality, and atheism and blasphemy were also legislated against.[69] The Puritan legal system was being modified, but was still highly influential.

In closing, let us look at the thought of John Witherspoon (1723-1794), president of Princeton University. Witherspoon would have liked for the *lex talionis* to be incorporated into American legislation:

> I make one particular remark, that though many things are copied from the law of Moses into the laws of modern nations, yet so far as I know none of them have introduced the lex talionis in the case of injuries, an eye for an eye, and a tooth for a tooth, etc. and yet perhaps there are many instances in which it would be very proper.[70]

This again demonstrates a rather high view of the Mosaic judicials, and that by a man very influential in the thought of the Founding Fathers of the United States of America, a man who signed the Declaration of Independence.

Later English Writers

Two authors come before our view in this section: Thomas Ridgeley and Thomas Scott. Both continued the earlier tradition of taking a high view of the judicial law. Ridgeley provides a list of seven kinds of judicial laws that expired with the coming of the New Testament era:[71]

1. The levitate and the inalienability of property.
2. The jubilee.
3. The six-year limit on slavery.
4. The sabbatical year.
5. The usury prohibitions.
6. The annual festivals.
7. The cities of refuge and the avenger of blood.

By inference, all other laws were binding. (It should be noted that Rushdoony and Bahnsen maintain the permanence of the six-year limitation on slavery and of the usury legislation, as well as at least some aspects of the jubilee and sabbatical year.) Ridgeley (c. 1667-1734) was an English Independent. His *Body of Divinity*, one of the few commentaries on the Westminster Larger Catechism, was published between 1731 and 1733. Later editions (the work was highly regarded and reissued several times) included notes from the hand of John Wilson, who comments in connection with Ridgeley's views:

> Dr. Ridgeley is of the class who appeal to the enactments of the judicial law; and he even seems to maintain that these enactments, just in the state in which they were made for the Israelites, are still in force. He does not anywhere say, in as many words, that the judicial law is permanently and universally binding; but, in several instances, when expounding the decalogue, and especially when teaching the results of transgression in the present life, he quotes its provisions in the same manner, and with the same drift, as if they were precepts of the moral law.[72]

Thomas Scott (1747-1821) was an Anglican minister who had been converted under John Newton. His extremely popular *Holy Bible with Notes* was issued in sections between 1788 and 1792. The following two statements were read in many households across Britain and America during the ensuing years.

> Making some allowance for the circumstances varying in different ages and nations, there is a spirit of *equity* in these laws, which is well worthy of being transfused into those of any state.[73]

> ... a full investigation of the subject would evince, that the laws enacted by him [Moses] were uniformly more wise, equitable, humane, mild, and salutary in their tendency, than the complex body of laws, even of the most civilized nations, nay of those where Christianity has most flourished. For the former bear *the evident stamp of a divine original*, the latter are tarnished by the infirmities and passions of our fallen nature.[74]

It is inconceivable that a man would have this view of the worth of the judicial law of God, and not want it to be enacted in his own homeland.

Southern Presbyterian Writers

We turn in conclusion to the thought of the two most excellent theologians of Southern Presbyterianism: James H. Thornwell and Robert L. Dabney. When the Confederate States of America were formed, in response to a perceived economic and atheistic threat from the Northern States, it was widely hoped that the new nation would be explicitly Christian. A petition was sent to the Congress of the CSA from the General Assembly of the Presbyterian Church in the CSA, authored by Thornwell, to that end. The proposed amendment to the CSA Constitution, to be added to the section providing for liberty of conscience, read:

> Nevertheless we, the people of these Confederate States, directly acknowledge our responsibility to God, and the supremacy of His Son, Jesus Christ, as King of kings and Lord of lords; and hereby ordain that no law shall be passed by the Congress of these Confederate States inconsistent with the will of God, as revealed in the Holy Scriptures.[75]

Thornwell argued that though "the will of God, as revealed in the Scriptures, is not a positive Constitution for the State,"[76] yet the State must believe the Scriptures "to be true, and regulate its own conduct and legislation in conformity with their teachings."[77] (Note that this is the position of Bahnsen and Rushdoony.) Beyond these general statements Thornwell does not go, yet his emphasis that modern civil law should be tied to and regulated by Scripture makes it hard to believe he could have held the kind of negative opinion regarding the Mosaic judicials that is sometimes encountered today. He was surely no "pluralist."[78]

Robert L. Dabney, like Ridgeley, nowhere in his works explicitly states that the judicial law of God is binding, yet seems to assume it as a principle in his writings. In his *Lectures in Systematic Theology* he cites the Older Testament capital punishments for murder, striking parents, adultery, and religious imposture, without any hint that he thought these had ceased to bind nations.[79] With respect to adultery, his statement is explicit:

> The law of Moses, therefore, very properly made adultery a capital crime; nor does our Saviour, in the incident of the woman taken in adultery, repeal that statute, or disallow its justice. The legislation of modern, nominally Christian nations, is drawn

rather from the grossness of Pagan sources than from Bible principles.[80]

This statement, especially in reference to "nominally Christian nations," makes it evident that, in Dabney's view, a genuinely Christian nation would draw its legislation from the law of God, including the penal particulars, rather than from pagan sources. *Dabney here explicitly disagrees with Calvin's notions of a "common law of nations."* Pagan sources are *contrasted* with Biblical law.

Dabney's view is further elaborated and brought into sharper focus in his discussion of the *lex talionis.*

> The application of the *lex talionis* made by Moses against false witnesses was the most appropriate and equitable ever invented. Whatever pain or penalty the false swearing would have brought on the innocent man maligned had the law followed the false witness unprotected, that penalty must be visited on the perjurer maligning him.

> Let the student compare the admirable symmetry of Moses' provision with the bungling operation of our statute against perjury. He discriminates the different grades of guilt with exact justice. We punish the perjurer who swears away his neighbor's cow with imprisonment, and the perjurer who swears away his neighbor's honor and life, still with imprisonment.[81]

Conclusion

Three matters of interest to modern Calvinists have emerged from this study. The first is that the apparent condemnation of the whole-law position by Calvin in his *Institutes* almost certainly does not apply to modern theonomists, who stand with Bucer, not with the Anabaptists. The second is that the Westminster Confession of Faith and the Catechisms do not condemn the whole-law position, but to a considerable degree presuppose it. The third is that during the period of Calvinism's greatest strength there were many, and often the most notable theologians were among them, who advocated the same position taken by Rushdoony and Bahnsen today.

This demonstrates that the theonomic-theocratic position is *not* "outside the Reformed tradition," as some have charged.

Earlier editions of this study have circulated here and there, and one verbal response has been made to it which requires attention at this point. It has been contended that, whereas these earlier Calvinists stressed that the "Mosaic judicials" could not be improved upon and thus should be followed, Bahnsen and Rushdoony argue from Matthew 5:17-19 that every jot and tittle of the Older Testament law is binding on Christians, save for the "ceremonial" laws, which the New Covenant altered. Bucer's argument, it is contended, is based on reason, while Bahnsen's is based on exegesis.

In reply we simply note that there is no conflict between these two routes, both of which lead to an identical conclusion. Both Bucer and Bahnsen (to continue to use these men as examples) hold that the judicial aspect of God's law is a revelation of his eternal standards. Both hold that these laws are binding on modern magistrates. The fact that Bahnsen's arguments are primarily exegetical while Bucer's are primarily rational only demonstrates what Christians have always maintained, that there is no conflict between Scripture and reason. One can divide Bucer from Bahnsen only by pitting reason against revelation.

Additionally, it should be noted that the whole-law position asserts that the judicial aspects of the law of God are part of the moral law, and thus are written on the hearts of all men (*Rom. 1:32*). Upon conversion, men stop suppressing the law written on their hearts, and the more men grow in grace, under the Spirit's influence, the more responsive to that law they become. The Reformation was a great movement of the Spirit. The fact that during the period after the Reformation, when Christianity was at a height, the judicial aspects of the law of God were widely regarded as binding is thus very significant. It indicates that there *is* moral equity in these laws, and serves as a general and indirect substantiation of the theonomic or whole-law position.

The fact that discussions of this subject in the past have not been as clear as today's discussion is becoming, only demonstrates the validity of the remark by William Cunningham, the eminent church historian, regarding the nature of theological controversy.

It holds most universally in the history of the church, that until a doctrine has been fully discussed in a controversial way by men of talent and learning taking opposite sides, men's opinions regarding it are generally obscure and indefinite, and their language vague and confused, if not contradictory.[82]

---

[1] Rousas J. Rushdoony, *Institutes of Biblical Law* (Nutley, NJ, 1974); Greg L. Bahnsen, *Theonomy in Christian Ethics* (Nutley, NJ, 1977).

[2] In *The Presbyterian Journal*, Aug. 31, 1977, 18.

[3] A treatment that borders on ridicule is G. Aiken Taylor, "Theonomy and Christian Behavior," in *The Presbyterian Journal*, Sept. 13, 1978, 9ff.

[4] Cf. note 1 above.

[5] These notions are set forth in germinal form in Meredith Kline, *The Structure of Biblical Authority* (Grand Rapids, 1972). Kline's theology is a neo-dispensationalism as rigorous as anything generated from the Scofieldian camp.

[6] Cf. note 1 above.

[7] No one has yet argued that it is against the "soprano" of the New Testament.

[8] Caruso's biography would be an exception, of course.

[9] Cf. Bucer, *De Regno Christi*, bk. 2, chap. 60, reprinted elsewhere in this issue.

[10] John Calvin, *Institutes of the Christian Religion*, trans. Ford L. Battles (Philadelphia, 1975), 4:20:14.

[11] John Calvin, *Commentaries*, trans. C. W. Bingham (Grand Rapids, 1950), *ad* Deuteronomy 22:22.

[12] Cited in Philip Schaff, *History of the Christian Church* (Grand Rapids, 1950), 8:791f., emphasis added. Calvin is referring throughout to Deuteronomy 13:6-10.

[13] *ibid.*, 792.

[14] Cf. Bucer, *De Regno Christi*, bk. 2, chap. 60, in the *Journal of Christian Reconstruction*, vol. 5, no. 2, Winter, 1978-79.

[15] From Bucer, *Scripta Anglicana*, ed. Conrad Hubertus (Basle, 1577); trans. John Milton in *The Judgment of Martin Bucer Concerning Divorce* (1644). Cf. *Complete Prose Works of John Milton* (New Haven, Yale, 1959), II, 422. Spelling and punctuation modernized and emphasis added. Further praise of Bucer by Calvin can be found in Calvin's prefaces to his own commentaries on Romans, Psalms, and the Gospels.

[16] Wilhelm Pauck, "Editor's Introduction to Bucer's *De Regno Christi*," in *Melanchthon and Bucer*, Library or Christian Classics XIX (Philadelphia, 1959), 157.

[17] Wilhelm Pauck, "Butzer and Calvin," in *The Heritage of the Reformation*, 1st ed. (Glencoe, IL, 1950), 88.

[18] *ibid.*

[19] Bucer, *De Regno Christi*, bk. 2, chap. 60, second paragraph.

[20] *ibid.*, bk. 2, chap. 28; trans. Milton. Cf. note 15. In *Milton's Prose Works*, II, 456.

[21] *ibid.*, bk. 2, chap. 60, first paragraph, trans. Pauck. Cf. note 16.

[22] B. S. Capp, *The Fifth Monarchy Men* (Totowa, N J, 1972), 169f.

[23] Philip Schaff, *The Creeds of Christendom* (Grand Rapids, 1966), III, 412f., 432.

[24] Miles Coverdale, *The Old Faith*, Parker Society edition (Cambridge, [1541] 1844), 47f.

[25] Schaff, III, 855.

[26] *ibid.*, III, 907f.

[27] Parker Society edition (Cambridge, 1850), Decade 3, 280.

[28] *ibid.*, 282.

[29] *ibid.*, 218.

[30] *ibid.*, 280f.

[31] John Hooper, "A Declaration of the Ten Commandments," in *Early Writings of Bishop John Hooper*, Parker Society edition (Cambridge, 1843), 376.

[32] Hugh Latimer, *Sermons*, Parker Society edition (Cambridge, 1844), 85. The quotation is taken from a sermon preached before Edward VI on March 8, 1549.

[33] J. W. Blench, *Preaching in England in the Late Fifteenth and Sixteenth Centuries* (Oxford, 1964), 274.

[34] Thomas Becon, *Catechism*, Parker Society edition (Cambridge, 1844), 310.

[35] *ibid.*, 311.

[36] *ibid.*, 312.

[37] For a summary of Puritan attitudes toward the law of God, cf. Bahnsen, *Theonomy*, Appendix 3.

[38] Capp, *Fifth Monarchy of Men*, 168f.

[39] Thomas M'Crie, *Life of John Knox* (Glasgow, [1811] 1976), 216.

[40] Thomas Cartwright, *Second Reply* [1575], cited in *Works of John Whitgift*, Parker Society edition (Cambridge, 1851), I, 270, emphasis added.

[41] Cited in Capp, 169.

[42] Rossell H. Robbins, *Encyclopedia of Witchcraft and Demonology* (New York, 1959), 382, emphasis added.

[43] William Perkins, *A Discourse on the Damned Art of Witchcraft*, in John Chandos, ed., *In God's Name* (New York, 1971), 135.

[44]Cf. Thomas Rogers, *Exposition of the Thirty-nine Articles*, Parker Society edition (Cambridge, 1854), 90.

[45] *Dictionary of National Biography* (Oxford, 1968), XIX, 120.

[46]Cf. Rogers, *Exposition*, 91.

[47] *Reformed Dogmatics*, trans. And ed. John W. Beardslee III (New York, 1965), 10.

[48] *ibid.*, 84.

[49]For a discussion of the views of Samuel Rutherford, the reader is directed to the essay by Richard Flinn, in the *Journal of Christian Reconstruction*, vol. 5, no. 2, Winter, 1978-79.

[50]John Owen, *Works* (London, 1967), VIII, 394, emphasis added. The Latin phrase means, "guardian, vindicator, and manager of the judicial law, and of the constitution of Moses."

[51]Cited in Capp, 171.

[52]Cf. Bahnsen, *Theonomy*, Appendix 3, consisting of an introduction by Bahnsen to Cotton's work, and of the text of Cotton's *Abstract*. These have been reprinted in the *Journal of Christian Reconstruction*, vol. 5, no. 2, Winter, 1978-79. For a corroboration of Bahnsen's opinion that the *Abstract* is really a later edition of *Moses His Judicials*, cf. Worthington C. Ford's discussion in the *Transactions of the Massachusetts Historical Society*, Second Series, XVI (October, 1902), 274-280.

[53]"How far Moses Judicials bind Mass[achusetts]," *Transactions of the Massachusetts Historical Society*, Second Series, XVI (October, 1902), 280-284.

[54] Thomas Shepard, *The Morality of the Sabbath*, in *Works* (Boston, 1853), III, 53f.

[55] *Compact Edition of the Oxford English Dictionary* (Oxford, 1971), I, 888.

[56]Shepard, III, 289, 340.

[57]John Eliot, *The Christian Commonwealth* (New York, 1972).

[58]Convers Francis, *Life of John Eliot* (Boston, 1836), 210.

[59]The office of *tithingman*, established in 1675, divided Massachusetts into groups of ten families for certain governmental purposes. Cf. Edmund S. Morgan, *The Puritan Family* (New York, 1966), 148f.

[60]Capp, 167f.

[61]Charles Hoadly, ed., *Records of the Colony and Plantation of New Haven from 1638 to 1649* (Hartford: for the Editor, 1857), 69.

[62]Thomas Hutchinson, *The History of the Colony and Province of Massachusetts Bay*, ed. Lawrence S. Mayo (New York, 1970 [1836-1864]), I, 371ff.

[63] *ibid.*, I, 367.

[64]Thomas Jefferson Wertenbaker, *The Puritan Oligarchy* (New York, 1947), 166.

[65] Hutchinson, II, 354.

[66] (New York: Johnson reprint, 1969).

[67] *idem.*

[68] Samuel Sewell, *Diary*, ed. M. Halsey Thomas (New York, 1973), 4.

[69] *ibid.*, 380.

[70] John Witherspoon, *Works* (Philadelphia, 1800), III, 356f.

[71] Thomas Ridgeley, *A Body of Divinity* (New York, 1855), II, 307f.

[72] *ibid.*, II, 386ff.

[73] Thomas Scott, *Holy Bible with Notes* (Philadelphia, 1807), at "Notes on Ex. 21:2." Emphasis added.

[74] *ibid.*, at "Practical Observations on Ex. 22:1-15." Emphasis added.

[75] James H. Thornwell, "Relation of the State to Christ," in *Collected Writings* (Edinburgh, 1974), IV, 549ff.

[76] *ibid.*, 553.

[77] *ibid.*, 552.

[78] On the supposedly Thornwellian concept of the "Spirituality of the Church," as well as on Southern Presbyterian theocratic views in general, cf. Jack P. Maddex, "From Theocracy to Spirituality: The Southern Presbyterian Reversal on Church and State," *Journal of Presbyterian History* 54 (1976), 438-457.

[79] Robert L. Dabney, *Lectures in Systematic Theology* (Grand Rapids, [1898] 1972), 402f.

[80] *ibid.*, 407f. See also his *The Practical Philosophy* (Mexico, MO, 1896), 362f.

[81] *The Practical Philosophy*, 513f.

[82] William Cunningham, *Historical Theology* (London, 1969), I, 179.

Volume 12, No. 2, 1989
Translation and Subversion
by Rev. R. J. Rushdoony

The publication of a new translation of the Bible should be an occasion for rejoicing. The availability of Scripture in a new language, or a fresh rendering in "modern dress" for people already possessing the Bible, can be of great importance in propagating the Faith. *The Faith*, this indeed is the central motive in many contemporary versions, but by no means all. At least two other motives are important factors on the contemporary scene: *first*, a financial motive and, *second*, an anti-Christian religious motive.

The Profit in Bibles

A profit motive is, in its place, a godly aspect of life, by no means to be condemned unless it transgresses the laws of God. Without faith, every aspect of life is under condemnation, all life then is out of focus, and things, in themselves pure, become impure in the hands of the ungodly.

As is well known, the Bible is the consistent best-seller. The annual sale of millions of copies makes it therefore a phenomenal sales item. Its potentiality as a money-maker is thus enormous, almost staggering to the economically minded imagination. But one very serious drawback exists: the Bible, in its most popular English form, the King James Version, is not subject to copyright. Any publisher can print it and enter into a highly competitive field where the margin of profit must be kept very low for competitive reasons. The handicaps thus are very real, although several publishers have regularly counted on their Bible sales for assured profits. Is it any wonder, therefore, that publishers, among others, have come to recognize the tremendous potentialities of a *copyrighted Bible*? A copyrighted Bible is thus a major bonanza to publishers and a financial and prestigious asset to scholars participating as translators and editors. Not every new translation has been a money-making scheme, but many of them have clearly had this motive as among their central ones. It is no wonder that new versions are thus often front-page news; the advertising and promotion behind a major version make it a financial asset to many media. *Possession* of a copyright is again a major affair and, in one recent case, was a subject of legal battle. Thus, the Revised Standard Version is copyrighted by the Division of Christian Education of the National Council of the Churches of Christ in the United States of America, and first published by Thomas Nelson and Sons in New York, Toronto, and Edinburgh. Because many evangelicals regarded this version as "Modernist" in character, in 1962, a "study" edition was put out by the A. J. Holman Company of Philadelphia, with 59 evangelical scholars giving their evangelical "imprimatur" to it by means of brief introductions and articles. *The unstated fact* is that, with every copy and every edition, the profit goes to the Division of Christian Education of the National Council of the Churches of Christ. The National Council has thus a source of income now entirely apart from any donations by member churches. It has an invested interest in a particular Bible. The use of this Bible is thus promoted in a variety of circles. It is used for responsive readings in hymnals and in Sunday school lessons. The Holman Study Bible was given away as a subscription premium by *Christianity Today*, ostensibly a voice of evangelical Christianity. "New Bibles" are big money and their by-products are likewise profitable. They are used in newer commentaries by permission to further their popularity and concordances suggest their durability. With all the money at stake in new versions, is it any wonder that people are urged, to their confusion, to believe in the necessity for new versions?

Revision, Translation, or Paraphrase?

It might be well to note here a further area of confusion. The Revised Standard Version claims to be a revision of the King James Version, *i.e.*, not a new translation but merely the King James corrected and modernized. Oswald T. Allis, in *Revision or New Translation* (Presbyterian and Reformed Publishing Company, 1948), has called attention to the fact that it is closer often to a new translation by unconservative scholars. In *Recent Revised Versions*, Dr. Allis extended his critique to the New English Bible.

New translations, moreover, tend to follow radical readings of erroneous or "wastebasket" texts in preference to standard readings.

With each new version, the number of departures from the Received Text is steadily increasing. The sales value of these new versions, judging by some promotional material, seems to depend on new and novel readings. There is, in the minds of some buyers at least, a premium on newness and on departures from the "old Bible." With some, there is almost a hopeful note that the newer Bibles might gradually convert "Thou shalt not commit adultery" to "Thou shalt commit adultery"! New versions, of various qualities of good and bad, are purchased by many persons almost as fetish objects and remain unread.

But many of the new versions are not *translations*: they are *paraphrases*. What is the difference? A translation is an exact and literal rendering of the original Greek or Hebrew into English. A paraphrase tries to put the original thought into modern thought forms. One of the most popular liberal paraphrasers today is J. B. Phillips. A paraphrase can be a very valuable help at times, but it can never substitute for a translation. Thus, Edgar J. Goodspeed renders Matthew 5:3, "Blessed are the poor in spirit," as "Blessed are those who feel their spiritual need." This is brilliant and telling; it gives us a vivid grasp of the meaning, but unfortunately Goodspeed, while giving us a few such gems, also neutralizes many of the basic theological terms of the New Testament with weak paraphrases.

The King James Version is not a paraphrase. It is both a revision of earlier translations in part and a new translation in its day.

Archaic Language

One of the charges consistently leveled against the King James Version is that its language is archaic and obsolete. The answer is a simple one: it is intended to be. In 1611 the King James Version was as "out of date" as it is today. Compare the writings of Shakespeare, Ben Jonson, King James I, and John Lyly with the King James Version and this becomes quickly apparent. The translators *avoided* the speech of their day for a basic English which would be simple, timeless, and beautiful, and they succeeded. Their version spoke from outside their age and tradition with elemental simplicity. Their wisdom here exceeds that of their successors. Nothing seems more ridiculous than an outdated "modern" translation. Let us examine William Mace, 1729, as he rendered James 3:5-6:

> The tongue is but a small part of the body, yet how grand are its pretensions! a spark of fire! what quantities of timber will it blow into flame? the tongue is a brand that sets the world into a combustion; it is but one of the numerous organs of the body, yet it can blast whole assemblies. Tipped with infernal sulphur it sets the whole train of life in a blaze.

In 1768, Dr. Edward Harwood's *Liberal Translation of the New Testament, i.e.*, a paraphrase, rendered Luke 15:11, "A certain man had two sons," as "A gentleman of splendid family oppulent fortune had two sons." This is clearly an extreme instance, but it does illustrate a point: if we consider our age and its requirements as *normative*, we can involve ourselves in absurdities. And such absurdities are not missing from the various versions. The critic Dwight Macdonald has called attention to some of these in the Revised Standard Version in a *New Yorker* article, "The Bible in Modern Undress" (*New Yorker*, Nov. 14, 1953, vol. XXIX, no. 39, 183-208). Macdonald comments on the R. S. V., by way of conclusion, "Whether it will be any more successful in replacing K. J. V. than the 1885 version was remains to be seen. If it is, what is now simply a blunder—a clerical error, so to speak—will become a catastrophe. Bland, favorless mediocrity will have replaced the pungency of genius" (208).

The issue is not that the Bible should speak our every-day language, for this involves debasement, but that it should be *understandable* and here, all arguments to the contrary notwithstanding, the King James speaks a language which, while sometimes difficult because the matter itself is so, is more often simple, clear-cut, and beautiful. Some modern versions are very helpful, but none equal the King James in its clarity and memorable beauty. The greatest single demerit of the King James Version is simply this: it is not copyrighted and, hence, no organization and no scholar can profit thereby.

A Trustworthy Translation

The question of a *trustworthy* translation is all-important, especially since novelty is increasingly characteristic of many new translations. Which translation is a trustworthy one?

At this point, it needs to be noted that all translations face certain perplexing problems. The meanings of certain Hebrew words are uncertain, and the exact identity of many plants and animals subject to debate. With these details, we are not concerned. The marginal readings of a good edition are helpful in clarifying meanings or giving alternate translations at difficult points.

The important question is in another area. What *text* of the Bible is being translated? In answering this question, let it be noted, we are departing from virtually all accepted scholarship. This however, does not trouble us, for, after all, the major break with "accepted" scholarship comes with acceptance of Christ as Lord and Savior, and the Bible as the inspired and infallible word of God.

Since the days of Westcott and Hort, textual criticism has applied to Biblical textual criticism a rigorously alien category of thought and "an essentially naturalistic method." (See Edward F. Hills' introduction to John W. Burgon, *The Last Twelve Verses of the Gospel According to St. Mark* [Jenkinstown, PA, 1959], 40f. and 66; and Edward F. Hills, *The King James Version Defended!* [Des Moines, Iowa, 1956].) This scholarship assumes man to be autonomous and ultimate rather than God; and it requires all documents to meet the same naturalistic tests with respect to their nature and history. Nothing which is not true or possible of Homer's *Iliad* can be posited thus for the Bible and its books. Moreover, this method is applied to the Bible with a certainty and omniscience lacking in the determination, for example, of composite authorship in Shakespeare's plays, where we often know he had collaborators.

As Hills has pointed out, the doctrine of the sacred origin and preservation of Scripture is a part of the "General doctrine of the Scriptures concerning the controlling providence of God." "He worketh all things according to the counsel of his own will" (*Eph. 1:11*). This providential preservation of the text, Hills has maintained, as an expert in New Testament manuscripts, is to be seen in the standard text of the New Testament translated in the King James Version.

It is not our concern here to enter into the intricacies of textual criticism, nor are we qualified to do so. But we are qualified to assert that most current criticism, both "conservative" and "liberal," rests on a *radically non-Christian philosophy* which cannot bear other than implicity or explicity anti-Christian fruit.

Another Religion in New Translations

Are the variations in the new translations simply minor differences in wording or do they conceal a new religion? To answer this question, let us examine Genesis 1:1, 2, first of all in three older translations: the King James (Protestant), the Douay (Roman Catholic), and the Holy Scriptures according to the Masoretic Text of the Jewish Publication Society (Old Testament, 1917, 1955, 1961); then let us examine *The Torah, the Five Books of Moses* (Jewish Publication Society, 1962) and the Doubleday Anchor translation, prepared by "more than 30 Catholic, Protestant and Jewish scholars" (*Time*, September 27, 1963, 48, 50):

> *King James:* In the beginning God created the heaven and the earth. And the earth was without form, and void; and darkness was upon the face of the deep. And the Spirit of God moved upon the face of the waters.

> *Douay:* In the beginning God created the heaven and earth. And the earth was void and empty, and darkness was upon the face of the deep. And the spirit of God moved over the waters.

> *Approved Version, Jewish Publication Society, 1917:* In the beginning God created the heaven and earth. Now the earth was unformed and void, and darkness was upon the face of the deep; and the spirit God hovered over the face of the waters.

> *Torah, 1962:* When God began to create the heaven and the earth—the earth being unformed and void, with darkness over the surface of the deep and a wind from God sweeping over the water—God said, "Let there be light"; and there was light. (*v. 3 included*)

> *Anchor:* When God set about to create heaven and earth—the world being then a formless waste, with darkness over the seas and only an awesome wind sweeping over the water—God said, "Let there be light," and there was light. (*v. 3 included*)

As Edward J. Young has noted in "The Interpretation of Genesis 1:2" (*The Westminster Theological Journal*, May, 1961), this passage has been used to try to introduce mythology into Moses' account.

The conservatism of the first three translations, especially the first two, is apparent. These are, of course, older translations. In the King James and Douay, Genesis 1:1 and 2 are three separate sentences and the first sentence is a separate paragraph. Now paragraphing is a form of interpretation in itself, as is sentence formation. To set "In the beginning God created the heaven and the earth" in a separate form is to declare in effect that this sentence is either an introduction to the account of creation, or a summary statement of creation, or both. It declares God to be the Creator, and then the *details* of the acts of creation are given to us.

But, in the Torah and Anchor versions, verse 1 is made into a *subordinate* clause, "When God began to create the heaven and the earth," and "When God set about to create heaven and earth." This now ceases to be a completed statement of fact. Instead, we are now told *what the condition of the universe was* "when God began to create," namely, that at least one segment of it was "a formless waste" and, as we learn subsequently, this "unformed and void" earth was *not created* but *developed* by God. As a result, instead of Biblical theism, we have the ancient pagan *dualism*, the co-eternity of God and matter. The great void of being, the unformed chaos of matter, always existed, in this philosophy, and God did not create it; he merely acted on it, with varying degrees of success. Thus, in the new "translations" of Genesis 1:1, 2, we have substituted for Biblical theism *an alien religion!* We have a god very different from and sharply limited in contrast to the God of Scripture. Translation here has become the vehicle of a new religion, the instrument of the proclamation of "other gods," an instrument of idolatry.

The net result of this new "translation" is, to repeat, another god than the God of Scripture. It is a god similar to that of illuminist tradition and of Masonry. The Cardinal of Chile, in *The Mystery of Freemasonry Unveiled*, described this god aptly:

> The god creator, or the god of Masonry, is not the God Creator of Christians. The Architect constructs the building with

materials which he did not make, but which he finds already made; the Creator constructs the edifice of the world, not with foreign or ready made substance but with materials which he himself made from nothing. (72)

It should be noted that the Torah Version gives the older accepted readings as footnotes.

In the Torah Version, "the spirit of God" in v. 2 becomes "a wind from God" and in Anchor it becomes "an awesome wind." The Holy Spirit is thus eliminated from creation.

In the Torah Version, Genesis 1:26 reads: "And God said, 'I will make man in My image, after my likeness.'" The footnote adds that this is, *literally*, "Let us make man in our image, after our likeness." This change is justified on the grounds that the Hebrew plural form here are simply "plurals of majesty." But the fact remains that the Hebrew text gives a plural form and that *Elohim*, a plural noun for God, literally *Gods*, takes, when used for Jehovah, a singular verb. Many Christian scholars have rightly seen in this an evidence of the *plurality* of the Godhead and of its *unity*, a definite witness to trinitarianism. Modern translators may disagree; but they have no right to mistranslate the text, which, as admitted, reads, "Let us make man in our image, after our likeness." Such novel and unwarranted renderings of words can be destructive of meaning and of doctrine. Thus, Genesis 3:15 reads, respectively, in Joseph Bryant Rotherham, in King James, and in the Torah version:

> *Rotherham, 1897:* And enmity will I put between thee and the woman, and between thy seed and her seed—He shall crush thy head, But thou shalt crush his heel.

> *King James:* And I will put enmity between thee and the woman, and between thy seed and her seed; it shall bruise thy head, and thou shalt bruise his heel.

> *Torah, 1962:* I will put enmity Between you and the woman, And between your offspring and hers; hey shall strike at your head, And you shall strike at their heel.

In the Torah Version by changing the number of "seed" or

"offspring" from singular to plural, the reference is radically changed in this prophecy. It can no longer mean Christ, who is singular, but refers to the plural offspring of the woman, to the faithful or to Israel. We are thus pointed to another Savior.

By such changes, often too slight for many readers to detect, new meanings are read into the Scripture, and another bible and other gods appear on the scene. And each new version, irrespective of its source, seems bent on surpassing the previous ones in its adoption of novelties.

An important consideration for Christians in evaluating new versions is this: consider the source. Can unbelievers, modernists, men with left-wing records, and men faithless to their ordination vows be expected to produce good fruit? Our Lord stated it clearly:

> Ye shall know them by their fruits. Do men gather grapes of thorns, or figs of thistles? Even so every good tree bringeth forth good fruit; but a corrupt tree bringeth forth evil fruit.
>
> A good tree cannot bring forth evil fruit, neither can a corrupt tree bring forth good fruit. (*Mt. 7:16-28*)

Volume 14, No. 2, 1997

A Presuppositional Approach to Ecclesiastical Tradition[1]

by P. Andrew Sandlin

Tradition is the living faith of the dead; traditionalism is the dead faith of the living.

Jaroslav Pelikan[2]

Introduction

"We Baptists don't believe in tradition," remarked a wily minister with a twinkle in his eye: "It's contrary to our historic position." That humorous anecdote underscores a crucial fact about tradition: it is unavoidable. All churches—all religions in fact—possess traditions. The most ardent Pentecostal or fundamentalist that eschews the very word, manifests religious tradition—Pentecostal or fundamentalist tradition if no other—in his religious practice, ecclesiastical or otherwise.

As Tonsor recognizes, the inevitability of tradition in general, the human phenomenon of which ecclesiastical tradition is but a single species, constitutes a chief factor in the eventual destruction of revolutionary ideologies, so potent is its cultural force, for "both nature and culture make nearly impossible the complete destruction of tradition."[3] Its force cements an otherwise atomistic society, and religion is one of its single key ingredients. It may seem odd, therefore, that a sector of Christendom so assertedly dedicated to the preservation of culture, Protestantism, would have such an apparently dim view of ecclesiastical tradition.

Almost all distaste for ecclesiastical tradition on the part of Protestants and radical reformers[4] issues from a reaction to the accumulated unbiblical traditions of Roman Catholicism and, to a lesser extent, Eastern Orthodoxy. It is difficult, in fact, to avoid the conclusion that the attitude toward tradition by the early reformers and subsequent Reformed orthodoxy was shaped almost entirely by a negative reaction to Romanism. However, if from our historical vantage point, our sixteenth- and seventeenth-century forebears lacked an objective, dispassionate assessment of tradition, we can forgive their iconoclastic fervor. They were convinced—as we should be convinced—that as an objective and authoritative truth deposit, Holy Scripture may have no rivals, as it did and does in Romanism.

To this point I have used the word *tradition* as though its meaning in this context were self-evident, but it is not at all clear that its definition even in such an ecclesiastical context is unequivocal. If, for instance, I say, "It is our church's tradition always to partake of the sacrament and communion *after* the public confession of sin and recitation of the Apostles' Creed," few Protestants would raise objection to either the designation of such actions as tradition or to the employment of the term in that context. On the other hand, if I remark, "Tradition requires of our church to offer homage to the Blessed Virgin and to venerate images," I would suffer more than raised eyebrows from a virtually all-Protestant audience.

In the first instance, tradition refers merely to the ordering of certain practices either mandated in the Scriptures or explicative *of* the Scriptures. The term *policy* or *practice* could not validly be substituted for tradition, because these actions and their ordering involve much more than discretionary activity. We believe the Bible *requires* public confession of sin and the partaking of the sacrament and *implies* the necessity of public profession of faith as well as the partaking of communion after such profession of faith and after the confession of sin. In the second instance, however, tradition seems to imply much more—it assumes there is some binding authority inherent in tradition itself, or perhaps even that tradition is an independent source of divine revelation, or at least in some way God's will.

The two usages employed above instance a distinction that the reformers and their immediate heirs understood, wittingly or not, and a distinction their Roman counterparts were less likely to observe. The Reformed recognized there is a vast difference between tradition as an inescapable feature of religion and tradition as an independent source of religious authority. This distinction, they judged, issued from Scripture itself.

Tradition in the Scriptures

Biblically, tradition is either that which is handed down from one person or one generation to another or, in its verb form, the act of handing down. Although tradition seems essential to the preservation of the Jewish faith (*e.g.*, *Ex. 12:26*f.; *Is. 59:21*), the Greek words communicating the idea of tradition in the New Testament are found rarely in the Septuagint and the word itself is not found in the Hebrew in the sense under consideration.[5] The majority of usages of the term *tradition* in the New Testament are unfavorable. Five times in Mark 7, for example, tradition (*paradosis*) is contrasted unfavorably with the message of the law; it constitutes a Judaic appendage to—and eventually a substitute for—God's inscripturated old covenant document. Christ reprimands the Pharisees thus: "Full well ye reject the commandment of God, that ye may keep your own tradition" (*Mk. 7:9*). In Galatians 1:14 St. Paul reminds the church of his misguided reverence for the Jewish tradition. In Colossians 2:8 he refers to and excoriates the spurious "revelations of the elemental spirits of the universe,"[6] perhaps a sort of gnosticism into which some of the Colossians had fallen.

The commendatory usage of tradition in Scripture seemingly always connotes the transmission and preservation of the Faith as disclosed in objective divine revelation. Hence St. Paul exhorts the believers to "keep the ordinances [traditions]" that he had transmitted to them (*1 Cor. 11:2*), to "stand fast, and hold the traditions which ye have been taught, whether by word, or our epistle" (*2 Thes. 2:15*).[7] The contrast between tradition favorable and unfavorable is that the content of the former is limited to the Scriptures themselves, while the content of the latter contains a mixture of Biblical and unbiblical dogma and regulations. On the face of it, this distinction seems not only too neat, but also too optimistic, as though the maintenance of tradition is nothing more than the preservation of the text of Scripture. It must be recalled, however, that the Scriptures speak with equal frequency and clarity of the transmission of the Faith itself. In St. Paul's exhortation to Timothy, "And the things that thou has heard of me among many witnesses, the same commit thou to faithful men, who shall be able to teach others also" (*2 Tim. 2:2*), the object of transmission seems to be not merely the divine revelation communicated to him, and the text of Scripture, but the Christian Faith itself. This is the obvious denotation in Jude 3, in which the writer notes that "the faith which was once delivered to the saints" must be defended against sly but pernicious attacks.

If we combine these two denotations of tradition, we derive a definition which conceives of it as the faithful transmission of the Christian Faith as circumscribed exclusively by the Holy Scriptures. (This is, I suspect, not coincidentally the idea the reformers had in mind.) The Bible again and again exhorts Christians to transmit the Faith untarnished and undiluted to their own generation and especially generations subsequent.

Tradition in the Patristic Church

It is not surprising, then, that the patristic church maintained a high view of tradition. Those are gravely mistaken, in fact, who assume that an indispensable role accorded to ecclesiastical tradition was a phenomenon emerging only in the later patristic church, as though the apostles and very early church fathers were nothing more than bare biblicists and that their immediate successors polluted the fount of primitive Christianity with human traditions. From almost the very first, "catholic tradition" was held in high esteem. Schaff observes of the second- and third-century church:

> Besides appealing to the Scriptures, the fathers, particularly Irenaeus and Tertullian, refer with equal confidence to the "rule of faith;" that is, the common faith of the church, as orally handed down in the unbroken succession of bishops from Christ and his apostles to their day, and above all as still living in the original apostolic churches, like those of Jerusalem, Antioch, Ephesus, and Rome. Tradition is thus intimately connected with the primitive episcopate. The latter was the vehicle of the former, and both were looked upon as bulwarks against heresy.[8]

Indeed, perhaps, the *chief* service to which the patristic church put tradition was as a bulwark against heresy. Florovsky notes of the orthodox battle with the early heresy of Arianism:

> The dispute with the Arians was centered again in the exegetical field—at least, in its early phase. The Arians and their supporters have produced an impressive array of scriptural texts in the defense of their doctrinal position. They wanted to restrict

theological discussion to the Biblical ground alone. Their claims had to be met precisely on this ground, first of all. And their exegetical method, the manner in which they handled the text, was much the same as that of the earlier dissenters. They were operating with selected proof-texts, without much concern for the total context of the Revelation. It was imperative for the Orthodox to appeal to the mind of the Church, to that "Faith" which had been once delivered and then faithfully kept. This was the main concern, and the usual method, of St. Athanasius.[9]

It is perhaps difficult for us moderns suckled on Renaissance and Enlightenment ideals and the resultant pluralism and atomization, to conceive of the importance the early church fathers attached to "one holy catholic church." Both the Great Schism between the East and the West, and the Reformation in the West, destroyed the unity of the Christian church. Previously a cardinal tenet of religions was the unity of the Faith in the church, preserved generationally in tradition. Tradition was not merely a correlate or appendage to the Faith of the church; it was in fact the very essence of the institutional representation of the church: "Pelikan notes that the orthodox consensus of tradition that shaped patristic Christianity—East and West—consisted of catholicity, confessionalism, and antiquity.[10] For example, 'In the usage of Eusebius, the terms orthodox, ancient, and ecclesiastical were almost interchangeable.'[11] The patristic church did not sharply distinguish between Scripture and tradition, the teaching of the apostles and that of the ecumenical councils, for it assumed the faithful transmission of Christian tradition was in fact nothing more than fidelity to Scripture itself. It did not seem to occur to them that what we Protestants term *sola Scriptura* could conflict with the views of the church catholic."[12]

Tradition in the Reformation and the Roman Response

In time, of course, such a conflict was apparent—at least to some willing to take on the authoritarian Papacy of medieval Romanism. It is not difficult to see how the *essential* devotion to tradition conduced readily to a devotion to tradition as an almost independent source of revelation, or at least an independent authority. This incremental emergency of an independently authoritative tradition coincided with an increase in the authority of the church, since the church was seen as the repository of the genuine Christian tradition. It was against this concept of tradition that the reformers' dictum of *sola Scriptura* was leveled.

The reformers did not depict Scripture as simply a valid form of inscripturated tradition and thus attempt to re-capture and sanitize tradition for a Protestant cause,[13] probably because they accepted the Roman definition of tradition as unwritten, in contradistinction to Scripture. When we peruse the writings of the reformers, in fact, we detect on the face of them what appears to be a quite distinct break with *all* doctrinal and ecclesiastical tradition. Calvin, for example, wishes to "fix the boundary of [the church's] wisdom where Christ has made an end of speaking" in his word,[14] and accords to the infallible Holy Spirit the place the Romanists accord to an infallible church. Yet it cannot be forgotten that:

> The phenomenon of Tradition ... had already become apparent in the theology of the Reformers in their acceptance of early church dogma, as well as in the crystallization of their own doctrinal Tradition in written creeds.[15]

Recall, moreover, that the reformers' frequent employment of the writings of the early church fathers to accuse the medieval Roman church of defection from true catholicism is itself a reliance on tradition. After all, if *sola Scriptura* entails the repudiation of all tradition whatsoever, an appeal to the church fathers hardly seems necessary.

The Roman Catholic Church codified its response to the Reformation hostility toward the authority of ecclesiastical tradition at the Council of Trent. In its fourth session it set forth the authority of oral tradition:

> ... seeing clearly that this [divine] truth and discipline are contained in the written books, and the unwritten traditions which, received by the Apostles from the mouth of Christ himself, or from the apostles themselves, the Holy Ghost

dictating, have come down even unto us, transmitted as it were from hand to hand: [the Synod] following the examples of the orthodox fathers, receives and venerates with an equal affection of piety and reverence, all the books of both the Old and New Testament—seeing that one God is the author of both—as also the said [unwritten] traditions, as well those appertaining to faith as to morals, as having been dictated, either by Christ's own word of mouth, or by the Holy Ghost, and preserved in the Catholic church by a continuous succession.[16]

This systemization of the regnant Roman idea of tradition reveals a subtle but obvious shift in the role of tradition from ancient catholic orthodoxy, which did indeed see tradition as an integral part of the Faith, recognizing it not only as the vehicle for the transmission of the Faith, but in some sense as the Faith itself, and did not equate it with separate, independent sources of authority. In fact, as Cunningham observes of the church fathers:

They speak, indeed, often of tradition, and traditions; but then it has been conclusively proved, that by these words they most commonly meant the sacred Scriptures themselves, and the statements therein contained.[17]

While this assessment because of its polemical context may be somewhat exaggerated, it points to an essential truth about the role of tradition in patristic Christianity—it was enveloped in a profound respect for the Holy Scripture as the only source of objective revelation and the final court of appeal. Cunningham reminds, moreover, that:

They [the fathers] sometimes appealed, in arguing against the heretics, to the doctrines and practices which had been handed down from the apostles, especially in the churches which they themselves had founded. But besides that there was more, not only of plausibility, but of weight, in this appeal in the second century than there could be at any subsequent period, it is evidence that they employed this consideration merely as an auxiliary or subordinate argument, without ever intending, by the using of it, to deny, or cast into the background, the supremacy or sufficiency of Scripture; and that they employed it, to prove the absolute and certain truth of their doctrines, as to disprove an allegation very often made then, as now, in theological discussion, that they were new and recently invented.[18]

That is, the fathers employed the unbroken consensus of the church as a weapon against heresy, not with the assumption that this tradition is objectively authoritative, but *with the assumption that a doctrine with historic attestation is less likely to be wrong than one of recent origin.* Herewith the general outlines of the patristic conception of tradition become clearer: since the Faith which the church espouses is founded on the infallible and authoritative word of God in Holy Scripture, that Faith is valid. Admittedly they were somewhat naïve in assuming that there could be no discrepancy between what the Bible itself actually teaches and what they believed (a naivete shared by some modern fundamentalists), but the early fathers cannot seriously be enlisted as predecessors of the Tridentine dogma that unwritten tradition occupies a place alongside Scripture as an independent, objective authority in the church.

A cardinal tenet of Reformed bibliology developed in reaction to the Roman exaltation of tradition is the *sufficiency* of Scripture. This tenet was given confessional expression by the great body of the Reformed church, of which the statement by the Westminster Confession of Faith that "nothing at any time is to be added [to Scripture], whether by new revelations of the Spirit, or traditions of men"[19] is but the most prominent example. A prime exponent of this tenet later in the seventeenth century was the Reformed dogmatist and polemicist Francis Turretin, who in characteristic fashion states: "[W]e [Reformed theologians] give to the Scriptures such a sufficiency and perfection as is immediate and explicit. There is no need to have recourse to any tradition independent of them."[20] Turretin argues for the sufficiency of the Scriptures on explicitly Biblical grounds.[21] He takes 2 Tim. 3:16, 17; Dt. 4:2; and Ps. 19:7 to teach the absolute sufficiency of Scripture; argues that "[n]o fit reason can be given why God should wish one part of his word to be written and the other to be delivered of spoken voice"[22]; and cites the fathers [!] in support of his view. He admits, however:

> ... we acknowledge that tradition is formal and active because the oracles of God were committed to the church as their keeper and proclaimer. But the tradition is not material and passive, implying some doctrine delivered in addition to the Scriptures (which we deny). So we have the Scriptures through tradition not as the source of belief, but only as the means and instrument through which they have come down to us.[23]

Turretin, then, accords tradition an *instrumental* function, the means by which the Scriptures and the Faith are preserved, but not the source of the Faith itself. Note too that he dissents not merely from the Roman Catholic view of the role of tradition, but from the actual Roman *definition* of tradition.

The question of the relative merit of tradition among the Reformed was also answered at length last century by the justifiably revered Princetonian Charles Hodge, who makes several concessions to the viability of tradition. First, he acknowledges that tradition appears within the Biblical revelation itself: "The revelation of God in his Word begins in a fountain, and flows in a continuous stream ever increasing in volume. We are governed by this tradition of truth running through the whole sacred volume."[24] Second, Hodge notes the existence of a "traditionary teaching flowing through the Christian Church from the day of Pentecost to the present time." This, according to Hodge, is "the common faith of the Church, which no man is at liberty to reject and which no man can reject and be a Christian."[25] By this description Hodge refers to what we call Christian orthodoxy. He justifies this use of tradition on two grounds: (1) that "what all the competent readers of a plain book take to be its meaning, must be its meaning," and (2) that since the Holy Spirit promised to lead his church into all truth, whatever they "agree in believing must be true."[26] Significantly Hodge contends that this "common faith" comprehends "only essential doctrines; that is, doctrines which enter into the very nature of Christianity, and which are necessary to its subjective existence in the heart, or which if they do not enter essentially into the religious experience of believers, are so connected with vital doctrines as not to admit of separation from them.[27] This view constitutes a sort of Reformed fundamentalism, apparently essential to ward of Papist contentions that tradition includes any number of unbiblical elements, as well as biblicist tenets that would undermine the Faith by appeal to the Bible.

Hodge, in addition, concedes doctrinal development: "All Protestants admit that there has been, in one sense, an uninterrupted development of theology in the Church, from the apostolic age to the present time."[28] He is intent, of course, to insist that the truths progressively affirmed were elicited from the text of Scripture itself—in other words, they were there all the time—in contradistinction to the claims of Rome that the church is endowed with the capacity and responsibility to posit new doctrine not found in Scripture. In fact, Hodge turns this concept of doctrinal development against Rome itself, validating Luther's somewhat novel understanding of an exclusively forensic doctrine of justification by appeal to doctrinal development.[29] He concludes that the church "understands the great doctrines of theology, anthropology and soteriology, far better now, than they were understood in the early post-apostolic age of the Church."[30] Naturally, one suspects Hodge is convinced additional light on doctrinal issues will emerge from the study of Scripture in time.

Although Hodge opposes the Roman Catholic concept of tradition on the grounds that (1) it cannot be proven that tradition was ever intended to serve as an independent authority, (2) that God never promised the sort of supernatural intervention in history that this view of tradition requires, (3) that there exists no ultimate criterion by which to differentiate spurious traditions from legitimate traditions, (4) that "common consent" as a form of tradition which Protestants do support is quite different from the view of tradition held by the Romanists, and (5) that tradition is not suited to serve as a rule of faith since it is not objective,[31] his clinching argument is that it "subverts the authority of the Scriptures."[32] He reminds his readers that it was precisely this undue stress on tradition that rendered the Pharisees so culpable by our Lord. Tradition therefore may become positively inimical to the Faith if it begins to undermine the authority of Scripture by serving as a rival authority.

The irony will not be lost on the astute listener that I have opted to cited three chief theologians from the Reformed tradition [!] in order to combat the Roman Catholic dogma that ecclesiastical tradition is vested with independent divine authority. However, the irony is mollified by the understanding that it is just *this* sort of use of tradition that is one of those uses that is not at all objectionable, since it is enlisted merely to argue that what the Reformed do believe is expressed in or deduced from Scripture.

Tradition in Modernist Protestant Thought

It is perhaps only in a recognition of the deleterious effects produced by a rationalistic usage of the dogma of *sola Scriptura* that the necessity of a valid and workable view of tradition becomes apparent. I take as an example a "conservative" (*i.e.*, somewhat neo-orthodox) liberal, Gerhard Ebeling, a church historian and dogmatician whose profound and brilliant treatment of the issue of the relation between Scripture and tradition is clearly heretical (it is well to remember that almost all heresy is profound and brilliant; profundity and brilliance are no impediments to—and are often the chief selling points of—heresy.)

Ebeling notes that it was only with the relatively recent emergence of the discipline of historical criticism that the problems inherent in the idea of tradition came to light. Of course, the reformers had leveled their criticisms at the use to which the Roman Catholic Church had put tradition, but their objections were largely unrelated to the nature of tradition itself. "It is only when criticism enables us to see the process of transmission in its true perspective," declares Ebeling, "that we become aware of the powerful influence exerted by Tradition, and can realize more clearly the part which historically conditioned traditions have played in history."[33] The phrase "historically conditioned traditions" carries the weight not only in Ebeling's comment but also in a theologically liberal attitude toward traditions in general. It presupposes the quite modern recognition that history is not objective; that religious traditions are colored by the cultural and philosophical climates of which they are a part; and that, consequently, it is impossible to address the concept of tradition apart from a consideration of these broader factors that allegedly influence religious tradition as much as religion itself. Not surprisingly, as a result of this enterprise, "the phenomenon of Tradition has been historicized and its validity called into question."[34] After all, if religious tradition is inextricably interwoven with cultural, philosophical, and other factors, it is quite possible that it is those "alien" factors, and not religion itself, that are most crucial in shaping the tradition.

As a result, historical criticism seemingly stripped away the pretensions of absoluteness in tradition and laid bare its inescapably historical and therefore relativistic character. Traditions were seen to be little more than human, and often self-serving, conventions, religious and noble conventions at times, but conventions nonetheless. Of course, in its earliest criticisms of tradition, the first disciples of Enlightenment sounded a lot like the reformers themselves, thundering against the Romanists who dared to add human tradition to the unadulterated word of God. However, what stands out as distinctive of the Enlightenment onslaught against tradition was that it was driven, not by a respect for the ruling authority of the word of God, but by an animosity for tradition itself. This animosity became painfully and flagrantly clear when it became evidence that Scripture and the Christian Faith are themselves tradition, and the more recent Enlightenment "historicists" like Ebeling overturn orthodoxy along with tradition. This is evidenced strikingly in Ebeling's observation that the reformers' denial of the authoritative role of tradition subverted the authority of Scripture itself.[35] Ebeling's assumption, of course, is that the traditional view of verbal inspiration is primarily a dogmatic—rather than strictly Biblical—facet of the Faith and therefore no less vulnerable to the criticism of tradition than any other dogma, holding as he does that "it would be . . . meaningless to attempt to deduce directly from Scripture a proof of the *sola Scriptura* principle, since such a proof, if it is to be convincing, must take for granted the very thing which has to be proved, namely, the canonical authority of Scripture."[36]

No less significant is Ebeling's reminder that the heirs of the formal principle of the Reformation—he lists Pietism, Enlightenment, and historical criticism—utilized this very principle of *sola Scriptura* to destroy Protestant orthodoxy:

> [W]e can see that each of these in its own way and within its own limits, adopts a relation to the points of view which were implicit in the principle of the orthodox dogmatic pattern itself. In this way they were committed to the hermeneutic

problem contained in *sola Scriptura*, and thus abandoned the standpoint of orthodox dogmatic, of which the hermeneutic principle consists....[37]

The cluster of modern approaches to the Bible set in motion both by an abstract and inorganic application of *sola Scriptura* and by Enlightenment has consequently served eventually to undermine both Biblical authority and the orthodox Faith. I speak most obviously of "higher criticism," or the historical-critical method, which has mesmerized even evangelical scholars.[38] Less obvious, though hardly less pernicious, is the hazard posed by "lower text criticism," which, as liberal Harold DeWolf notes, cannot be isolated from "higher" historical criticism. He is perplexed that conservatives are solicitous to employ the very form of ("lower") criticism intimately tied to "higher" criticism which eviscerates the orthodox Christian Faith.[39]

We should never be lured therefore into assuming that a "high" view of Scripture, or even of the necessity of an intently exegetical theology, constitutes *ipso facto* a sound relation to Christian orthodoxy. In this context, Ebeling notes what may seem to us today as an odd, reserved, and even obscurantist approach of some of the early fathers to exegesis and the exegetical arguments of heretics:

> There was no expectations whatsoever [in the patristic orthodox view of tradition] of new and revolutionary insights from scriptural exegesis.[40]

I cannot resist the temptation to interrupt the citation to point out that it is the *liberal* theologian criticizing ancient catholic *orthodoxy* on the ground that the latter is not sufficiently exegetical. He continues:

> Here, once again, we encounter the confusion of the results of the process of tradition with the original content of tradition. Therefore it becomes questionable whether the appeal to the apostolic writings can render any service whatever in the controversy with heresy, that is to say, at the point at which reliable knowledge of the apostolic tradition becomes a crucial problem. Tertullian renders a very skeptical judgment about the possibility

of persuasion by scriptural exegesis in dogmatic controversies. Ultimately opinion is pitted against opinion, and nothing is decided. Suspicion is aroused by the fact that it is precisely the heretics who desire to wage the struggle on the field of the Scriptures and appeal to the word of the Lord, "Seek and you shall find." Tertullian opposes the view that a person who believes still has anything more to seek. As he formulates the matter in a surprising antithesis, it is faith that brings salvation, and not the searching of the Scriptures....We must have this faith if we wish to occupy ourselves with the Scriptures in any meaningful way at all. This is the reason we should not allow ourselves to become engaged with the heretics in any exegetical dispute whatsoever. Heretics have from the outset no right to the Scriptures because they do not have the true faith. Scripture [according to Tertullian] is not the criterion of what we are to believe, but faith is the criterion of how we are to understand Scripture. Faith is the only normative and necessary guide to interpretation ... The battle of the early Catholic fathers for the apostolic writings as the source of knowledge of the apostolic tradition ends, paradoxically, in the sacrifice of Scripture as a decisive authority. At the moment at which the authority of the New Testament canon began to be accepted, it already no longer functioned as a decisive critical norm for the determination of the apostolic tradition.[41]

I must assert tendentiously that what we perceive in Tertullian's attitude toward the heretics is what we may term a presuppositional approach to the relation between Scripture and tradition. Not surprisingly, it displeases Ebeling, for it contains "a historical error, because the tradition which claims to be apostolic did not stem from Christianity alone."[42] In other words, he dislikes the fact that the orthodox did not allow exegesis of Scripture to rule in their debate with heretics, but rather *presupposed* the validity of orthodoxy on the contested points. Ebeling the liberal would rather have had the orthodox appeal to Scripture *alone*, seemingly the Protestant principle. Whereas Ebeling, no doubt, opposes this presuppositional approach of the orthodox for the very reason they employed it: it prevents the overturning of orthodox doctrine by exegetical appeals to Scripture. Indeed, it is a ploy of an arid, "scientific" liberalism to exalt exegetical theology at the expense of a dogmatic and systematic theology.[43]

A Presuppositional Approach to Ecclesiastical Tradition

Ebeling pinpoints the manifold flaws and inconsistencies of the more recent Roman Catholic conception of tradition, chief among which is its decisions to eviscerate its very own Tridentine decrees on the authority of tradition by the dogma of the assumption of Mary, for whose acceptance on traditional grounds no argument could credibly be made.[44] Ebeling is equally solicitous, however, to criticize the Protestant doctrine of *sola Scriptura*, suggesting, "the fact that the phenomenon of tradition becomes a theological problem in a very compelling way in the form of the scriptural principle [of *sola Scriptura*] can be overlooked only so long as we view the New Testament canon as being from the outset a divinely inspired book, a priori distinct from every other type of tradition."[45] But this is precisely the historic, orthodox view of Scripture, and thus the numerous problems a consideration of tradition apparently poses for Scripture are valid only on the presupposition that Scripture is not in fact the revealed word of God. Ebeling is convinced that to affirm the orthodox view of Scripture is perforce to assert:

> That the Bible ... represent[s] an ontologically quite different type of literature, subject to fundamentally different conditions of development and, hence, also to different rules of understanding and interpretation than is the case with any other human literature. But then what shall we do with the historical relativity of the Bible and the humanity of its language? If we understand God's revelation as revealed doctrine, then what we finally have ... is the difficult situation of a doctrine of inspiration which erects a wall around the Bible and instead of risking an interpretation of the Bible, basically only recites it. Such a doctrine understands the Bible not as a message to the world but as a secret teaching for the initiated.[46]

Ebeling is contending, of course, that the orthodox doctrine of the inspiration of Scripture must be jettisoned if Scripture is to retain relevance for modernity. In typical neo-orthodox fashion, he wishes to shift revelation to the subjective-objective *event* of the divine-human encounter.[47] That his abandonment of the orthodox view of inspiration may destroy any sort of Biblical authority whatever and so render irrelevant [!] any question of the relevance of Scripture as the word of God has perhaps not occurred to Ebeling. Moreover, the suggestion that the orthodox view of inspiration which absolutizes a time-bound document cancels the possibility of history- and culture-transcending relevance can be argued only on the grounds that God does not control history and shape culture. It is altogether sensible, however, to assert that a document immersed in human language, culture, and history may constitute the infallibly revealed word of God if language, culture, and history are divinely shaped, among other designs, for the purpose of conveying the very word of God (cf. 45–46).

Nonetheless, the most important lesson we can learn from the theologically liberal agenda of sequestering Scripture from all tradition is that it must of necessity culminate in the repudiation of orthodox Christianity itself. Thus, in a series of lectures in 1953 Ebeling noted:

> This Protestant orthodoxy, which did not recognize its historical relativity and for this reason alone could maintain that it was absolutely and unchangeably orthodox, disintegrated once and for all during the course of the eighteenth century with the advent of cultural changes which did away with the historical foundations of that orthodoxy. If today someone overlooks this and still thinks he can call himself orthodox, he is nevertheless no longer orthodox in the sense of Protestant orthodoxy ... And if anyone believes today that he can uphold the orthodox doctrine of inspiration and make it the shibboleth of orthodoxy, he is simply not aware that he does this in quite another fashion than did orthodoxy. Within Protestant orthodoxy the doctrine of verbal inspiration has meaning only because of the metaphysical Aristotelian presuppositions which orthodoxy drew upon ... Of course, those who today emphatically uphold the orthodox doctrine of inspiration do not know or understand anything about this philosophical background which attaches to the classic orthodox doctrine of inspiration and the sacrifice of which would reduce the doctrine of verbal inspiration to nonsense. Similarly, it is nowadays considered orthodox to keep theology free from every connection with philosophy, while the characteristic trait of classic orthodoxy was the intensive employment of philosophy

for theology, specifically the Aristotelian scholastic philosophy which at that time reigned in equal measure in Catholicism and Protestantism. This is the fundamental reason why Protestant orthodoxy no longer exists even as a possibility; these Aristotelian intellectual presuppositions are no longer taken for granted as general and obvious truths.[48]

Despite the ignoble condescension with which he paints the exponents of orthodoxy, Ebeling is quite justified in alerting us to the serious naivete of modern conservatives who wish "to keep theology free from every connection with philosophy." The accuracy of that charge, however, does not extricate him from self-defeating traps of his own inventions: (1) If the orthodox Protestant view of Scripture must be scrapped in the twentieth century because of the demise of the "metaphysical Aristotelian presuppositions which orthodoxy drew upon," what prevents us from contending with logically equal force that *Ebeling's* theories must be scrapped because there is every reason to suspect that the historicism on which they presently rest will one day be disproven (in the parlance of Gilbert Chesterton, he ends up undermining his own mines); most importantly, however, (2) if we must jettison the orthodox Protestant view of Scripture because it presupposes an "alien" philosophical orientation, how can we justifiably stop with the view of Scripture? Why not debunk the entire Christian message? For it no less than the orthodox Protestant view of Scripture was conceived inextricably in historical circumstances and its writers fashioned their doctrine on the anvil of "alien" philosophies. One thinks immediately of St. John's *logos* doctrine, with its patently Hellenic cast. May we argue that the *logos* doctrine is no longer crucial for the Faith? This is precisely the tack of modern and post-modern liberalism in general, docetically shearing away the historical kernel from the supposed transcendent message of the Faith, and finally being left with . . . nothing. This inclination to attack orthodoxy on the grounds that it consists of alien (usually Greek) philosophical elements is unfortunately not limited to the neo-orthodox and theological liberals. Eminent evangelicals like Clark Pinnock have jumped into the fray, denying the timelessness, immutability, omnipotence, and omniscience of God on the grounds that the orthodox understanding of God rests on Greek philosophical suppositions, while, according to Pinnock, the Bible contradicts orthodoxy. Pinnock wants to be a biblicist in opposing orthodoxy.[49]

The beguiling nature of the proposal to isolate the message of the Christian Faith from tradition is highlighted in Ebeling's penetrating questions:

> Must not all theological reflection be conservative in the sense that it holds irrevocably fast to the traditional witness to Jesus Christ, and at the same time progressive in the sense that it witnesses to the freedom of the Christian kerygma from the very limited and transient form of the secular and cultural situation? ... Can theological reflection ever be positive and conservative in the sense of a basic, unreserved, and uncritical acceptance of anything that advances a claim to be a witness to revelation? Similarly, can theological reflection ever be progressive and liberal in the sense of theory of progress derived from a philosophy of history or in the sense of a criticism of tradition which is itself basically very uncritical, because it lacks self-criticism and considers its own position absolute?[50]

The first impulse of those schooled in the Reformation dictum of *sola Scriptura* is to applaud the insights of each of these questions. Does not the declaration that the power of the Christian message must be emancipated from "every limited and transient form of the secular or cultural situation" inspire every orthodox Protestant to stand up and cheer? Do we not equally wish to assert the freedom of the word of God over all historical human systems? Is not this the essence of *sola Scriptura*?

That it should give us pause that these words are uttered by an enemy of the orthodox Christian Faith is not merely *ad hominem* reasoning. For this Enlightenment effort subverts the Christian message by seemingly exalting the Christian message at the expense of the tradition of which it is a part. It does, paradoxically, by so immersing the Christian message in tradition that it can relativize that message just as it relativizes everything else—except of course, its own bold assertions, its protests to the contrary notwithstanding. It says that because the gospel is itself a tradition, but because that tradition is relative and not inherently authoritative, it can function in any number of traditions, even if those traditions are not orthodox.[51]

It is possible then to posit not only post-Biblical tradition, but Scripture itself as the sort of tradition so imbedded in "alien" philosophical suppositions as to render them useless to succeeding generations. The orthodox response to that agenda is to assert that the Hellenic character of the New Testament, for example, not to mention the Greek language itself, was a specially designed vehicle for conveying divine propositional revelation. Similarly, though in a derivative and subordinate sense, the "scholastic" form of Protestant orthodoxy is the divinely shaped milieu for an accurate expression of Reformed truth. It does not follow that this scholastic *form* is infallible or beyond criticism any more than the Greek language and Hellenic thought-forms are infallible and beyond criticism. They are both, however, suitable for functioning as vehicles to convey, in the case of Greek, the infallible word of God, and, in the case of "scholasticism," the fallible but accurate doctrinal formulations of seventeenth-century Protestant orthodoxy. This Protestant view patently assumes something about God: He controls history.

A Presuppositional View of the Relation between Scripture and Tradition

To discover a viable Reformed view of the relation between Scripture and tradition, I believe it necessary to appeal to the writings of an individual seemingly far removed from the controversy, the late Reformed apologist Cornelius Van Til. What, indeed, has Van Til to do with this issue? The answer is, plenty. For an understanding of his epistemology, anthropology, and apologetics furnishes a distinctively Reformed—and, more importantly, Biblical—answer to these vexing questions. Particularly critical for the issue of the relation between the authority of Scripture and the role and inevitability of tradition is his interpretation of the Reformed philosophy of history. Van Til's philosophy of history is an aspect of his broader philosophy of religion, in which the doctrine of predestination occupies a vital role. Indispensable to Van Til's apologetic is the statement in answer to Question 7 of the Shorter Catechism, that God "foreordained whatsoever comes to pass." Thus, for Van Til, primary contingency in the universe is an impossibility.[52] Secondary contingency arising from secondary causes is an inevitability and preserves an authentic human responsibility, but Van Til follows the Reformed tradition is affirming that the existence of every aspect of the universe derives from God's decree. Moreover, this decree is not impersonal.

It is designed for a specific purpose, and thus natural revelation of which history is a vital part serves God's covenantal designs:

> Natural revelation, we are virtually told, was from the outset incorporated into the idea of a covenantal relationship of God with man. Thus every dimension of created existence, even the lowest, was enveloped in a form of exhaustively personal relationship between God and man. The "ateleological" no less than the "teleological," the "mechanical" no less than the "spiritual", was covenantal in character.
>
> Being from the outset covenantal in character, the natural revelation of God to man was meant to serve as the playground for the process of differentiation that was to take place in the course of time ... The forces of nature are always at the beck and call of the power of differentiation that works toward redemption and reprobation. It is this idea of a supernatural-natural revelation that comes to such eloquent expression in the Old Testament, and particularly in the Psalms.
>
> Here then is a picture of a well-integrated and unified philosophy of history in which revelation in nature and revelation in Scripture are mutually meaningless without one another and mutually fruitful when taken together.[53]

Christian tradition is one aspect of natural revelation. It was never intended to operate independently of Scripture, and vice versa. We immediately detect in this schema the possibility of a solution to the apparent impasse between what are often judged to be the competing claims of Scripture and tradition. Scripture and nature (of which human history and tradition as an aspect thereof are a part) are complimentary—not competing—aspects of divine revelation. It is not a question of Scripture *versus* tradition, but of Scripture *and* tradition, in proper relation, as indispensable elements of a single overarching covenantal divine plan.

Since history flows under the decree of the sovereign God,

and since his church is a leading agency in the advancement of his kingdom, God suits the events of history to serve his purpose for the church, as Singer, a disciple of Van Til avers:

> Like the birth of Christ, so the Church, that great company of the elect, that institution at the very heart of the historical process in all ages, is the great divide of history to which all other events relate. Scripture also indicates clearly that all events in both ancient and modern history, refer in some way, known to God alone for the most part, to the life and work of the Church. These events are not only related to the birth of Christ, but have an immediate bearing on the Church in their own day. They all serve God's purpose as regards His will for the elect, for it is through this divinely ordained institution, the Church, that the events of history derive their meaning and purpose.[54]

Since tradition has "an immediate bearing on the Church," we can expect not merely that it operates according to God's sovereign decree (as indeed does all of history), but moreover that it is specially suited to serve as an enrichment to the church. Of course, this is not to say that tradition occupies the *same* role as Scripture in the church, only that it occupies a role *no less than* Scripture in the church. They are both divinely suited to the ends for which they were intended. It is only when man intrudes himself autonomously into this impeccably balanced divine relationship that it becomes insuperably problematic. Indeed, both Roman Catholic traditionalism and theologically liberal reductionism suffer from the same religious ailment, the exercise of autonomy.

The decree of papal infallibility, for instance, is only the logical corollary of an institution committed to the view that it is the exclusive representative of God on earth. When the Council of Trent reified its view of coordinate sources of objective authority (Scripture and unwritten tradition), what it was really asserting was that it was an autonomous religious institution and the agency of divine revelation on earth because it considered itself the infallible, institutional guardian of divine truth and the infallible arbiter of the meaning of Scripture. In this action it belied its commission of the original sin, the sin of autonomy. Van Til, significantly enough, reduces the error of Romanism in its

supraexalted view of tradition to the sin of autonomy and
concomitant denial of divine predestination:

> The bearing of this conception of tradition on the questions of
> authority and its relation to reason must now be drawn. The
> hierarchy of the church in general, and of the pope in particular,
> is not to be thought of as itself subject to the final and
> comprehensive revelation of God. There is no place anywhere
> in the whole of Roman Catholic thought for the idea that any
> human being should be wholly subject to God. On the contrary,
> the position of Rome requires the rejection of the counsel of
> God as all-determinative.[55]

No less does Van Til oppose the idea of human autonomy
pervasive among modern man, chief among whom is the theological
liberal, who, as Ebeling, undermines the authority of Holy Scripture
by reducing it to a culturally conditioned human document:

> As the idea of a closed canon [*i.e.*, in Reformed orthodoxy]
> seeks to identify something as absolute in a sea of relativism, so
> it separates this identified object from all relations of significance
> with human experience. It sets off the Bible as a mechanical
> something over against human experience. It wants the Bible to
> be the standard of human life. It lifts this standard of life out of
> contact with life and then expects it to have an all-important
> bearing on life. It wants all of life to be regulated rationalistically
> by a hard and fast pattern that is not adjustable as human
> experience accumulates.
> Thus the idea of the sufficiency of Scripture as well as that
> of its necessity is charged with being both irrationalistic and
> rationalistic. This charge is based upon the assumption of the
> ultimacy of man. Thus man's ultimate irrationalism requires that
> he charge the Christian position with rationalism because it holds
> to God who controls all things. Thus man's ultimate rationalism
> requires that he charge the Christian position with irrationalism
> because it holds that God controls all things by his counsel that
> is itself above and prior to and therefore not involved in the
> "relativity" of history.[56]

Contrary to Ebeling, therefore, the affirmation of verbal
inspiration and Christian orthodoxy is possible, not in spite of the

fact that they are expressed in philosophical thought forms alien to modern culture, but because the thought forms in which these dogmas were explicated were specially designed by the all-controlling God of history to serve that very purpose. The fatal flaw of the view of Ebeling and other "historicists" is not that Scripture and orthodoxy are "historically and culturally conditioned," for they surely are, but that God specially conditioned history and the cultures to serve as the vehicle for supernaturally revealed truth and its ecclesiastical solidification. The thought forms in which this "tradition" is expressed, no less than the Hebrew thought forms in which the Old Testament was expressed and the Greek thought forms in which both the New Testament and ancient catholic theology were expressed, were predestined by God as the Author of history to effect his purposes for his church. The "historicists" must posit both Scripture and orthodoxy as relative so they can posit *themselves* as absolute.

The relativization of orthodoxy on the grounds of "historical and cultural conditioning," therefore, is seen simply to be an extension of the expression of human autonomy. To assert that history and culture relativize orthodoxy is to assert that God does not control history. The Calvinist can recognize the valid subordinate role of tradition precisely because he knows God is in control of history. Predestination secures the derivative role of ecclesiastical tradition. To be sure, this does not legitimize all tradition of all kinds, for God has not chosen to speak infallibly in human tradition as he has in Holy Scripture. Tradition does not fulfill the same role in the church as does Holy Scripture, the latter of which is the touchstone by which all human ideas, practices, and traditions are tested.[57]

It will be perceived that this Van Tilian approach—that is, a consistent Reformed approach—conduces a great deal to the correction of the error of the subordination of Scripture to tradition and the church by the Roman Catholics on the one hand, and the subordination of Scripture and orthodoxy to cultural and historical relativism on the other. For we contend that since the predestinating God "controls whatsoever comes to pass" and that history is the "playground" for God's processes, no aspect of the temporal may be absolutized. Romanism absolutizes tradition, and therefore the church, as the arbiter of interpretation. Enlightenment liberalism (self-contradictorily, of course) absolutizes the fact of historical conditioning. By contrast, Reformed orthodoxy recognizes God and his revelation as absolute. Since God creates history as the "playground" for his purposes, we can have confidence that the historical (and, therefore, cultural and philosophical) bed in which both the Biblical revelation,[58] and, in a subordinate sense, catholic and Reformation orthodoxy rests is divinely created as the subjective vehicle for the objective communication of the Scriptures and transmission of the Faith.

Further we can follow both the early orthodox fathers and Hodge in boldly positing "the common faith of the Church," that is, "certain fixed doctrines among Christians . . . which are no longer open questions."[59] They are no longer open, in fact, to the possibility of refutation by exegesis, for we believe that the God who controls history has so superintended our forefathers that the doctrinal formulations that they hammered out on the anvil of controversy are in fact essentially what the Westminster Confession of Faith terms "good and necessary consequence" of scriptural statements. Like Tertullian, therefore, we do not open exegetical debate with heretics who wish to employ *sola Scriptura* to obviate orthodoxy, not because the Scripture is not absolutely authoritative and sufficient, but because the God who controls history has allowed his church to elicit from the absolutely authoritative and sufficient Scriptures the incontrovertibly fundamental doctrines of the Christian Faith.

Objections

Opponents of predestination will naturally object to the interpretation of the role of tradition set forth in this essay. That such an opposition rests the orthodox formulations of the Trinity and christology on nothing more than the determinations of man spawned by chance should give them pause. The most egregious result of a denial of a Reformed view of tradition on the basis of a denial of predestination, however, is that it undercuts the Christian Scriptures and Faith themselves no less than orthodox tradition. For if God cannot or will not secure an accurate interpretation of the core of the Faith in history by the church we have no reason to believe he could or did secure the inspiration and infallibility of the Scriptures. If divine predestination is denied, the universe rests on chance; and if the universe rests on chance, the Christian Faith is a mockery and we are of all men most miserable. This denial of Christian predestination is always hypocritical, however, for as Rushdoony remarks, "[P]redestination is an inescapable concept . . . This belief [a denial of predestination] has not been held by any religion or philosophy, although it has been nominally professed as a means of undermining some particular faith . . . [W]hen the doctrine of predestination is denied, it does not disappear. Where denied to God, predestination then accrues to some other agency, nature, man, or the state."[60]

Other critics may suggest my view absolutizes tradition, that it comports more easily with what Neibuhr[61] has depicted as the "Christ of Culture" view than with the Augustinian and Calvinistic "Christ the Transformer of Culture" view. Such an objection represents a serious misreading of the essay. To assert that traditional core orthodoxy is divinely shaped is not to argue that the cultures (much less their assumptions and mores) in which such orthodoxy arose and in whose thought forms and terminology that orthodoxy is expressed are infallible. It is merely to assert that since God is the Lord of history no less than eternity he has created the cultures in such a way that they may function as suitable conduits for the expression of orthodoxy. Nay, he pointedly *designed* such cultures for such function. Biblical Faith and orthodoxy are therefore not the servants of human culture. Rather, human culture, under the predestinating hand of God, is the servant of Biblical Faith and orthodoxy.

Ardent Protestants may argue that this idea assumes *ipso facto* the validity of all tradition and a concomitant dissolving of *sola Scriptura*. This assumption is equally false. The thesis comprehends only, as Hodge notes, the traditional beliefs constituting the core elements of the Faith: mainly orthodox trinitarianism and christology, *sola Scriptura* and *sola fide*. The conclusion of this essay insinuates not merely that the decisions of the church catholic addressing matters other than core elements of the Faith are not binding and that decisions by separate bodies within Christendom (Romanism, for example) are not to be classed as authoritative,

but also that even the valid, divinely shaped tradition of which the
early church councils are comprised is ever subordinate to Holy
Scripture, the "only rule of faith and practice." This, in fact, is the
view expressed in the Westminster Confession (ch. 1, sec. 6):

> The whole counsel of God, concerning all things necessary for
> his own glory, man's salvation, faith, and life, is either expressly
> set down in scripture, or by good and necessary consequence
> may be deduced from scripture: unto which nothing at any time
> is to be added, whether by new revelations of the Spirit, or
> traditions of men. Nevertheless, we acknowledge the inward
> illumination of the Spirit of God to be necessary for the saving
> understanding of such things as are revealed in the word; and
> that there are some circumstances concerning the worship of
> God, and government of the church, common to human action
> and societies, which are to be ordered by the light of nature and
> Christian prudence, according to the general rules of the word,
> which are always to be observed.

Thoughtful critics may infer that the Reformed perspective
on tradition here set forth is a two-edged sword inasmuch as, if
practiced consistently, it necessarily commits Reformed believers
in the future to decisions of ecclesiastical consensus at variance
with historic orthodoxy. Two observations militate against this
objection: First, the recognition of the subordinate authority of
universally orthodox tradition in no way commits one at any time
to affirmation of any dogma at variance with explicit Biblical
teaching. The Bible alone is ultimately authoritative. Second, the
Reformed hold that since God controls history, a consensus decision
of the church undercutting historic orthodoxy is an utter
impossibility; God has promised to preserve his church not from
all error, but from such error as would eviscerate the Faith itself
(*Mt. 16:18; Ac. 20:29, 30; Eph. 5:27*).

Most misguided are the objections of (usually liberal, but
occasionally cultic) antitraditionalists, whose pretended neutrality
is a patent farce. As noted in the introduction, tradition is an
inescapable concept; and even those religions, ideologies, and
cultures decrying tradition—instanced hyperbolically but
frighteningly in George Orwell's *1984*—create their own tradition,
if it is nothing more than the attempt to obliterate tradition.

Conclusion

It is a distinctively Reformed—and *only* distinctively Reformed—approach that can offer adequate solutions to the question of the relation between Scripture and tradition as they function in the church. It is Calvinism's unswerving allegiance to the sovereignty of God as exercised in his work of the absolute predestination of "whatsoever comes to pass" that furnishes a key to the solution to this thorny issue. Scripture alone is the infallible and objective authority in all spheres of life. Yet God has promised not only the preservation of the church, and the Scriptures as its covenant document,[62] but also orthodox doctrine itself. This Reformed view generates not merely assurance about the accuracy of what we now believe, but also confidence of increasing confessional unity and uniformity among the true church catholic. We can possess such confidence precisely because God controls history. I conclude with an apposite citation from Van Til:

> The message of Christianity must ring out clearly in the modern tumult. If Christianity is to be heard above the din and noise of modern irrationalism and existentialism, it must think in terms of its own basic categories. If it has to import some of its materials from the enemy, it cannot expect effectively to conquer the enemy. It is the Christian Faith that alone has the truth; this should be its claim.[63]

---

[1] A slightly shorter version of this paper was delivered at the 1994 Conference on Revival, Reformation, and Reconstruction in Warsaw, Ohio. I must emphasize that this essay is a tentative attempt to come to grips with an extremely complex—sometimes convoluted—issue that has engaged some of Protantism's most adept minds. Consequently, I would be presumptuous to depict this paper as a definitive contribution to the issue of the relation between Scripture and tradition in the Reformed Faith.

[2] Jaroslav Pelikan, *The Emergence of the Catholic Tradition* (University of Chicago Press, 1971), 9.

[3] Stephen J. Tonsor, "The Inevitability of Tradition," *Modern Age*, Spring, 1994, 229.

[4] By radical reformers I refer to the Anabaptists, Quakers, Pentecostals

and, to a certain extent, fundamentalists. Further, it almost goes without saying that objection to ecclesiastical tradition is a hallmark of cults.

[5] Charles B. Williams, "Tradition," in ed. James Orr, *The International Standard Bible Encyclopedia* (Grand Rapids, 1939), 5:3004.

[6] K. Wegenast, "Teach, Instruct, Tradition, Education, Discipline," in ed. Colin Brown, *The New International Dictionary of New Testament Theology* (Grand Rapids [1978], 1986), 3:775; cf. this sound, succinct discussion of the etymology of the Greek terms for tradition.

[7] "Before 2 Thess. 2:15 is seen as a classic proof-text for the Roman Catholic principle of tradition (namely both written and oral tradition), it should be borne in mind that *paradoseis* here does not consist of a fixed canon or writings handed down and supplemented by oral tradition, but refers to the apostles' written and oral admonitions to the church, which the church has duly accepted (cf. 2 Thess. 3:6)," *ibid.*, 774.

[8] Philip Schaff, *History of the Christian Church; Ante-Nicene Christianity* (Grand Rapids, 1910), 525.

[9] Georges Florovsky, *Bible, Church, and Tradition: An Eastern Orthodox View* (Belmont, MA, 1972), 80.

[10] Pelikan, *op. cit.*, 332-339.

[11] *ibid.*, 336.

[12] Andrew Sandlin, "Orthodoxy," *Calvinism Today*, October, 1993, 22.

[13] Gerhard Ebeling, *The Word of God and Tradition*, trans. S. H. Hooke (Philadelphia, 1964), 108. The two works by Ebeling cited in this essay require a much more extensive treatment than the limitations of the topic of this essay admit.

[14] John Calvin, *Institutes of the Christian Religion*, Bk. 4, Ch. 8, Sec. 13.

[15] Ebeling, *op. cit.*, 104.

[16] Philip Schaff, *The Creeds of Christendom* (Grand Rapids [1931], 1990), 2:80.

[17] William Cunningham, *Historical Theology* (Still Waters Revival Books, Alberta [1882], 1991), 1:186. The general thrust of this assessment has been verified by Kelly: " . . . [T]he reader should be placed on his guard against an ambiguity inherent in the word [tradition]. In present-day idiom 'tradition' denotes the body of unwritten doctrine handed down in the church, or the handing down of such doctrine, and so tends to be contrasted with Scripture. In the language of the fathers, as indeed of the New Testament, the term of course conveyed this idea of transmission, and eventually the modern usage became regular. But its primary significance . . . *viz.* authoritative delivery, was originally to the fore and always remained prominent. Hence by tradition the fathers usually mean doctrine which the Lord or His apostles committed to

the Church, irrespective of whether it was handed down orally or in documents, and in the earlier centuries at any rate they prefer to employ other words or phrases to designate the Church's unwritten traditional teaching ... [W]hile Scripture (*i.e.*, the Old Testament) and the apostolic testimony are formally independent of each other, these fathers seem to have treated their contents as virtually coincident," J. N. D. Kelly, *Early Christian Doctrines* (New York, 1960 ed.), 30, 31, 34. Note in addition the comments of Herman Ridderbos, *Redemptive History and the New Testament Scriptures* (Phillipsburg, NJ, 1968), 15-24.

[18] Cunningham, *loc. cit.*

[19] *Westminster Confession of Faith*, Ch. 1, Sec. 6.

[20] Francis Turretin, *Institutes of Elenctic Theology*, trans. George Musgrave Giger (Phillipsburg, NJ, 1992), 136.

[21] *ibid.*, 136-138.

[22] *ibid.*, 139.

[23] *ibid.*, 142.

[24] Charles Hodge, *Systematic Theology* (Grand Rapids, 1981 reprint), 1:113.

[25] *ibid.*, 113, 114.

[26] *ibid.*, 114.

[27] *ibid.*, 115.

[28] *ibid.*, 116.

[29] *ibid.*, 118.

[30] *ibid.*

[31] *ibid.*, 122-128.

[32] *ibid.*, 128.

[33] Ebeling, *op.cit.*, 105.

[34] *ibid.*

[35] *ibid.*, 106.

[36] *ibid.*, 114, 115. cf. 119.

[37] *ibid.*, 114.

[38] J. Ramsey Michaels observes: "Most evangelicals who teach the Bible at the college or seminary level have made their peace with biblical criticism to a degree that was never possible in the older Fundamentalism. Careful attention has been given not only to biblical languages and the historical-grammatical understanding of what the biblical texts say, but to hermeneutics, that is, the attempt to translate the biblical message into categories which address today's questions and concerns. This has led to a disinterest in prooftexting and a candid acknowledgment that priority has been assigned to some aspects of the biblical revelation over others. It has also fostered attempts to distinguish critical theories about the Bible which are arbitrary and speculative

from those which genuinely illumine our understanding of how God's Word took shape in history," Michaels, "Inerrancy or Verbal Inspiration? An Evangelical Dilemma," in ed. Roger Nicole and Michaels, *Inerrancy and Common Sense* (Grand Rapids, 1980), 51. The extent to which the historical-critical method has subverted the Faith in evangelicalism is chronicled in Harold Lindsell's troubling, if flawed, accounts *The Battle for the Bible* (Grand Rapids, 1976) and *The Bible in the Balance* (Grand Rapids, 1979), ch. 7 and *passim.*

[39] Harold DeWolf, *The Case for Theology in Liberal Perspective* (Philadelphia, 1959), 51, 52. For a fuller treatment of this subject, consult Theodore Letis, "B. B. Warfield, Common-Sense Philosophy and Biblical Criticism," *American Presbyterians*, Vol. 69, No. 3 [Fall, 1991], 175-190.

[40] Gerhard Ebeling, *The Problem of Historicity*, trans. Grover Foley (Philadelphia 1967), 49.

[41] *ibid.*, 49, 50.

[42] *ibid.*, *53.*

[43] *idem.*, *Word*, 140.

[44] *idem.*, *Historicity*, 53-60.

[45] *ibid.*, 61.

[46] *ibid.*, 72. Ebeling's argument may cause us to give pause over an unlimited, abstract, and "scientific" application of the historical-critical method to the exegesis of Scripture, for it is difficult to argue with the contention that if the Bible is a unique and supernaturally inspired book, we can expect that our method of interpreting it cannot be identical to the method employed in interpreting every other book. Pelikan notes: " . . . when the problem of the relation between Scripture and tradition became a burning issue in the theological controversies of the Western church, in the late Middle Ages and the Reformation, it was at the cost of the unified system. Proponents of the theory that tradition was an independent source of revelation minimized the fundamentally exegetical content of tradition which had served to define tradition and its place in the specification of apostolic continuity. The supporters of the sole authority of Scripture, arguing from radical hermeneutical premises to conservative dogmatic conclusions, overlooked the function of tradition in securing what they regarded as the correct exegesis of Scripture against heretical alternatives," Pelikan, *op. cit.*, 119. It is not at all clear that the reformers understood that what we refer to as grammatical-historical exegesis may be employed to undermine orthodoxy, nor did they assume that their exegesis was tendentious with reference to orthodoxy.

[47] Ebeling, *Historicity*, 74-80.

[48] *ibid.*, 30, 31.

[49] Clark Pinnock, "Between Classical and Process Theism," in Ronald Nash, ed. *Process Theology* (Grand Rapids, 1987), 313-327. We should not be led into overlooking Pinnock's deviation from orthodoxy by his recent conversion to certain tenets of Reconstructionism; see Robert V. Rakestraw, "Clark H. Pinnock: A Theological Odyssey," *Christian Scholar's Review*, XIX:3 [March, 1990], 263. American evangelical Jack Rogers attributes different views among evangelicals on the sufficiency and reliability of Scripture to philosophical influences. See Jack Rogers, "The Church Doctrine of Biblical Authority," in ed. Rogers, *Biblical Authority* (Waco, TX, 1977), 22-44.

[50] Ebeling, *Historicity*, 32.

[51] *Idem., Word*, 146.

[52] Cornelius Van Til, *The Defense of the Faith* (Phillipsburg, NJ, 1967 ed.), *passim.*

[53] *Idem.*, "Nature and Scripture" in ed. N. B. Stonehouse and Paul Woolley, *The Infallible Word* (Philadelphia, 1946), 259-261.

[54] C. Gregg Singer, "The Nature of History," in ed., Carl F. H. Henry, *Christian Faith and Modern Theology* (New York, 1964), 231. See also Singer, "A Philosophy of History," in ed. E. R. Geehan, *Jerusalem and Athens* (Phillipsburg, NJ, 1971), 334, 335.

[55] Van Til, *Defense*, 138.

[56] *Idem., A Christian Theory of Knowledge* (Phillipsburg, NJ, 1969), 65. Van Til's criticism of G. C. Berkouwer's later approach to Scripture involves a repudiation of the "cultural conditioning" argument. See Van Til, *The New Synthesis Theology of the Netherlands* (no location: Presbyterian and Reformed Publishing Company, 1975), 62-77.

[57] To those who argue that a recognition of obvious error in ecclesiastical tradition in the process of the transmission of the Faith from generation to generation refutes the claim that tradition can function as a subordinate authority, I offer Van Til's response to those who argue that since the autographs of the Bible have not come down to us infallibly "we have no identifiable revelation of God after all." He notes: "There would be no *reasonably reliable* method of identifying the Word of God in human history unless human history itself is controlled by God. The doctrine of Scripture as self-attesting presupposes that whatsoever comes to pass in history materializes by virtue of the plan and counsel of the living God. If everything happens by virtue of the plan of God, then all created reality, every aspect of it, is inherently revelational of God and his plan. All facts of history are what they are ultimately because of what God intends and makes them to be. Even that which is accomplished in human history through the

instrumentality of men still happens by virtue of the plan of God. God tells the stars by their names. He identifies by complete description. He knows exhaustively. He knows exhaustively because he controls completely ... Such a view of God and of human history is both presupposed by, and in turn presupposes, the idea of an infallible Bible; and if such a God is presupposed then it is not a matter of great worry if the transmissions are not altogether accurate reproductions of the originals. Then the very idea of 'substantial accuracy' or 'essential reliability' has its foundation in the complete control of history by God. Then it is proper and meaningful to say that God in his providence has provided for the essentially accurate transmission of the words of the original.

"Without such a view of history as wholly controlled by the plan of God the idea of an essential dependability would be without foundation. If history is not wholly controlled by God, the idea of an infallible Word of God is without meaning. The idea of an essentially reliable Bible would have no foundation. In a world of contingency all predication is reduced to flux," Van Til, *Theory*, 28, emphasis in original. What is said here of the "essential dependability" of the extant texts of Scripture may be said equally about tradition. The assumption of divine control of history renders unnecessary an infallible or infallibly preserved tradition. That it be reliable is sufficient.

[58] Benjamin Warfield defended against attacks on the inspiration of Scripture that the differences of authorial style militate against Biblical inspiration by noting that the same God who inspired the writers controlled them and history in such a way as to secure that their spontaneous writings constituted his inspired word. See Benjamin Warfield, *The Inspiration and Authority of the Bible* (Phillipsburg, NJ, 1948), 156-158.

[59] Hodge, *op. cit.*, 114.

[60] Rousas John Rushdoony, *Salvation and Godly Rule* (Vallecito, CA, 1983), 345.

[61] H. Richard Niebuhr, *Christ and Culture* (New York, 1951).

[62] See Edward F. Hills, *The King James Version Defended!* (no location: The Christian Research Press, 1956).

[63] Van Til, *Theory*, 23.

Volume VIII, No. 2, 1982

The Atonement Analyzed and Applied

by Rousas John Rushdoony

Expiation and Atonement

The terms *expiation* and *atonement* are very similar. Atonement means the reconciliation of two parties who have become estranged. Expiation is the act of payment, restitution, and restoration whereby atonement is made. When we speak of making atonement, we thus speak of both expiation (the restitution) and atonement (reconciliation).

The most serious mistake we can make with reference to expiation and atonement is to assume that these are ecclesiastical concerns whose sole reference is to a particular institution, the church or Christian synagogue, and its doctrine of Christ. Because the Triune God is maker of heaven and earth and all things therein, all men inescapably have to do with God at every point, act, word, and thought in their lives. As such, they are either in obedience to God, or in disobedience. Whether or not men believe in God, they are inescapably tied to him in all their being. Man's sin and unbelief is a moral or ethical fact; man's being is metaphysically the creation of God. By his sin and unbelief, man makes himself morally estranged from God and at war with God. Metaphysically, however, man still remains totally God's creation and creature, so that, in spite of himself, man cannot depart an iota from the conditions of his life and being as they are ordained by God.

As a result, when man sins, he seeks ethical or moral separation from God and indeed claims a metaphysical separation as his own god (*Gen. 3:5*). The fact remains, however, that man is still God's creation, and everything he does will manifest that fact in spite of himself. Thus, because man was created in God's image to serve him as his subduer over the earth, the condition of man's life is the law-word of God. Whenever and wherever man transgresses God's law, his whole being will demand and seek expiation. Having been created responsible to God, man will seek to discharge that responsibility, even though the form of it is now perverted and evil. Thus, *first,* man continues to seek dominion and to subdue the earth (*Gen. 1:26-28*), although now his quest is turned towards the kingdom of man rather than the kingdom of God. However, all that the ungodly accumulate will only serve God's kingdom (*Is. 61:6*) and the lot of the ungodly will be frustration and failure. *Second,* in his sin, man will inescapably seek to make atonement, even though he may deny in the process that he is either guilty of sin or is seeking to justify himself. Thus, man becomes his own judgment, because his whole being, as the creation of God, will serve God: To be God's creation means to serve God, whether willingly or unwillingly. Because we are totally God's handiwork, in all our being we manifest his purpose and judgment, so that, in our sin, we judge ourselves by our waking and sleeping, our thoughts and our dreams, in our eating and drinking, in our work, rest, and play, in every way we manifest his judgment on our sin.

Asaph tells us, in Psalm 76:10, "Surely the wrath of man shall praise thee: the remainder of wrath shalt thou restrain." Alexander commented:

> The very passions which excite man to rebel against God shall be used as instruments and means of coercion. See . . Ps. xxxii.9. And so complete shall be this process, that even the remnant of such passionate excitement, which might be expected to escape attention, will be nevertheless an instrument or weapon in the hand of God. This last idea is expressed by the figure of a girdle, here considered as a swordbelt. So too in other cases the verb *to gird* is absolutely used in the sense of girding on a sword. See . . Ps. xlv. 3, and compare Judges xviii.11, 2 Kings iii.2.[1]

The Prayer Book Version renders the first half of this verse, "The fierceness of man shall turn to thy praise." Kirk commented, "All rebellion against God's will must in the end redound to God's glory: it serves to set His sovereignty in a clearer light (Ex ix. 16)."[2]

Expiation and atonement are thus inescapable facts. A distinction must be made, however, between that which meets God's requirements, and that which man, in spite of himself, renders as a means of escaping guilt, although without success. *First,* legitimate expiation and atonement meet and fulfill God's requirements. To make atonement legally means thus to do so in the manner prescribed by God in his word, and in no other way. Because it is God's law which all sin violates, it must be God's law alone which sets the terms of reconciliation. No thief, adulterer, or murderer has any legal or moral grounds to set the terms of his forgiveness and reconciliation. He does not make the law, and he has no legitimate bargaining power with respect to it. *Second*, illegitimate expiation and atonement are man's attempts to remove the penalties for sins on his own terms, in his own way, and in his own time and place. In all false expiation and atonement, there is no lack of suffering and punishment, far greater indeed than in legitimate atonement, but there is no release.

Hell is the end result of all illegitimate expiation and atonement. The reprobate, insistent on their own way and their own will, give themselves over to eternal self-justification. They are thus totally past-oriented and past-bound, endlessly rehearsing their sins and endlessly justifying themselves (*Lk. 16:19-31*). There is neither community nor work in hell, only endless memory and unending and determined self-justification.

Heaven is the habitation of those whose sins are legitimately expiated and for whom atonement is accomplished by Christ. The memory of their sins is blotted out even by God (*Is. 43:25*), so that they are freed from the guilt of the past and are future-oriented in this world, and eternity-oriented in the world to come. They now work, with no curse to hinder or frustrate their activities (*Rev. 22:3*), because their reconciliation is real and total (*Rev. 22:4*).

Legitimate and illegitimate expiation and atonement are in two directions, God-ward and man-ward. *First*, all sin is an offense against God, and all sin requires restitution to God. This is the theological aspect of making atonement. The terms are strictly specified by Scripture. *Second,* sin also is man-ward, in that people are robbed, killed, raped, injured, slandered, despoiled by fornication and adultery, defrauded, and so on. Restitution must be made also to man, and this is the anthropological side of making atonement. Civil forgiveness follows such restitution, even as theological forgiveness follows restitution to God. Here again the terms of restitution and restoration are specified by God's law-word.

False religion offers illegitimate expiation and atonement, and false civil orders offer illegitimate expiation and atonement. Examples of the latter are the prison system, rehabilitation programs, psychiatric treatments, and so on, all very much with us.

When false religion and false civil government offers men false expiation and atonement, the social order begins to disintegrate. It may talk about love, brotherhood, and community, but it will be marked by hatred, enmity, and social warfare. Men will be at war with themselves and with other men, torn apart by self-hatred and a hatred of the world and life. Illegitimate expiation and false atonement in church and state mean that the social order begins to exhibit the marks of hell, and there is neither peace nor community.

Ancient Rome recognized the necessity of atonement for social stability and order, and hence it required that all citizens be present for the annual lustrations. The only exemptions allowed were military, and the soldiers gained atonement by proxy. Rome recognized the *necessity* for expiation and atonement, but it sought these things on false grounds and hence failed to gain them.

Today, the same things are sought by means of laws, political action, and psychiatry. If anything, the results are becoming more disastrous now than they were then. Thus, expiation and atonement are matters of great concern, of heaven and hell, of life or death, and any person or society neglecting them will pay the price of self-destruction.

Our Atonement by Jesus Christ

At the heart of Christian faith is the fact that sinful man, incapable of making atonement to God, is redeemed by the atoning work of Jesus Christ. This great act is set forth typically in the Old Testament sacrificial system, and it is to the Old Testament we must look first for its meaning. We are told of man's fall, and the subsequent course of mankind (*Gen. 3-5*). Man as a sinner cannot render unto God that holiness and righteousness which is God's due. Lawless man is in all his being anti-God and is no more capable of faith in God and obedience to God's law than is a dead man capable of dancing a jig. Paul in Romans 3:9-20 stresses the total inability of man to justify himself by self-righteousness. The sinner's self-righteousness compounds his sin.

Salvation is entirely the work of the Triune God through Jesus
Christ. Because it is entirely God's work, it is academic to discuss
whether or not man can exercise his supposed free will. If God is
man's creator, man's will, and all his being, is the handiwork of
God and a part of his plan. For Arminians to assume some area of
independence for man is to assume that God is not wholly God,
and that man constitutes an area of independence from God in
the universe.

Moreover, the atonement, as we meet it in Leviticus, is a
covenant fact. The sacrificial system did not render expiation and
atonement for all men but for covenant man, Israelite and non-
Israelite. Those whom God chose as his covenant people were at
one and the same time those who were redeemed and for whom
intercession was made. There is no hint of universalism in the Old
Testament with respect to the efficacy of sacrifice. In Psalm 87, we
have the procession of foreigners into Zion, and, of all of them it is
said, "This and that man was born in her" (*Ps. 87:5*), and this fact
of being born into citizenship in the Jerusalem of God is of God's
choosing: "The LORD shall count, when he writeth up the people,
that this man was born there" (*Ps. 87:6*). "The people" can be
translated "the nations." God is portrayed as choosing the peoples,
individuals from all nations, and by his sovereign choice decreeing
their rebirth and their reconciliation. To be *born there* means to be
born into the covenant by God's sovereign grace. Particular persons
are saved, but no man is saved in abstraction from either Christ or
Adam. We are redeemed *out of* and *from* the humanity of Adam
into the new humanity of Jesus Christ. Our salvation is thus both
individual and particular and at the same time an aspect of the
universal fact of Christ's new humanity and new creation: the old
man or old humanity of Adam is sentenced to death and is
abolished, and the old world is sentenced to death also. Those
who are chosen and elected to redemption are transferred from
one world and humanity to another. Those who are ordained for
reprobation are elected to self-expiation and self-justification, to a
cycle of sado-masochistic activities. There are two humanities and
two kinds of expiation and atonement.

We cannot separate the facts of atonement and regeneration

except for theological analysis: in life, they are inseparable. No man is regenerate without Christ's atonement, and only the regenerate are atoned for through Christ. To speak of Christ having died for all men as individuals (rather than all men, *i.e.,* all peoples, races, tongues, and tribes) is in essence the same as saying that Christ has regenerated all men, an impossible statement.

Can we limit this by saying Christ opened up the *possibility* of atonement and regeneration for all men? Emphatically not, because the cross did not constitute a possibility but *the fact* of expiation and atonement. Moreover, there can be no *possibility* outside of God without a denial of God. *All the possibilities* of atonement in the cross were and are of God's sovereign choice and predestination. The idea of a universal atonement dethrones God and enthrones man.

The world-wide nature of God's kingdom is set forth in Psalm 87. It develops the thought of Psalm 86:9,10:

> All nations whom thou hast made shall come and worship before thee, O LORD: and shall glorify thy name.
> For thou are great, and doest wondrous things: thou art God alone.

Thus, the very psalm which restricts the kingdom of God to those born by God's choice into the covenant speaks of God's sovereign grace to the Gentiles. Leupold titles the psalm "The Glorification of Zion by the Adoption of the Gentiles."[3] The universalism of the faith is eschatological: it is not a universal atonement but a world-wide dominion by God's sovereign and efficacious grace.

Psalm 87 declares that the foundation of the true Zion is of God. A catalogue of some of Israel's enemies follows, but these enemies are now by rebirth the people of God's covenant. *All God's people,* including singers and the players on instruments, cry out to God with joy, "All my springs are in thee" (*Ps. 87:7*). They do not rejoice because they chose the Lord, but because he chose them (*Ps. 87:6*). It is not their free will they celebrate but God's sovereign grace: "All my springs are in thee."

The atonement is universal in the sense that men of every race and nation are among the redeemed. In this sense, "all men" are included in God's election. It is not universal if *all men* as individuals are meant. Christ's expiation and atonement have reference to his covenant people. Scripture tells us that Jesus Christ suffered and died for his sheep (*Jn. 10:11, 15*), his church (*Ac. 20:28; Eph. 5:25, 27*), his people (*Mt. 1:21*), and the elect (*Rom. 8:32-35*), and this was in terms of an eternal and efficacious purpose by the omnipotent God. "The world" is to be reconciled to God (*2 Cor. 5:19*) because it is to be recreated, whereas the reprobate are cast out as false heirs (*Mt. 21:33-41*). The re-made and new world and the regenerated humanity in Christ shall live forever in the joy of their Lord, and in the glory of the resurrection. An atomistic view of man can lead to the Arminian view of the atonement, but any view which takes seriously the sovereignty of God, and the covenantal nature of man's relationship to God, will reject that view. Significantly, Arminians do reject both God's sovereignty and covenantalism.

Lawless man makes himself his own god and law and denies God and his law. To be redeemed means to believe in and obey God, to be subject to his absolute government. Expiation and atonement reconcile us to God's sovereign rule and government, so that, as Berkhof points out, atonement is closely tied to intercession:

> The great and central part of the priestly work of Christ lies in the atonement, but this, of course, is not complete without the intercession. His sacrificial work on earth calls for his service in the heavenly sanctuary. The two are complementary parts of the priestly task of the Saviour.[4]

Both atonement and intercession, priestly tasks, are inseparably tied to Christ's royal task, government: The government is upon his shoulder (*Is. 9:6*). Only those who are subject to his government by his sovereign grace are at the same time those for whom he makes intercession with the Father. And those for whom he makes intercession are those whom he has made atonement for in his mercy: they are the covenant people. The reprobate are in covenant with death and hell (*Is. 28:15*).

There are thus two covenants, two humanities, and two kinds of atonement. Those who are the reprobate find their atonement

and self-justification in sado-masochistic activities. Those who are
the elect of God in Christ are called out of this fruitless and self-
defeating atonement to Christ's efficacious work. They move from
self-government to God's government, from self-made laws to
God's law, from talking to themselves to praying to God through
Christ, and from the covenant with death and hell to the covenant
of God in Christ.

Vicarious Sacrifice

An ancient Greek religious rite gives us an insight into the
widespread existence of vicarious sacrifices and penalties:

> ... the *Thargelia*, a festival of Apollo at Athens, included a
> peculiar rite in which one or two men (*pharmakoi*) were first fed
> at the public expense, then beaten with branches and leeks, and
> finally put to death. The connexion with Apollo was not very
> marked; it seems rather to be an ancient rite which had to do
> with the safety of the ripening crop. Nor does it presuppose the
> Divine anger, though doubtless more stress was laid on such a
> ceremony in time of famine or pestilence, when men felt that
> their gods were angry with them. It was primarily a means of
> removing any taint of evil which might bring danger to men or
> destruction to their ripening crops. Because rites of this character
> were out of line with the development of Greek religion from
> Homer onward, it is perhaps safe to regard them as survivals
> from a very early period. In themselves they shed little light on
> the present question, except as they indicate that men feared the
> possible anger of their gods, and possessed means to allay the
> anger itself. Still these rites of riddance must be taken into
> account as the source of later purificatory rites, and perhaps as
> the starting-point of propitiatory sacrifice.[5]

Fairbanks gives us an evolutionary perspective, and hence what
he describes is a very primitive rite in his eyes which historical
development made obsolete.

Such vicarious sacrifices are readily found all over the world,
among Aztec and other Indians (human sacrifices), and evidence
is not lacking of the prevalence and persistence thereof.

These earlier *forms* of vicarious sacrifice have indeed often given
way as cultures have developed and grown sophisticated, but this

by no means gives us any ground for assuming that the fundamental motive in these rites has disappeared or abated.

In dealing with the fact of *motive*, it is necessary to begin by calling attention to the *tainted* motives of fallen man. Man, as sinner and covenant-breaker, approaches all things from the standpoint of his rebellion. This means that, even when he accepts his guilt, he in effect denies it. He can ascribe guilt to the environment, other people, or to God, and he can do so directly, or, by admitting guilt, he can still do so indirectly by insisting that the conditions of his life made sin likely or inevitable. Thus, Epicurus insisted that the world poses a moral dilemma: if God wishes to prevent evil and cannot, then God is impotent. If God could prevent evil and does not, then God is evil. Thus, as Epicurus framed the problem, God was in either case indicted and man absolved, and man had every "good" reason to reject God as evil or to rule him out of the universe as impotent or dead.

When man is guilty, or feels guilty, he suffers. When he suffers, he resents the fact that he does, and he is determined that others should suffer also. For him the world is out of joint because he himself is, and someone must pay for this. Vicarious suffering and sacrifice is demanded by covenant-breaking man, ancient and modern, as a means of satisfying his own outrage at being made to suffer. When Cain was angry at God, he killed his brother Abel, and Lamech (*Gen. 4:23-24*) made clear that "whoever wrongs me in the least forfeits his life."[6] The "wrong" could be a fancied one: Lamech made himself the judge, and others a vicarious sacrifice to his own assertion of autonomy. The motive in all non-Biblical vicarious suffering and sacrifice is thus a tainted and evil one. Basic to man's life, politics, and religion is this effort to lay his own guilt upon others. Even in masochistic self-punishment, there is a strong sense of the evil and oppressive world of God and man which "requires" such suffering. The masochist is an injustice collector, to use the apt phrase of Dr. Edmund Bergler. The world and God are to him dispensers of injustice, and he is the perpetual and long-suffering victim.

It is clear thus that vicarious suffering and sacrifice is a part of the life of fallen man. The masochist suffers, he believes, because God and man are evil, and he is their appointed and innocent victim. The sadist, on the other hand, lays his guilt on others and requires them to accept the role of a vicarious sacrifice.

But a still deeper motive is also always present. All men who are covenant-breakers are not only tainted in their motives but guilty men as well. Although they may consciously deny or excuse their guilt, in their hearts they know that they are guilty. It is thus guilt, injustice, or unrighteousness which leads them to suppress the knowledge of God (*Rom. 1:18-21*). They are guilty in relationship to God and his law; they seek to make themselves gods and their own sources of the determination of good and evil, of morality and law (*Gen. 3:5*). Denying God is basic to their denial of guilt. If there be no God, then man cannot be an offender against a myth, a non-existent thing. Basic to atheism is the flight from guilt and responsibility.

However, man is God's creation, and every atom of his being witnesses to God, as does all creation. There is thus for him no escape from the witness of God (*Ps. 139*). At every hand, he is confronted by God, God's claims on him, and his guilt before God. Man thus stands guilty in all his being, and inescapably so, as long as he is a covenant-breaker.

Sigmund Freud saw man as inescapably guilty, and he held that, until the problem of guilt were solved, religion and priestcraft could never be abolished. Guilty men would seek somehow to find relief through religion, and some sort of religious atonement. The abolition of religion could only be properly effected by reducing guilt to a scientific problem and explaining it away as a survival of man's primitive past and of ancient drives within his unconscious being.[7] The practical effect of Freud's solution was to create a new priestcraft to deal with the problem of guilt, psychoanalysts, with psychologists and psychiatrists also engaged in a like task.

Man seeks, in his sin, a sin-bearer to bear the burden of his guilt. Hence, vicarious sacrifice is basic to his outlook. "Someone must pay," he believes, and pay heavily for the suffering of others. The masochist seeks himself as the vicarious victim. He makes atonement for his own guilt by means of masochistic activities, but, even in so doing, he is eloquently protesting against God and life for requiring so great a price.

Bergler has spoken of the habit of masochists of pleading guilty to the lesser offense. His meaning is Freudian, but his insights are often telling. Even the guilty pleas of sinful man are an indictment of God and life. The sado-masochists deny the sin, resent the guilt, and charge the real offense to God, life, and man.

Thus, the doctrine of vicarious sacrifice is not evaded by denying Biblical faith. It remains, in a warped and evil form, because it is inescapable. Whenever and wherever man denies God and his word, he replaces it with an imitation thereof. All the categories of life are God-created and God-ordained. Man cannot escape them; in his sin, he perverts them.

God's law has penalties for sin. These penalties are fixed and unchanging. The sin of man requires eternal death. Man is incapable in his sin of pleasing God, or of offering an acceptable sacrifice or atonement. Man cannot make a personal atonement to God, or place God in his debt by any works or acts. His creation was of grace, and his life is incapable, apart from God's grace, of ever pleasing God. Even in his faithfulness, he is still an unprofitable servant (*Lk. 17:10*). Only through the vicarious sacrifice of God the Son, who takes upon himself the death penalty for the sins of his elect, can there be a remission of sin and guilt. All atonement in Scripture is by vicarious sacrifice, first set forth typically in the appointed clean animals (*Lev. 1:4; 16:20-22; etc.*), and then by Jesus Christ (*Is. 53:6, 12; Jn. 1:29; 2 Cor. 5:21; Ga. 3:13; Heb. 9:28; 1 Pet. 2:24*).

Vicarious sacrifice is inescapable. In covenant-breaking man, it means sado-masochistic activities; it means punishing various classes, races, or peoples as the guilt-bearers for the rest of society. It means a politics of guilt and hatred, and a constant social revolution, as one group after another seeks to absolve man and society of guilt by punishing a chosen "evil" class or group which is made responsible and guilty for man's sins and problems.[8] The failure of churches to understand the meaning of vicarious sacrifice and the *freedom* it creates has been disastrous to man and society. The presence of covenant-breaking forms of atonement is always a menace to man and society.

Imputation

Perversity has long been native to man's disposition, in ways great and small. Men seem to prefer unhappiness, because they go to such great lengths to ensure its persistence and presence.

Literature in particular manifests extremes of perversity. Catullus, in pre-Christian Rome, is a very obvious example. Modern man is also marked by a penchant for unhappiness and perversity, by a desire to create conditions whereby he can accuse God and man of treating him unfairly. His greatest pleasure is often in this triumphant charge of injustice. He collects injustices as though injustice were gold, and then he finds even greater pleasure in charging God and man with unfairly and unjustly visiting them upon him. In humorous fashion, the cartoonist Charles M. Schulz has Lucy declare:

> When you feel down and out
> Lift up your head and shout,
> Someone's going to pay for this!

There are times when the hatred of happiness, prosperity, success, light, and peace are openly expressed. Usually, however, man claims to want all things good while willfully working to ensure the triumph of evil. In effect, man says, because I am evil and dark, let there be only darkness.

Is this an overstatement? Let us then glance at a student poem for confirmation, H. E. Sheleny's "Hate":

> The dismal rain comes down
>   And taps against my window pane
> Like so many little demons
>   Striving to steal in and possess
> My soul. I love the Rain.
>   The Darkness cascades over me
> As if to engulf me in a torrent
>   Of fear. I love the Dark.
> The Sun warms me. It brightens
>   The world. It SEEMS to offer hope.
> I hate the Sun.[9]

The point is ably and powerfully made. The Rain and the Dark are dismal, like little demons, and they seek to steal and possess the soul. They are compared to a torrent of fear. Yet "I love the

Dark," *i.e.*, evil, fear, the demonic, and so on. The Sun gives light and warmth and offers hope; ergo, "I hate the Sun."

Man not only chooses evil, but he also chooses suffering. He seeks to justify his continued rebellion against God and his preference for evil by indicting God for injustice in making man suffer so greatly. The greater man's suffering for sin, the greater his self-justification and his sense of self-righteousness before God and man.

Theologians have rightly distinguished between *original* sin and *actual* sins. Original sin is the evilness or sinfulness of fallen man in all his being. It is the common attribute of all who are in the humanity of Adam. This sin or depravity is total in that it is the governing fact in his nature which colors his mind, will, emotions, actions, and all his being. Just as a tiger is always a tiger, so a member of the humanity of Adam is inescapably a man whose being is not merely marked by but is in essence governed by original sin, the desire for autonomy from God as a self-ordained God. Actual sins are particular acts in violation of God's law. A new-born babe is without actual sins; it is marked by original sin.

In the atonement by Jesus Christ, this fallen man dies in Christ and is made a new creation in him. His actual sins are atoned for, and his old life and nature are sentenced to death and then made a new creation.[10] Regeneration and justification accompany the atonement. Without them, actual sins would be dealt with only, but the sinning man would remain unchanged.

Jesus Christ, "the Lamb slain from the foundation of the world" (*Rev. 13:8*) is he in terms of whom God makes all things new (*Rev. 21:5*). Not only does he remove sins from creation, but he removes the fact of sinfulness or rebellion and regenerates all things in terms of himself into the renewed image of God. This means a life of the knowledge of and obedience to God, of righteousness or justice in all our ways, of holiness or separation and dedication to him in all our being, and it means also a life of dominion, man under God bringing every area of life and thought into captivity to Jesus Christ.

This freedom of the believer is accomplished by Christ's atonement. The sins of the redeemed man, or of the man who is by grace singled out for redemption, are *imputed* to Jesus Christ;

they are laid to his charge, entered into his account, so that he assumes the penalty of death for us. But this is not all: through him and in him we have the *remission* (*aphesis*) of sins. Our sins are forgiven; restitution is made for them by Jesus Christ, and there is a dismissal of sins and a release. The remission of sins means that we stand before God as pardoned men. The atonement effects a *legal* change in our status before God.

But a pardoned murderer or revolutionist is still a law-breaker at heart. Not so the redeemed man. At the same time, he is *regenerated,* made a new creation, by the Holy Spirit through Christ, so that the pardon is received by the new man; it gives new life to one who is newly raised from the death of sin.

To remit the sins of the ungodly is to compound evil. Humanists, denying God's law, insist that love and forgiveness can win over a criminal and change his life. The result has been the proliferation of crime and a growing decay of society. The criminal remains a criminal still, and all that the humanistic remission of sins accomplishes for him is a greater freedom to commit crime, to sin.

All offenses against God's law require death. If we do not have the death of Christ as our vicarious substitute, we have the certainty of death at the hands of Christ as King and Judge. Those who commit capital offenses against God's law with respect to human society should face death at the hands of a godly government as well.

It is Christ's atonement which saves the sinner. The atonement does not simply make salvation possible: it makes it actual, because it secures and seals an unchanging and irrevocable salvation. What Christ does cannot be undone, and whatever work he begins in a man, he carries through to its eternal fulfillment and glory.

The perversity of man in warring against God is replaced by a delight in doing God's will, and rebellion and unbelief are replaced by faith and obedience. Without imputation, there is no redemption. The denial of imputation implies a humanistic faith in the self-sufficiency of man and his ability to save himself. In Romans 5:12 Paul tells us:

> Wherefore, as by one man sin entered into the world, and death by sin; and so death passed upon all men, for that all have sinned.

Here as elsewhere man's inability to grasp the full meaning of God's truth no more nullifies that truth than a man's blindness obliterates the sun from the heavens. Paul makes clear that our solidarity with Adam is a very real fact. Adam's sin and fall mean "that all have sinned." Adam is our federal head or representative man. As all tigers and hyenas are no less tigers and hyenas from Adam's day to ours, so we are no less begotten in Adam's image, and in his own likeness (*Gen. 5:3*).

Adam's sin is thus imputed to all men. This is the *legal* fact. All of Adam's race are a part of a war against God, and so death is "passed upon all men," *i.e.*, the sentence of death, for all sinned in Adam. Just as a man's liability for damages becomes the liability of his family residing with him, and of his property and income, so the liability of Adam becomes the liability of his race and the earth they inhabit. This is the *legal* fact.

The physical and moral fact is that all of Adam's race are begotten in his image. We are not told how this moral rebellion is transmitted, but we are told that it is basic to our very conception (*Ps. 51:5*).

Imputation is basic to our condemnation, and to our pardon. Even as Adam is the head of the new humanity. Murray cited the parallels and the contrast ably:

> We cannot grasp the truths of world-wide significance set forth in this passage unless we recognize that two antithetical complexes are contrasted. The first is the complex of sin-condemnation-death and the second is that of righteousness-justification-life. These are invariable combinations. Sin sets in operation the inevitable consequents of condemnation and death, righteousness the consequents of justification and life, and, as is obvious, these are antithetical at each point of the parallel.[11]

The godly man thus moves in terms of Christ and his law-word, Christ's righteousness or justice. His sentence of death was just, and his redemption an act of sovereign grace. Accordingly, the redeemed man becomes an instrument of Christ's redeeming power and of his righteousness or justice. Christ as the true and new man puts into force man's calling (*Heb. 10:5-19*), which David of old set forth in Psalm 40:7-10:

> Then said I, Lo, I come: in the volume of the book it is written
> of me.
> I delight to do thy will, O my God: yea, thy law is within my
> heart.
> I have preached righteousness in the great congregation: lo, I
> have not refrained my lips, O LORD, thou knowest.
> I have not hid thy righteousness within my heart; I have
> declared thy faithfulness and thy salvation: I have not
> concealed thy loving-kindness and thy truth from the great
> congregation.

Even as we once did the works of Adam, so now we do the works of Christ; we are governed by his word and his spirit. This means that we who are now alive in Christ are also alive to his law-word and to his spirit. Christ's work being perfect, and his power extending to every realm, he does what no human judge can do: his legal pronouncement of pardon and remission of sins is accompanied by his regenerating power and a new life that delights in obeying the Lord. Alexander's comment on Psalm 40:7 is very good:

> The reference is here to the Law of Moses. *Written of me* is by
> some referred to prophecy, by others to the requisitions of the
> law. The literal meaning of the Hebrew words is *written upon
> me, i.e.,* prescribed to me, the *upon* suggesting the idea of an
> incumbent obligation. "Enjoined upon me by a written precept."
> This is clearly the meaning of the same phrase in 2 Kings xxii.13.
> Thus understood, the clause before us may be paraphrased as
> follows: - "Since the ceremonies of the Law are worthless, when
> divorced from habitual obedience, instead of offering mere
> sacrifice I offer myself, to do whatever is prescribed to me in the
> written revelation of thy will." This is the spirit of every true
> believer, and is therefore perfectly appropriate to the whole class
> to whom this psalm relates, and for whom it was intended. It is
> peculiarly significant, however, when applied to Christ: first,
> because he alone possessed this spirit in perfection; secondly,
> because he sustained a peculiar relation to the rites, and more
> especially the sacrifices of the Law.[12]

The redeemed man thus has the Lord as his federal head, a program for dominion through God's law, and a freedom from perversity into joyful and willing obedience through faith. He has undergone a legal change by imputation and remission. He has a new life by Christ's regenerating grace and power.

Because Jesus Christ is very God of very God as well as very man of very man, our salvation is the work of eternity, not of time, and of the Creator, not of the creation. It stands thus impervious to the workings of men and history, and it abides eternally. Without imputation, man is trapped in history and its sin and death. In Jesus Christ we have our glorious and eternal salvation, victory in time and eternity.

The unregenerate impute sins to man and to God. Sado-masochism means that a man's sins are imputed to other men, or to one's self in a charade of self-pity which accuses God, but, in either case, there is an implicit and explicit imputation to God and to other men. Injustice-collecting has basic to it imputation. The injustice collector collects injustices as a means of increasing his misery and his tally of indictments against God and man. If the masochist suffers, it is suffering as a means of indicting others and of affirming a basic innocence behind the confessions to lesser offenses.

Those who charge the doctrine of imputation as representing a lower morality must face this "paradox": humanistic, sado-masochistic imputation is a flight from moral responsibility and accountability, whereas the Biblical doctrine goes hand in hand with a true confession of sin and guilt, and a new life of moral responsibility. Humanistic morality imputes sin to God, the environment, society, capitalism, communism, and so on, rather than facing man's responsibility honestly. It brings in imputation, not to redeem man from his sins, but to absolve him falsely. Biblical imputation goes hand in hand with the sinner's full awareness of his offense against God. In Scripture, those whose sins are imputed to Christ do *not* impute the guilt of sins to him. They freely confess their sin and guilt. It is the offense and the death penalty which is imputed to Christ, and by means thereof the elect are redeemed and pardoned. Those whose sins are imputed to Christ confess their sin and guilt: they do not impute them to their parents, the environment, capitalism, their teachers, or anything else. Rather, they are *delivered* from such false imputation.

False imputation began with the fall. Adam imputed his sin to Eve and to God: "The woman *whom thou gavest* to be with me, *she gave me* of the tree, and I did eat" (*Gen. 3:12*). Eve imputed her sin to the tempter: "The serpent beguiled me, and I did eat" (*Gen. 3:13*). Ever since then, imputation of this false and evil variety has been basic to the life of man. The Bible thus does not give us a strange or novel doctrine: it gives us the only valid and moral form of imputation, one basic to moral responsibility and to legal accountability in a just moral order.

Sacrifice

False imputation has almost the status of a science today. The source of evil is regularly traced to a group, class, or race. Capitalism, communism, the military-industrial complex, Puritanism, the blacks, whites, and so on are seen as the root causes of evil in the world. More sophisticated forms in psychoanalysis and psychiatry impute sin to our parents, our environment, our "primitive" ancestors, and so on. The psychiatrist, modern man's new priest, does not ask for a confession of sins which acknowledges sin in the way that the confession of the Office of Compline does:

> I confess to God Almighty, the Father, the Son, and the Holy Ghost, and before all the company of heaven, that I have sinned, in thought, word and deed, through my fault, my own fault, my own most grievous fault: wherefore I pray Almighty God to have mercy on me, to forgive me all my sins, and to make clean my heart within me.

The psychiatric confessor receives confession in order to impute guilt to some other person, thing, event, or cause than the confessing person. There is absolution by false imputation: the confessing person's guilt is transferred and imputed to another person or cause. Basic to modern psychiatry and psychology, as well as to its politics and sociology, is an essential environmentalism. Environmentalism is simply a form of imputation, and the modern world is governed by this false doctrine of imputation. Since all of us are both the victims of this environment, and, at the same time, the environment for all other people, we thus impute our small quota of sin and guilt to others and also have imputed to us the sins of our entire age and world. In every way, man is the loser! Moreover, he exchanges a true for a false sense of responsibility: he imputes personal sins to others while assuming sins that are not his own.

Eugenics and the emphasis on heredity do not solve the problem of imputation: they transfer the problem to the past, which cannot be changed, and offer hope only in distant generations yet to come.

But this is not all. False imputation requires a false sacrifice. Someone must pay the penalty for the sin and guilt, and the net result is that, in humanistic societies, social energies are directed, not towards godly reconstruction, but towards making the guilty class or group pay the penalty. Since the accused group has a different idea of who should be sacrificed for the social good, the result is civil conflict and sometimes blood-letting. False imputation requires a continual sacrifice of the offenders, and the more grievous the conflict, the more bloody the sacrifice.

In Biblical imputation, the sinner must fully recognize that the sins imputed to the sacrificed are *his own*. The evangelical formula is, "Christ died for *my* sins," not for sin in general, nor for *our* sins, but *mine*. Sin does not belong to the environment, to capitalism, communism, nor our parents. It is personal, and it is *mine*. In the words of the Office of Compline, it is "my fault, my own fault, my own most grievous fault." Biblical imputation is also the birth of responsibility. The truly redeemed, as against false professors, are *responsible* persons. Biblical imputation transfers us from the irresponsibility of the fallen Adam and from his false imputation [" *The woman thou gavest* to be with me, *she gave me* of the tree, and I did eat" (*Gen. 3:12*)], to godly responsibility. Instead of imputing guilt to others, we assume the *responsibility*, we find in Christ our atonement by his vicarious sacrifice and our freedom from sin and guilt, from irresponsibility, and from false imputation.

The sacrificial system of the Bible sets forth this principle of responsibility and imputation. All sacrificial animals had to be clean animals or birds, bullocks, goats, sheep, dove, or pigeon (*Gen. 8:20; Lev. chapts. 1, 11, etc.*). Thus, the *first* aspect of sacrifice is that the offering had to be clean, *i.e.*, kosher as food and hence an animal of usefulness. *Second*, the animal had to be without blemish (*Lev. 1:3, 3:1, 2:17-25; Dt. 15:21, 17:1; Mal. 1:6ff.*). If a herd animal, it was to be a male for certain offerings, as the burnt sacrifice. It could not be a sick or old animal but only one in every way unblemished and valuable. *Third,* it had to be a domestic animal. Some wild animals are clean, but the wild animals are not man's property (*2 Sam. 24:24*), and the sacrifice begins with the surrender by the sacrificer of what is his, and from the best of his possessions. The wild animals are already God's (*Ps. 50:10-11*). Unlawfully acquired property could not be offered to God (*Dt. 23:18*). The unbloody offerings, cereals, flour, oil, wine, fruits, etc., were all products of man's labor and hence again were man's property and exacted a price, a sacrifice from man. The sacrifice involved the best from man's possessions and the best to God.

Fourth, the thing sacrificed represented the sacrificer and, on the Day of Atonement, represented also his sin and guilt. Aaron confessed all the transgressions of Israel and placed his hands on the sacrificial animal, the scapegoat (*Lev. 16:21-22*). The laying on of hands represents a transfer, as of the Spirit (*Num. 27:18; 2 Tim. 1:6, etc.*), and it was probably normal practice in all sacrifices.

Thus, the Biblical sacrifices involved a transfer of sin and guilt to a vicarious sin bearer or substitute. The sacrifice had to be a part of the life and possessions of the sacrificer, of his best. There was thus an identification with the death, a confession of sin and guilt, and thus a strong and full sense of responsibility together with gratitude to God that an unblemished substitute was ordained by God.

The sacrificial victim thus belonged to the condemned and was a substitute. Paul tells us that Jesus Christ is our passover lamb, sacrificed for us (*1 Cor. 5:7*). Christ appeared "to put away sin by the sacrifice of himself" (*Heb. 9:26*). He, as the Adam of the new creation, dies for his elect and effects their atonement, a change in their *legal* status from men sentenced to death to pardoned and free men; he changes their *moral* status by making them a new creation by regeneration; and he changes their *family* status by making them sons of God by the adoption of grace.

False imputation breeds not only irresponsibility, an inability to face up to sin and guilt, but false sacrifice. All who are members of the humanity of Adam are ever involved in looking for sacrificial victims. Whatever the problem or offense, a sin-bearer is sought out as the scapegoat. Whereas with the Biblical scapegoat there was a personal and total confession of sins, and all men as sinners were individually and nationally to see themselves as guilty *before God* for their transgressions, humanism sees things differently. The offense is in essence *against man*, because its definition of law and of sin is man-centered. Man then must make atonement to man and be sacrificed to man. Sin is not seen as the human condition of the entire humanity of Adam but as an attribute of a class, group, or race. The sin-bearer and scapegoat is then a guilty segment of humanity which must be made the victim, *i.e.*, the capitalists, communists, blacks, whites, male chauvinists, and so on. Then all men see the problem as the sin and guilt of *the other* group, and all men try to effect atonement and salvation by sacrificing all other men. History then becomes, as it has been, a bloody battleground. Politics becomes in the hands of humanists the art of providing scapegoats and sacrificial victims.

The word *sacrifice* comes from the Latin *sacrificium, sacer*, holy, and *facere*, to make, so that it means that something is forfeited or destroyed in order to re-establish a communion and to make holy the sacrificer.

This Christ does for us. As Chytraeus wrote:

> The *efficient principal cause* of Christ's sacrifice is the will of God's Son, who voluntarily turned upon Himself the wrath of God against sin and underwent abuse and dreadful torments of soul and body, so as to make satisfaction for the sins of the human race and, with the placation of God's wrath, restore righteousness and eternal life to men. John 10:15: "I lay down My life for the sheep." Isa. 53:7: "He was sacrificed because He Himself willed it." Ps. 40:8: "I have delighted to do thy will, O my God."[13]

Because Biblical imputation and sacrifice go hand in hand with responsibility, and atonement is also accompanied by regeneration, Christ's sacrifice does make holy. Humanistic sacrifices intensify sin. To illustrate, racism is today a major sin in the eyes of humanists. Thus, where whites have been in the past guilty of racism, and of victimizing other races, they must now be victimized and sacrificed to make atonement for their ancestors' sins.

But the human condition outside of Christ involves *total*

depravity, i.e., every aspect of the individual is governed by the fall and sin, and every people, tongue, tribe, and race is affected totally by sin. Thus, to stay with racism, no oppressed race has ever lacked its own form of racism as well as the full complement of sins. One group may be culturally richer in its inheritance, but both oppressor and oppressed have a common problem. Exchanging places does not solve that problem, nor does the idea of equality, which is, together with inequality, an abstraction and a meaningless myth when applied to the concrete and actual situations of men and races. As there are differences between members of one family, so there are also between members of one nation, or one race. Abstractions only complicate the concreteness of human problems.

If man's problem is sin, then political abstractions and political attempts to solve problems by finding victim groups are dangerously false, nor do they solve the root problem. Political scapegoats are found, and the problem is intensified, because it is falsely dealt with, in that irresponsibility is fostered. Laws can no more abolish racism than they can abolish sickness, death, or bad weather.

How then can we deal with racism? We recognize, *first* that there is a basic division in humanity, between those who are of Adam, and those who are of Christ. *Second*, those who are of Christ are only those who manifest the works of Christ. "By their fruits shall ye know them" (*Mt. 7:20*). The regenerate do not live by man's law and mores but by God's word and law (*Mt. 4:4*). In terms of God's word and law, they seek the reconstruction of all things. If we pinpoint the evil as racism, communism, or capitalism, we may or may not deal with actual evils, but we do so then from a perspective which is false and in itself evil. We fail to see sin in its true nature. We become self-righteous, and, if we deal with actual victimization, our answer is to transfer victimization to another group. Humanistic peace treaties lay the foundations for the next war, and humanistic solutions become the fabric of the new problems, because in essence they involve false imputation and require false sacrifices. These sacrifices do not make holy: they pollute humanity. Christ's sacrifice redeems the humanity of the new Adam and makes it righteous or just. As Paul says:

> But now the righteousness of God without the law is manifested,
>   being witnessed by the law and the prophets;

> Even the righteousness of God which is by faith of Jesus Christ
> unto all and upon all them that believe: for there is no
> difference:
> For all have sinned, and come short of the glory of God:
> Being justified freely by his grace through the redemption
> that is in Christ Jesus:
> Whom God hath set forth to be a propitiation through faith in
> his blood to declare the remission of sins that are past,
> through the forbearance of God.
> To declare, I say, at this time his righteousness: that he might
> be just, and the justifier of him which believeth in Jesus.
> *(Rom. 3:21-26)*

Man's obedience to the law, if that were possible, could not effect man's salvation. The justice or righteousness of God, to which the law and the prophets witness, requires the penalty of death upon sin. All men are sinners, and none are righteous in and of themselves. The atonement and justification of the people of Christ is thus not of themselves but of Christ. By means of his atoning sacrifice, he effects the remission of our sins and makes us legally righteous before God. Christ's is the one true sacrifice for sin.

Where a false sacrifice or victimization for sins is effected, a false order and a false peace are created. If one problem is alleviated, it is only to create another. In the humanistic worldview, we are all of us victims, and we are all of us victimizers, because we belong to a group, race, class, or profession someone can find responsible and hence guilty for their plight. Men endlessly document their humanistic doctrines of imputation in order to "solve" problems of poverty, racism, war, class conflict, crime, and all things else. Because of our extensive social interlocks, all these solutions have a semblance of truth. The roll-call of "facts" is an endless one. We are thus guilty of racism, and we are also the victims of capitalism, socialism, fascism, or communism. We are alternately victim and victimizer and always more and more the slaves of the civil government which seeks atonement by imputing sins falsely to these various factors. Politics becomes the art of imputation so that some group or class may be sacrificed in order to save society. False imputation destroys society, however, because it leads to false victimization, to making another group the scapegoat. In the Bible, the people had to identify themselves with the scapegoat. It was the sin of *all* the people which the scapegoat bore. In humanism, others are the scapegoats, and all sins and problems are imputed to them. The consequence is self-righteousness and hypocrisy, and also social anarchy and civil conflict. In trying to victimize one group, all are sacrificed; by failure to confess total depravity, sin is magnified and given status as good politics and sound sociology. False imputation leads to false sacrifice, and the result is death, not life.

The Unatoned

The unatoned, those who have no redemption in Jesus Christ, cannot live without atonement. They seek that atonement in sado-masochistic activities. "A large percentage" of prostitution is concerned with meeting the demands of sado-masochism.[14] Politics provides a fertile area of activity for many sado-masochists. We are told of Lloyd George "that he reduced those who worked with him to nervous wrecks, almost as a way of charging himself with energy."[15] The treatment of employees and associates in the world of business and labor unions is rich in sado-masochism. Our literature has become pathological, and its prominent figures are perverse in their natures and writings.[16]

Those outside of Christ seek, consciously or unconsciously, an atonement by means of their own sado-masochistic plan. But, without Christ's atonement, men are trapped in their own cycles of self-punishment, pleading guilty to the lesser offense, and to sadism, ascribing the greater and real offense to others. This sado-masochism will manifest itself in every area of our lives, and it will lead to a politics of self-abasement and self-destruction, combined with an ascription of ultimate sin and offense to a class, religion, race, or group. Sado-masochism separates men from reality to fantasy; it creates what Warner rightly calls the urge to mass destruction, often presented as the salvation of man and the world.[17]

It leads not only to a non-productive and suicidal life, but also to fear. Out of a background of police and detective work, O'Grady saw clearly, "Fear is the tax that conscience pays to guilt."[18]

The unatoned seek atonement, *usually unconsciously,* in sado-masochistic activities, through fantasy, politics, marriage, religion, social work, and so on, polluting all that they touch.

Consciously also, they recognize that sin must be atoned for, somehow removed. Massive and costly political and social efforts are demanded and instituted in order to remove sin, and we have the politics, sociology, and psychotherapy of sado-masochism on all sides. Sin somehow must be erased.

Another common effort was early favored by Reik: everybody sins, so let us all forgive one another and thereby undermine the seriousness of sin. Of course, such a reading of sin is humanistic. If man could forgive and wash away the *guilt* of sin, then long ago all guilt would have been abolished, and men would be sinning without guilt or fear. But sin is a violation of God's law, and the sinner cannot abolish either God or his law, and his guilt therefore remains.

The problem of guilt will not go away. John Ciardi, in commenting in 1962 on the Adolf Eichmann case, wrote, "For the question 'Who is guilty?' might better become 'Who is not guilty?'" He had been in an air crew responsible for massive destruction in Tokyo during World War II. He commented:

> But what if Japan had won and it turned out to be Japanese judges who tried the case? What could I have offered in my own defense but, one by one, all of Eichmann's arguments: I was only a cog—the smallest kind of cog, in fact, one of the four gunners who rode at least fifty feet away from the controls and bomb switches. I only obeyed orders—when I had to. It was my duty— alas. But in the end what could I plead to that—happily—never- convened court but "guilty as we all are"?[19]

All are guilty, and there is no remission of sins. Humanism begins by trying to abolish sin and guilt and ends by making it inescapable and ineradicable. By denying the fixed and eternal law of God, it substitutes for it man's law, which becomes quickly totalitarian and provides no hope of escape.

Thus, Dr. Lorand sees "the demonic, dark side" of man as the primitive, primordial, and *personal.* It is Freud's id and ego. Our hope for Dr. Lorand is in the superego, our socialized part. "We are constantly witnessing a struggle in our psyche, recognizing hostile and antagonistic powers in perpetual battle with the socialized part of our personality, our censor."[20] This means, when developed to its logical conclusion, salvation by total socialization by means of the totalitarian state.

The unatoned may be in the church, and they may be in the world at large. In either case, their lives have no valid direction. As Jude observed, all such men are rebels against God's authority; they are the living dead, "twice dead"; they are like "wandering stars" having no orbit. They are "trees whose fruit withereth," and they are "clouds without water" (*Jd. 10-13*).

The unatoned, being aimless, are also the bored. They seek "something new" as a substitute for becoming a new creation. Thus, a letter by a Miss B. L., aged 20, wrote of an affair of over 18 months with a married man of 30. Every sexual experiment was tried by this "happy" couple, and then boredom apparently set in. "Nothing else to try. Can you help us? We seem to be looking for something new all the time."[21] Luke comments on the decadent Greek thinkers of Paul's day, noting, "For all the Athenians and strangers which were there spent their time in nothing else, but either to tell, or to hear some new thing"(*Ac. 17:21*).

The unatoned may deny both sin and guilt, but they remain guilt-ridden sinners whose lives manifest their lack of peace and their troubled conscience. Having no peace, they are at war with God's peace, and they are troublers of the peace of this world. "There is no peace, saith the LORD, unto the wicked" (*Is. 48:22*).

The Atoned

One of the great proclamations of Scripture sounds forth in Romans 5:1, 2 which, while specifically referring to justification, sets forth the power and the privilege of the atoned:

> Therefore being justified by faith, we have peace with God
>   through our Lord Jesus Christ:
> By whom also we access by faith into this grace wherein we stand,
>   and rejoice in the hope of the glory of God.

Because our atonement, our reconciliation to God, and our justification are totally the work of God through Jesus Christ, our security is firmly grounded in the Lord, and we have peace. We are released from guilt into faith, grace, joy, and hope.

Peace with God is an impossibility on man's terms, or by man's works. The sinner cannot find peace nor a clear conscience. Because he is a guilty man, he is deeply and thoroughly involved in sado-masochism and is in flight from reality. He seeks escape in the fantasy world of fiction, entertainment, and self-pitying indulgence, because there is no escape in reality. He is a self-doomed and willfully blind man.

The atoned, however, have *peace with God*. They are delivered from the ennervating power of guilt into the freedom of godly action. True faith thus is alien to charnel-house theology; instead of bewailing mortality and concentrating mournfully on the dead bones of its fallen estate, it works joyfully in Christ to do his will. The Great Commission does not ask us to spend our days mourning over past sins and what we once were but to go forth in Christ's power, commanding all nations of the world by "*teaching* them to observe all things" which our Lord commands, and to baptize them into the new creation (*Mt. 28:18-20*).

Calvin, in speaking of the life of the atoned, declared, in commenting on Romans 4:20:

> All things around us are in opposition to the promises of God: He promises immortality; we are surrounded with mortality and corruption: He declares that he counts us just; we are covered with sins: He testifies that he is propitious and kind to us: outward judgements threaten his wrath. What then is to be done? We must with closed eyes pass by ourselves and all things connected with us, that nothing may hinder or prevent us from believing that God is true.[22]

The atoned do not evaluate themselves in terms of either their pride or their guilt: God is true, and God declares them to be reconciled in Jesus Christ, to be atoned and justified by his sovereign grace.

Atonement thus means freedom. It is freedom from sin and guilt, and from the fallen humanity of the first Adam. We are freed from an endless dwelling on the past, the mark of hell, and are given a life of hope, power, and glory. The atonement is God's great Emancipation Proclamation. It releases us from the slavery of sin and death into the freedom of righteousness and life.

This means the ability to *rest*. There is neither rest nor peace for the wicked (*Is. 48:22*). It is the mark of hell to be endlessly concerned with the past, trying to re-arrange, edit, and alter past events (*Lk. 16:20-31*). The redeemed work to alter the present and the future by means of God's law-word. Moreover, being heirs of *life*, they can *rest*, one day in seven, one year in seven, two years at the end of forty-eight years. Those who are the living dead cannot rest: life is always running out on them and, with unceasing and sleepless activity and fretful self-indulgence, they try to seize life, but without joy, peace, or rest.

True rest and true work go together. Godly rest is productive of faith, energy, and action, and godly work is marked by joy, peace, and rest. Thus, the atonement also means the ability to *work* productively and effectively, because we know that our labor is never vain or futile in Christ (*1 Cor. 15:58*).

The life of the atoned is also deliverance from the delusions and fantasies of a man-centered world. A woman in Moravia's *The Empty Canvas* epitomizes this reduction of reality to the limits of a person's thinking, so that the real is what man conceives it to be, and nothing more. Asked, "What do you believe in?", Cecilia answers:

> In nothing. But I don't mean I didn't believe in it because I thought about it, and realized that I didn't believe in it. I didn't believe in it because I never thought about it. And even now I never think about it. I think about any sort of thing, but not about religion. If a person never thinks about a thing, it means that for him that thing doesn't exist. With me, it isn't that I like or dislike religion, it just doesn't exist.[23]

This is the logic of modern philosophy come to fruition. The protagonist in the novel echoes a common opinion, a good illustration of sado-masochism, as he recalls an opinion that:

> Humanity is divided into two main categories; those who, when faced with an insurmountable difficulty, feel an impulse to kill, and those who, on the contrary, feel an impulse to kill themselves.[24]

The unatoned are caught in some form of this internal dialogue.

Because they are guilty, they know the power of guilt over themselves, and they use guilt to control others. Husbands and wives try to make each other feel guilty as the means of governing one another. A guilty person is unfree and is essentially incapable of consistent independent action. Preachers commonly preach to heighten a sense of guilt in their congregations. Supposedly this is done to further holiness, but holiness comes with faith and growth in obedience, not growth in the paralysis of guilt. Politicians use guilt heavily to control people: citizens are made to feel guilty for all the ills of the world and their country so that they might surrender more power to the state. The politics of guilt and pity is the politics of totalitarian humanistic statism.

Where control by guilt prevails, legalism does also. Man-made rules are imposed rigorously, and law proliferates in church and state. Even "free sex" groups impose rigid rules and find violations unforgivable. Because man is ultimate for all such people, man's rules are basic. Fear of offending other persons, *fear of man*, is then basic, so that a double guilt governs such men. *First*, there is the guilt before God, who made them, and whose laws are implanted in every atom of their being. *Second*, because man is made his own god, there is guilt and fear before man, lest others be offended or despise the law-breaker, or rule-breaker, as an outcast, as socially unfit.

The atoned are free from the burden of sin and guilt because they are legally and personally redeemed by the atonement effected by Jesus Christ. Their salvation is grounded in an effectual, objective, and legal act by God the Son. Pietistic religion undermines that objective legal fact. As Aulen noted, "the watchword of Pietism was New Birth ... rather than Justification— that is to say, the word chosen was one that described a subjective process."[25] The new birth is very important, but its importance rests on the background of an objective and unchanging legal act by Jesus Christ. To stress the *results* of that act rather than the act itself is to place the emphasis on man. The result, too, has been a weakening of the objective legal fact. Because priority is given to man in pietism, man then assumes a place of sovereignty: God's legal act, the atonement, is then available to all who of their own free will *choose* Christ. The result is an ineffectual legal act made effective only by man's personal choice. As G. B. Long observes tellingly:

> This author sees no purpose, benefit, or comfort in a redemption that does not redeem, a propitiation that does not propitiate, a reconciliation that does not reconcile; neither does he have any faith in a hypothetical salvation for hypothetical believers. Rather, he has faith in a redemption which infallibly secures the salvation of each and every one for whom it was designed, namely "the children of God that were scattered abroad" (*John 11:52*), which is such a multitude of sinners declared righteous that no man can number them. God forbid, therefore, "that I should glory, save in the cross of our Lord Jesus Christ" (*Gal. 6:14*).[26]

It is a real and objective law, which is broken by sin. That law is not a mere code which represents a human demand: it is the word which sets forth the righteousness of the living God. Our redemption from the *penalty* of the law for sin is Christ's word. We are not, as Murray pointed out, redeemed from the law itself, because the law is summed up as our obligation to love the Lord our God with all our heart, mind, and being, and our neighbor as ourselves. "It would contradict the very nature of God to think that any person can ever be relieved of the necessity to love God with the whole heart and to obey his commandments."[27]

The atoned are redeemed from the *penalty* of the law into the *power* of the law. The law expresses the righteousness of God, and it is the means to dominion (*Dt. 28*).

Our religious experiences are thus at best hardly secondary to the supreme importance of God's great act, the atonement. The atonement is the charter of man's freedom.

---

[1] Joseph Addison Alexander, *The Psalms, Translated and Explained* (Grand Rapids, Michigan: Zondervan, 1864), 323.

[2] A. F. Kirkpatrick, *The Book of Psalms* (Cambridge, England: Cambridge University Press, 1906), 455.

[3] H. C. Leupold, *Exposition of the Psalms* (Columbus, Ohio: The Wartburg Press, 1959), 621.

[4] Louis Berkhof, *Systematic Theology* (Grand Rapids, Michigan: Eerdmans, 1946), 367.

[5] James Hastings, editor, *Encyclopaedia of Religion and Ethics*, vol. V (Edinburgh, Scotland: T. & T. Clark, [1912] 1937), 651.

[6] U. Cassuto, *A Commentary on the Book of Genesis*, Part 1 (Jerusalem, Israel: The Magnes Press, The Hebrew University, [1961] 1972), 243.

[7] See R. J. Rushdoony, *Freud* (Nutley, New Jersey: Presbyterian and Reformed Publishing Co., [1965] 1975).

[8] See R. J. Rushdoony, *The Politics of Guilt and Pity* (Nutley, New Jersey: The Craig Press, 1970).

[9] *Crest*, vol. II (Orange Coast College, Costa Mesa, California), 20.

[10] See Robert L. Dabney, *Christ our Penal Substitute* (Harrisonburg, Virginia: Sprinkle Publications reprint, 1978).

[11] John Murray, *The Epistle to the Romans*, vol. I (Grand Rapids, Michigan: Wm. B. Eerdmans, 1959), 179.

[12] J. A. Alexander, *The Psalms, Translated and Explained* (Grand Rapids, Michigan: Zondervan, 1864; reprinted), 180.

[13] John Warwick Montgomery, editor, translator, *Chytraeus On Sacrifice* (St. Louis, Missouri: Concordia, 1962), 80f.

[14] Perry Whittacker: *The American Way of Sex* (New York, NY: G. P. Putnam's Son, 1974), 190.

[15] Aurens Uris, *The Frustrated Titan, Emasculation of the Executive* (New York, NY: Van Nostrand Reinhold Co., 1972), 97.

[16] See the examples given in Otto Friedrich, *Going Crazy, An Inquiry into Madness in Our Times* (New York, NY: Avon Books, [1975] 1977).

[17] Samuel J. Warner, *The Urge to Mass Destruction* (New York, NY: Greene & Stratton, 1957).

[18] John O'Grady and Nolan Davis, *O'Grady, The Life and Times of Hollywood's No. 1 Private Eye* (Los Angeles, California: J. P. Tarcher, 1974), 206.

[19] John Ciardi, "Manner of Speaking," in *Saturday Review*, July 7, 1962.

[20] Dr. Sandor Lorand, M. D., in the "Preface," to Arthur Zaidenberg, *The Emotional Self* (New York, NY: Bell Publishing Co., [1934] 1967), 14f.

[21] Dr. Harold Greenwald and Ruth Greenwald, "Nothing Left," *The Sex-Life Letters* (New York, NY: Bantam Books, [1972] 1973) 446.

[22] John Calvin, *Romans*, 180.

[23] Alberto Moravia, *The Empty Canvas* (New York, NY: Farrar, Straus and Cudahy, 1961), 272.

[24] *ibid.*, 302.

[25] Gustaf Aulen, *Christian Victor* (London: Society for Promoting Christian Knowledge, [1931] 1937) , 150.

[26] Gary D. Long, *Definite Atonement* (Nutley, New Jersey: Presbyterian & Reformed Publishing Company, 1966), 65.

[27] John Murray, *Redemption—Accomplished and Applied* (Grand Rapids, Michigan: Eerdmans, 1955), 49f.

Vol. 13, No. 1, 1990-91

The Covenant and the Character of a Nation

by J. A. Wermser

Translated by Gilbert Zekveld

Editor's Note: The following was written sometime between 1850-1860 by J. A. Wermser, bailiff in Amsterdam, Holland from 1842 until he died in 1862. He was a close friend of the great Dutch historian, statesman, and publicist Guillaume Groen van Prinsterer (1801-76), the founder of the Anti-Revolutionary Party. A compiler of Wermser's essays said that he was "one of those men who with all their strength and talents labored in order to call his church and his people back to the faith of the fathers during the Reformation." The essay presented here, originally titled "Concerning Infant Baptism," is a recent original translation from the Dutch. It was written at a time, notes translator Zekveld, when virtually the entire population of The Netherlands, except Jews and Anabaptists, were baptized as infants. The author expresses concern over why so few recognized how the covenant promises of God for new life and community, which are sealed in baptism, were designed to have a liberating, unifying, and transforming effect on church and society.

Christianity and the Nation

Originally the nation was not Christian, and as such, Christianity was not part of its history. Since that time, Christianity has become part of its history and Christianity has become national. But another foreign power at enmity with the gospel and Christianity, the power of liberalism, has touched and wounded Christianity . . . but has not conquered it. We do not deny that the revolution has become part of our history, but we maintain that the nation which at one time changed from a non-Christian to a Christian nation is not ready to change its Christian character for an atheistic character.

Skeletons

Skeletons are not useless. Even a skeleton has power to resist;

it has some independence. A skeleton is not superfluous but has evidence that it belongs to a body, or used to belong to one.

The skeletons of church, the day of rest and infant baptism, if indeed these institutions have become skeletons, do show us how much we have wasted, and what the situation is we shall meet with if we do not think of restoration.

That I present the church and its confession, the Sabbath, and also infant baptism to you as skeletons I blame on those who take pleasure to see these institutions as skeletons.

I am not afraid to draw this picture, and I will take it for granted that all these institutions may be skeletons. And even so, they show me that church and Sabbath and infant baptism do not only belong to the flesh, but are part of the more solid backbone and so belong to the certainty (steadfastness) of Christianity. And I know that no one shall think little of the system which gives him shape, even though it is only a skeleton.

Searching Theology and Narrow-mindedness

I think it praiseworthy that the scientist works independently, but at the present time it is very much to be regretted that he does not find this independence as a student of Christ. I would almost say, in order to give expression to what I mean, that science in its modern liberal direction is not baptized. That is to say that modern liberalism did not die with Christ, neither is it raised with Christ . . . hence its collision with the baptized church that lives and receives divine wisdom, because the living church died with Christ also concerning her own wisdom.

Furthermore, without question, there are within the Reformed churches people of a sickly and narrow-minded persuasion, which do not freely experience the liberating and redeeming power of the death and resurrection of Christ. It is with this persuasion that the sickly side of theological science is mainly of one mind, although they claim not to agree.

The church as a whole must and does live and is fed from a common good, but both the narrow-minded and modern theological science seek their sustenance often in that which each individual discovers rationally. Modern theology overlooks the truth, and concerns itself primarily with searching; [on the other hand,] many members of the church seem to think they possess unique information not given to other believers. Both are wrong— [truth is] not that which is discovered after eighteen centuries, but that which has been the common good of God's people during eighteen centuries. Truth is not knowledge which is obtainable by a few, but that which may be obtained by all. It is not to be caught up in the third heaven as Paul was, but God's grace in Christ, in which the whole church participates. It is that by which everyone (the learned and the unlearned) must be saved. Believers are not saved by that which is distinct, but by that which they have in common.

Unity and Catholicity of Divided Church Saved in Baptism

When we do appreciate this at all, we see that it witnesses against all one-sidedness and narrow-mindedness. For baptism requires that the one baptized shall improve upon his baptism until it appears in its full strength. It also requires that we see the baptism of others as an institution that asks for our help, that others too may come to the full recognition of the truth. There are circumstances in which, in order to keep the truth and to have no communion with the sins of others, division and removal become necessary. But in doing so, we must be very careful and not hurt any more than is necessary.

In as much as we deny anything good in others, we hurt ourselves and rob ourselves of any contact to influence others and help others. This is especially true with a view to acknowledging each other's baptism; when we have an objective view of baptism, we have a right and an obligation to admonish others to walk as baptized people.

Being exclusivistic and being conscientious are not the same. The first always draws back, is passive. With its limited appreciation of God's grace, it has no means to fight unrighteousness. The other, quite to the contrary, leans upon God's promises, is active, spreads itself, appreciates what is good in others and is victorious in its battle against the rule of misconception and unrighteousness.

Narrow-mindedness is always without fruit, and has always been an overflowing fountain of misconception and wrong-doing in the church. Therefore, it is important to remember that baptism in all of Christendom is a common foundation of a consecrated life, and it gives us the right and calls us to exhort concerning doctrine and walk, wherever needed. And as we appreciate our own baptism, we shall be earnest and serious in admonishing those that are baptized with us but err or are indifferent. As it is at present, the one does indeed acknowledge the baptism of the other, but without taking it seriously. This should be much different when we would realize that as Christians we have claims and duties toward each other, the claims and duties of those who are baptized into the name and service of the Father, the Son, and the Holy Spirit.

"Baptized Heathens"

This is a very unhappy expression but is said of the majority of the nation, because of its falling away in doctrine and conversation, and almost nobody is troubled by it; it saddens but a few. We have become used to it, and because of our misconception concerning baptism, we restrict Christianity to those that are knowingly converted unto the Lord. We have become used to the idea that someone's Christianity begins with his conversion. But what was he during the time between his [infant] baptism and conversion? A Jew? A heathen? And why are your children baptized before you hear of their conversion? Is it so that they could be baptized heathens? Is that so very important? What were you, yourself, before you were converted to the Lord? Was your baptism nothing, a witness of your dislike of the Lord, of his grace, of his service?

Concerning all kinds of heathens, even of cannibals, many will feel some pity, and many would even help by giving in order that those may hear the gospel. But, concerning our own people that are estranged from the Lord and his word, we do often feel dislike and hate; and many a time these people are left to themselves. It is possible that their ancestors were more shining believers than we are ourselves, and we know that baptism as a seal of the covenant of grace cannot be broken from God's side. By the same token, it may be that very soon your own children will be part of those we call baptized heathens.

Because of this, it is necessary that when we desire that

our children and grandchildren may be sanctified unto the Lord, it is not enough to bring them and the next generation up in the fear of the Lord. But it is also absolutely necessary that our national environment and our national institutions must be Christian, in order that divine truth shall have a public face, and the means of grace shall be maintained and kept all around us.

Questions That Dishonor the Lord

Those who are baptized are, in their baptism, assured in every way of God's grace; they are overwhelmed by it. And the Reformed churches teach that those who are baptized, as they grow up, are bound to receive further instruction in these things. This instruction, sad to say, is often not given. It is even so that some believers teach their children something entirely different; and because of this, they err themselves, and others with them. There are those in the church who are very carefully searching for whom Christ died, and furthermore whether or not there is a well meant offer of grace, or is it perhaps an offer not well meant?

When children are a few days old, they are baptized, and every time with the declaration that the Lord Jesus died no less for them than for adults. But when these same children become adults and when they as men and women make up the church, they are afraid to believe this declaration that was said of them when small, when baptized. People are afraid to say of adults what is still being said of infants that are being baptized. And quite often the best sermon is said to be suspect, because the pastor tells the adults what was already said of them when infants, namely that in Christ we have the washing away of our sins! When as infants we can ask for nothing, because we know nothing, the judgment of others may be somewhat mild, and such an infant is placed upon a foundation of grace; but when he has become an adult, we become very serious and ask the question: did Christ die for him?

And still we continue to baptize children (the children of those of whom we are in doubt whether or not Christ died for them) proclaiming thereby that they are "received in grace" and are "heirs of God and his covenant." Instead of instructing these children in the doctrine of the Lord, very often the thing is turned around and the child is taught to doubt the promises given in its baptism, and the grace of God is made out to be something that is not certain. What was certain in their baptism becomes uncertain when they grow up!

The Christian Day of Rest and the Uncovered Head

The Christian nation, with its day of rest as the symbol of rest restored by the reassurance of Christ, stands over against the Israelite with his day of rest begun in creation and covenant of work, which culminates in our Lord's death. The Christian nation stands with the head uncovered when it prays and when it takes an oath (the servile Israelite to the contrary stands with his head covered, not so much as an evidence of reverence—for the Jew is not irreverent when he covers his head). [The Christian uncovers his head in prayer] as a token of the redemption in which he confesses to be a partaker and because of which the Christian, as he stands redeemed, may appear thus before God as a free man.

Confusion

The confusion in the heart of man is never greater than when, being illuminated by God's Spirit, he becomes aware of his guilt on the one hand and aware of the power of Christ's sacrifice on the other. For some time, he will not be able to give all these new realities a place in his life and thinking. So also, is a Christian nation.

The cause of that confusion in the individual and by a people, at which we so often marvel, is very simple. The truth concerning our sin, redemption, and sanctification are not hard to write down on a lifeless sheet of paper. The human heart, however, is not like that. There we find debates and wrestlings taking place down into the depths of the human will and mind. There in its application, the Holy Spirit battles against the prince of darkness; it is the same battle that Christ experienced in his death and resurrection, to bring us salvation. The fight against sin and darkness causes confusion all the time. And a condition of relative peace and regularity, be it in a people or individual, cannot be born but in proportion to the Christian awareness as it emerges out of the confusion.

What Does Baptism Seal?

Many think they are Christians because they believe they are such, that they are believers. This is a subjective approach and we are called upon to believe in the Triune God, the object of our faith.

Baptism, administered to adults or children, never seals unto us that we are believers, but it seals what we have in God. The Lord does not tell us merely to believe that we love him, but the Lord requires us to acknowledge [his love]. He says and seals what he will be for us and waits patiently for our answer.

The Baptists are wrong when in baptism they seal subjective grace, and therefore only administer baptism to adults, because no one except the one who is baptized can know whether he/she possesses grace and is a believer; the church waits until it is told and accepts the confession in Christian charity. When someone is being baptized upon the ground of subjective faith, he does not receive a seal of God, but rather seals himself. Such a seal will be uncertain, and should be often repeated, as it rests upon the changing moods and convictions of the one baptized concerning his state of grace and is not grounded in sovereign grace and God's faithfulness.

Baptism administered to adults or infants who as yet do not belong to the church, never seals that which we have within, but always that which we have (or may have) in God. Faith is not faith because we believe first, but because our hope is in God. It is exactly because of this that baptism has the character of a seal, is a pledge, and is the beginning of a covenant relationship between God and man, and of life which has its foundation in the death and resurrection of Christ. The object of our faith is certain and immovable. So it should be possible for the subjects, the individuals, the churches and people to free themselves, by faith in the object, from boundless confusion and develop into Christian awareness.

The Doctrine of the Reformed Church is Pre-eminently Generous

The doctrine of the Reformed church sets all those baptized, without distinction, upon a foundation of overflowing grace and in an absolute covenant relationship with the Triune God. We must see by whom this commonly received baptism is appreciated or not appreciated and so make a distinction. All those baptized are called upon to examine themselves whether they live as covenant-keepers. Abounding grace and perfect redemption are in baptism assured and sealed unto us by a Triune, covenanting God. What is so dangerous in believing this? Is it not much more dangerous not to believe this because of being narrow-minded or indifferent? Far from believing that all those baptized are taken up in a one-sided covenant, they are to the contrary admonished and obliged unto a new obedience. And here too we see evidence of the Biblical character of Reformed doctrine. "With Thee is forgiveness, that Thou mayest be feared" (*Ps. 130:4*).

New Obedience

The old obedience to the covenant of works was not obeyed because fallen man could not and would not be subject to God's law. The covenant of works was broken by man, and resulted in death and slavery. In all his attempts man was a slave and could not escape death. The Lord requires a new obedience because in baptism he seals unto us that he accepts us as his children and heirs; a new obedience which, for both young and old, begins with the life of the resurrection in Christ, because he suffered and died for our sins in our place, a new obedience—when we "let the Lord work in us by his Holy Spirit" (*Heidelberg Catechism, Question 103*), "imparting to us that which we have in Christ, namely the washing away of our sins and the daily renewing of our lives" (*from the form for infant baptism*).

When we are stingy concerning forgiveness, redemption and grace, new obedience is altogether impossible. New obedience proceeds only from yielding self to redemption, as it exists in forgiveness and sanctification. There is no regeneration and renewal by the Holy Spirit, other than that which results in the dying of the old man, a dying with Christ by faith in his atoning work; and in a resurrection of the new man, a resurrection with Christ, by faith in his resurrection for our justification.

The Future of Baptism

The future of circumcision was in the atonement which Christ was to bring in his own sacrifice. When that future had come, circumcision came to an end. But where circumcision came to an end, there baptism began. The future of baptism lies in the complete application of the obtained redemption, when the whole church, by the power of the blood of the everlasting covenant with soul and body completely regenerated, shall stand before the Lord.

A Narrow and Abstract View of the Doctrine of Predestination

The doctrine of predestination is expressly revealed in the Bible. However, the Lord does not teach us an abstract doctrine of election so that we as children of dust and time would afflict ourselves by attempting to climb up into heaven to find whether we are personally chosen unto salvation or not. To the contrary, God in his eternal predestination, which belongs to his right of majesty and flows out of his eternal sovereignty, in order that we would be able to understand, has introduced his covenant of grace into time and his economy into this world, that we may hold on to this covenant of grace and *in this way* may climb up to know our predestination.

But what reveals itself to the contrary to those of a limited persuasion? A one-sided appreciation of an abstract doctrine of election and an almost complete denial of the covenant of grace, continuing to contemplate God's eternal counsel, and an almost complete ignorance concerning the [application of the] covenant of grace [in time]; placing self in a beginningless eternity, while we are children of time which has a beginning. The result of this is that not one truth is rightly appreciated; least of all the truth which they think most important. Because of this narrow view, they neglect the covenant of grace. And the nature of faith, God's leading with humanity and the strength and character of the means of grace are hard to be recognized. What should the world and even the churches as they exist be taught to believe? That people are saved when they are elected? The question remains: how shall I know that I am elect? Why do we read in God's word of his judgments and his blessings upon earth, that he threatens and is angry, that he blesses and makes promises to lead men to repentance? Is it not so that God knows that only the elect shall be

saved? What are the means of grace in relation to an immediate
predestination? A maybe? A lottery where some gain a prize, but
the majority remains as it is? A lottery ticket which makes it
possible, but in no way certain, that the prize I love so much shall
be mine?

The Lord has placed us in his covenant of grace in order that
we by his grace, and in communion with him, shall be comforted
and *walk* in the future hope of eternal glory. Increasingly we should
learn to understand that the means as well as the results are the
fruits of his free and eternal election; and that the way for us to
come to full assurance of faith is by *the life of faith itself.* But the
narrow-minded take away this infallible certainty, which the Lord,
to help us, has laid in the covenant of grace, and they place the
convicted sinner directly over against an abstract predestination.

What to do now? There is no end of doubt concerning a
personal share in the grace of God. The certainty which the Lord
has given us here on earth, and still gives, is being taken away by
the self-willed obstinacy of man, and nothing remains but to climb
up into heaven and to look for immediate and extraordinary
assurances, that one has found grace in the sight of God.

The invention of a whole system of special assurances, sealings,
revelations and appearances, of which not one is valid, has become
the result. Because of this, too many of God's dear children are
being kept in great uncertainty concerning their salvation.

The Vine

The church, seen in its true strength as an institution of the
Lord, is the body of Christ. To be incorporated into that body is to
be incorporated into Christ himself. The child is by baptism
incorporated into the holy catholic church. He is being placed from
nature into grace. As a child of Adam, he comes to baptism in
order that he shall rise from baptism as a child of God. And so
Christ has been objectively given to this child as well as to all the
church, with all the means of grace (*Heilsgoederen*).

In order that this grace may enter a tender and young branch
subjectively, this branch is bound to acknowledge God's fatherly
goodness and mercy, which the Lord in objective but, nevertheless,
very positive grace, has been pleased to give. The future of this

young branch, as of all the other branches, is pictured in the words of Jesus:

> I am the true vine, and my father is the husbandman. Every branch in me that beareth not fruit he purgeth it that it may bear more fruit. Now ye are clean through the word which I have spoken to you. Abide in me, and I in you. As the branch can not bear fruit of itself, except it abide in the vine; no more can ye, except ye abide in me. I am the vine, ye are the branches; He that abideth in me, and I in him, the same bringeth forth much fruit: for without me ye can do nothing. If a man abide not in me, he is cast forth as a branch, and is withered; and men gather them, and cast them into the fire, and they are burned. (*Jn. 15:1-6*)

The church is not made up of individuals who believe. No, the church of all the earth (all those baptized in the name of the Triune God, the catholic Christian church, continuation, extension, and development of the church) is an organic, continually developing whole of which Christ is the life and power. It brings forth strong and living branches as well as weak and dead branches.

Children who have been recently baptized, as well as growing children, are the tender branches in Christ, the vine. We do not know whether they will remain in him, whether they shall bear fruit or not. God Almighty, who works all things after the counsel of his own will, knows whether they shall remain in him and bear fruit or shall fall away. We rejoice that the Holy Spirit has taken them in distinction of millions of children of Jew and Gentile, and has incorporated them into Christ as branches of the vine through baptism.

Is it not better to pray with the Reformed church that the Lord may protect these branches, and rule them by his Holy Spirit; that he may grant that these children be nurtured in the Christian faith and godliness, in order that these tender branches, just ingrafted into Christ, but not rooted in him, may grow and increase in the Lord Jesus Christ; that they shall not be dry but green and living branches; that they may show this by recognizing his fatherly goodness and mercy which he has shown us and all of his church by giving Christ to us, and us to Christ?

A Sad Peculiarity

It is a sad thing in our day that we should take God's institutions, which he shall certainly maintain and uphold for those who believe, and change and deform them into a caricature, and after this to ask the question: "Do you believe this?"

Many have made an attempt to take the glorious day of rest, the symbol of the relation between heaven and earth, and make it into a day of pleasure and play, and then ask the faithful: "Is God pleased to make this special day, a day of being idle and lazy?" In the same way, unbelievers in the church have blamed the church for unbelief, superstition, and the unrighteousness of their own kind, and made a mockery of the church by asking if being just a member of the church has saving power. It is the same with baptism, especially the baptism of infants. We do not believe that baptism has any subjective, grace-bringing power. The child is the same after baptism as it was before; with this distinction, that now it is sacramentally laid down and surrounded by the never-failing promises of God. And that it does not seek its salvation in Adam, but in Christ; not by nature but by grace.

The groundwork has been laid; all it has to do now is to adhere to further development in order "that it finally be presented without spot among the assembly of the elect in life eternal."

Vol. I, No. 2, 1974

Power From Below

by Rousas John Rushdoony

One of the basic lusts of fallen man is for power, but, more accurately, his desire is for autonomous power. Man was created by God to exercise dominion over the earth (*Gen. 1:26-28*) in knowledge, righteousness, and holiness, and basic to that task is the use of godly power. But the use of power in subordination to God and in submission to his word is alien to man in revolt. Man, seeking to be his own god, and to determine good and evil for himself (*Gen. 3:5*), wants power in independence from and in defiance of God.

Historically and religiously, men have looked to power from above, and, in a variety of religions, men have looked to the gods for power. Non-Biblical religious worship, while no less an aspect of man's revolt against God, was still marked by a belief in a higher realm of spirits and powers whose aid it was held to be wise to seek. These higher beings could be allies of men, if properly approached. Temples of pagan antiquity were not places of worship, corporate or private, but places for transactions with the gods. The favor and help of these higher powers were sought in a particular venture, activity, or area of personal concern. If the insurance, protection, or help of the particular god or temple proved unsatisfactory, the individual took his business elsewhere and bought security or insurance at another temple or shrine. In all these cults of antiquity, and of various cultures to the historical present, the reality of a higher world of beings was assumed. It was believed, of course, that these higher beings were only different in degree from men, and that a continuity existed between men and the gods. As against the Biblical doctrine of the uncreated Being of God, and the created nature of man and the universe, pagan religions held to the great chain of being doctrine. All being is one being, the differences being one of degrees between the gods and men, and between men and all other creatures. The idea of continuity militated against worship in anything resembling the Biblical sense. All the same, this higher world, however different in nature than the Biblical view, was held to be real.

The culmination of modern philosophy, beginning in Descartes and coming to focus in Kant and Hegel, led to Darwin and the doctrine of evolution. This doctrine had deep roots in pagan antiquity and the belief in the great chain of being and was a logical development of it. It did, however, militate against any higher world. Both the old pagan doctrine and the Biblical Faith were ruled out. Man was held to be alone in a meaningless universe which was a product of blind chance. There was no sentient power, no mind or purpose beyond and above man, only blind and evolving energies and forces.

Power from above was thus eliminated from the universe, in both its Christian and its pagan versions. Moreover, in looking at *the power in man*, it became apparent that mind, in terms of evolution, had to be ruled as a shallow-rooted late comer. The older and more basic forces in man lay below the surface, and Freud located them, as did others, in the unconscious, in the subterranean within man. There followed what Dr. Cornelius Van Til has described as integration downward into the void: man was re-interpreted in terms of the child, the child in terms of primitive man, primitive man in terms of a mythological animal past, and so on. Culture began to seek vitality in the subterranean, in what lay below modern, civilized man. Primitivism in the arts became synonymous with vitality. A jungle beat in music with an abandonment of reason became a symbol of power, and, in every area, the downward quest for power was held to be the only means of escape from sterility and impotence. The perverted, lawless, primitive, and chaotic became equated with power.

All of this was a relentless development of the logic of the modern myth. *Power from above* having been denied as a myth, modern man became involved in a desperate search for *power from below*. The earlier means of this quest of power from below was psychoanalytic, psychiatric, and artistic. It also became political, and a new breed of leaders from below began to dominate the twentieth century—Lenin, Stalin, Hitler, Mussolini, and their paler counterparts in the democracies. Democracy itself was an enthronement of power from below: *vox populi, vox dei.*

The quest, however, soon took occultist directions. The human scene failed to manifest sufficient power. The source of power being the subterranean, modern man, by definition concluding that God and "the above" are dead, felt that what lies below must indeed by very powerful. The result has been the rise of magic, witchcraft, Satanism, and related interests.

Satanism is not new, and its past history is an ugly one, but the new Satanism is the most vicious yet, and potentially the most dangerous. The Biblical Satan is a creature who seeks to be God and is fully aware of the existence of God (*Jas. 2:19*). His program is a reasoned one: *First*, man is to be his own god, determining good and evil for himself (*Gen. 3:5*). *Second*, man should be freed from all testing and judgments and given cradle to grave security. If man needs bread, the stones should be made bread (*Mt. 4:3*). *Third*, faith should be totally unnecessary; man should be able to walk by sight and God should prove all things for man's benefit (*Mt. 4:6*). *Fourth*, rightness is an attribute of the creature, and the creature should be worshipped and served rather than God (*Mt. 4:8-9*).

The new image of Satan is a product of Darwin and Freud. *First*, he is not a creature made by God but a dark force evolved out of chaos and essentially is chaos. There was never thus any higher status for Satan, but a totally subterranean one, a creature of chaos, not of God. *Second*, the new image of Satan is of a totally mindless, irrational, perverse being whose existence is total terror to the rational in man. The new Satan is the utter contradiction of reason, whereas the Biblical Satan is an example of fallen and totally depraved reason. It should not surprise us that some of the new Satanists lose their reason and become themselves mindless. *Third*, because no power exists above by definition, total power is held to exist below, and the result is a growing evidence that there is a strong tendency to believe in the omnipresence and even omnipotence of Satan. Satan is held to be everywhere, operative in all situations, and hence to be reckoned with at all times. It is surprising how far this idea has infiltrated the churches. Too few churchmen remember that Satan, like themselves, is a creature, capable only of a local appearance, *i.e.*, able to be in only one place at a time. Only God is omnipresent and omnipotent.

Power from below, whether feared or courted, is thus very much a part of modern man's faith. That power can reside in inanimate nature, as in the stars, and hence the revival of interest in astrology. It can reside in magic and witchcraft, or in other related practices, but, in any case, it is *power from below.*

The result of such a faith can only lead, as it already has, to a greater faith in raw and primitive violence as against reason. We can only expect, until this faith is shattered, a steady intensification of violence, crime, and revolution. *Power from below* means that normal sexuality is regarded as sterile and inhibited, and violence, rape, and perversion are thus regarded as raw and true power in the sexual realm.

It also means a greater stress on mindless religion, as witness the so-called charismatic movement, an emphasis on mindless experience as power. The charismatic who learns to babble insanely in what is no tongue at all has no answer therein to moral and intellectual problems, but he "witnesses" eloquently to others of the feeling of "power in the Spirit," power which is in essence a cultivation of what is mindless and subterranean.

In the world of films, television, novels, student riots, and political revolutions, power is held to come from below. The answer to all problems is violence. Problems are all held to be solvable if only enough violence and mindless force is applied. In the world of television, killings and brutal beatings solve all problems, and, in the world of the revolutionist, the same great faith in the healing force of violence, power from below, is in evidence.

The world thus is in crisis. *Power from below* is a faith which insures the triumph of mindlessness and violence. No calls for law and order can stem this intense faith of the new pagans. The so-called religious revivals of recent years have only been a part of the same ugly faith. Instead of "turning on" with narcotics, the call is for "turning on" with Jesus. Instead of the narcotic "trip," the "trip" with Jesus (and the "great Trip," the Rapture) are offered, so that religion is made a part of the same tradition as the pagan creed, and mindlessness is not challenged.

Only a full-orbed and intelligent orthodoxy, stressing the sovereign and Triune God, the doctrine of creation, and the sovereign grace of God in salvation, can do justice to the fact of *power from above.* Anything short of God's total claims is a deception.

Volume 13, No. 2, 1994
Covenant Salvation: Covenant Religion vs. Legalism
by Joseph P. Braswell

"Legalism" is a word that is much abused. For example, some use it to designate an overemphasis upon *rules* that govern behavior. Of course, "overemphasis" is a relative term with point of reference to how much emphasis the person making the judgment personally feels should be placed upon standards of behavior. In the extreme form of this way of understanding legalism, one is a legalist if he believes that one can formulate binding, *objective* moral prescriptions of right and wrong acts, for Christians are "led of the Spirit," not under law. Of course, any reduction of Christian life to an abstract set of rules is a serious error (but equally so is the reduction of it to existentialist subjectivism). It is wrong to emphasize standards to the exclusion of goals and motives. Nevertheless, in the interests of clarity, we must note that legalism is not the same thing as a deontologically reductionistic *moralism* in the realm of *sanctification* (and such a *reductionist error* is not the same thing as, and should not be confused with, a legitimate "third office" of the law as moral standard in Christian ethics).

Another way of defining legalism is to view it as the attempt to gain *justification* by lawkeeping. Whereas *moralism* is a position with respect to *sanctification, legalism* is a position with regard to *justification.* This approach is far more in line with the historic sense of the term within Reformational debates about the doctrine of justification. The Reformers meant by the term the error of attempting to *earn* God's favor by means of good works that possess an *intrinsic merit* according to a principle of "pure justice." Legalism is thus a doctrine of justification by works-righteousness, an attempt to be good enough to measure up to the standard of the law as the principle of judgment for the verdict of justification.

Yet there still remains a good deal of unclarity and confusion in this definition. If we designate the Adamic covenant of creation as a "covenant of works," as many Reformed continue to do, we must ask whether Adam was supposed to be a *legalist.* If the obedience required of him was to function as the meritorious ground of his justification (in something of the manner of *congruent merit*), then it qualifies as the sort of "works-righteousness" we condemn as legalism, something that would *earn* him, according to the terms of the covenant, eternal life. Moreover, is Christ as the "Second Adam" a legalist?

We obviously mean something more by legalism than just a works-righteousness basis of justification as that is understood within what has traditionally (but perhaps erroneously) been called the covenant of works. Is it then the attempt by *fallen* man (in need of redemptive grace) to stand once again (illegitimately) in that original covenantal relation, thus exempting prelapsarian Adam and Christ from the charge of being legalists? Does such a view of *seeking* God and hungering to please him, however misguided and naïve, adequately express the *sinful* (and therefore *antitheistic*) nature of legalism?

I will argue below that we cannot understand legalism by any reference to the original covenant, for it is not a doctrine of justification by the law of *God*, but one of justification by the law of *autonomous man*. To see this, we must first realize what the law of God is, and what it is not.

The "Bare Law" Abstraction

The traditional Protestant-Reformational view of the law's "second office"—its unyielding demand for absolute and flawlessly *perfect* fulfillment and consequent *unfulfillability* in a postlapsarian situation—is an abstraction. This "charge" must be correctly understood for what it truly is. All theologizing—all concept— formation, analysis, and interpretation—involves varying degrees of abstraction. We must be sensitive to the *limited legitimacy* of abstractions as arising only within a particular context and addressed to a specific concern. To assert that a given theological proposition is an abstraction by itself says nothing and certainly in no way impugns it.

This assertion does, however, underscore a potential danger. For an abstraction is *misused* if it is confused for a real state of affairs, if such concepts are reified and regarded as though they represent how things are in and of themselves, independent of all perspective and interpretational schemata. We may call such confusion the error of abstractionism, and Protestant interpretation has often been guilty of such abstractionism in its view of the law.

For example, John Murray, better than most Protestant exegetes before him, recognized that a *covenantal* perspective on the law— the law as *covenant torah*, in its original and divine intention—did not stand in any way opposed to grace, but flowed out of a context of grace. In order to square this recognition with more traditional Protestant interpretation (the law/gospel schema, focusing on the "second office"), he proposed that Paul in Romans 10:5 was speaking of an abstract concept of "*bare law*."[1]

Murray of course believed that the Judaism of Paul's day had committed this abstraction, that the Jews were legalists who had reduced *torah* to pure *ethos*.[2] Only in this way—out of context— could the law stand opposed to grace as a *works-principle*. Regardless of whether we find Murray's exegesis of Romans 10:5 convincing (I personally do not),[3] he has underscored a problem still not appreciated by the majority of Reformed exegetes: that the Protestant "second office" view does not capture the contextualized old covenantal view of the law of Moses.

We find this failure to appreciate Mosaic law as covenantal wisdom-instruction for life, this *abstractionist* view of Mosaic *torah* as "bare law" in traditionalist interpretation of Galatians 3 as well, and this again causes exegetes to read Paul's statements in terms of the unfulfillability thesis. For example, F. F. Bruce simply dismisses the possibility of the Judaizers raising as an objection to Paul's argument in Galatians 3:10 (as understood by Protestant traditionalists: the unfulfillability thesis) that it is based on an abstraction.[4] According to the traditional Protestant interpretation of Galatians 3:10,[5] Paul cites Deuteronomy 27:26 in order to argue that anyone who does not keep every jot and tittle of the law *flawlessly* is accursed; thus, justification by law-fulfillment (works-righteousness) is impossible. Yet the *torah* does not teach what Paul allegedly is arguing. For one thing, the Deuteronomy passage used to support the unfulfillability thesis does not intend anything of the sort in context, but, more importantly, the argument is pure *abstractionism*. It removes the law out of its covenantal context which includes provision for atonement and forgiveness.

The Mosaic covenant was through and through a covenant of *redemptive grace* that, through the sacrificial system, made merciful provisions for the sins and shortcomings of the covenant people that they could be restored to right standing and be blameless before the law. Only by abstracting "bare law" out of the integral *covenantal context* of *torah* could Paul's argument stand, but then it is *irrelevant* to the situation he addresses, for the Judaizers would need only to appeal to the *covenantal harmony* of law and grace (*i.e.*, the old covenantal sacrificial system fulfilled in the Christ-sacrifice of the new covenant as the basis to deal with imperfect law keeping). Since the intention of *torah* is wholly determined by its place in the Mosaic covenant, it was *never* intended to assert any such impossible demand for absolute perfection as we find asserted by the unfulfillability thesis, and, were Paul to claim otherwise, he would be guilty of gross distortion of the law's true meaning that makes his argument's major premise too controversial for his argument to be cogent in the problem-situation to which he supposedly addresses it.

In order for Paul's argument to work, it must be able to demonstrate some discontinuity—some incompatibility—between the old covenant situation and that of the new covenant, some principle that makes continued allegiance to *torah* incompatible with allegiance to Christ. This point, it is obvious, cannot be based upon opposing the principle of law to grace, which is irrelevant abstractionism, but must be a redemptive-historically qualified discontinuity of old covenant situation *as such*[6] to the advent of the new covenant as a new redemptive-historical economy that cannot be reconciled with continued allegiance to the Mosaic economy *in toto*. That incompatibility revolves around the exclusively *Jewish* covenantal nomism that is irreconcilable with the universally inclusive new-covenantalism in which there can be neither Jew nor gentile. *Torah* sets forth a "wall of separation," marking the identity of the Jews as a holy people *distinct* from gentiles who are outside the *torah*-fence, but in Christ Jews and gentiles become united as one holy people. The boundary lines drawn by the *torah* are incompatible with the new covenantal boundary lines drawn by the extension of the promise to the gentiles in Christ. One need not become a Jew (one of the *torah* people, bearing the peculiar identity-markers of the Mosaic covenant) in order to be in Christ.[7]

To return, however, to the main thesis of this essay, the heresy of legalism rests upon an abstract view of the law that sees it as *bare law*, as isolated from its redemptive-covenantal context. As such, it is a fundamental disobedience, a *radical rebellion* against the Lord of the covenant. God's covenant as such is rejected and law is viewed *autonomously*. "Bare law" rests upon a presupposition of *pure justice*, an autonomous justice-in-itself that is independent of God, that stands over and above God as an impersonal principle to which he too is subject. In order to understand better the true nature of this heresy we must investigate that religious principle which legalism expresses in opposition to the kingdom of God. We must investigate the antithesis between theism and antitheism.

Covenant Keepers versus Covenant Breakers

Reformed theology has generally revered Augustine as a theologian of grace. It is often said that he rediscovered Paul and incorporated Paulinism into his soteriology. Usually, this is said in reference to Augustine's predestinarianism and antipelagianism. For, according to the Calvinist reading of his letters (especially Romans), Paul is a staunch advocate of original sin and total depravity. He is opposed to all human efforts—works—and affirms the absolute sovereignty of God's free and unconditional election by grace. And Augustine, in his opposition to Pelagius, made appeal to these alleged elements of Pauline theology.

However, the heirs of the Reformation will quickly add that Augustine did not follow through in his Paulinism to include Paul's forensic doctrine of justification by faith. Augustine remained a Catholic, holding to a view of medicinal grace and of justification as a transformational process of renewal at work within the saints to make them righteous. It is only with the Protestant Reformation that Paul's alleged imputational view of justifying righteousness comes into its own.

Augustine's Paulinism is to be found at a deeper level, however. It is to be found in the Pauline *antithesis*. It is at this point that it seriously challenges the Lutheran view of justification by faith as well as subsequent Catholicism. Paul presents us with an absolute

contrast of belief and unbelief as two mutually exclusive and
diametrically opposed principles that can also be expressed as
obedience and *disobedience.* These stand in antithesis like light against
darkness, God against idolatry, Christ against Belial, righteousness
against unrighteousness. Paul certainly does buy into a principial
total depravity that views unbelievers as at enmity with God, haters
of God empowered by *Sin* (hypostatized as a God-opposing,
demonic force that has enslaved humanity to its dominion) to every
act of defiance and rebellion. Paul's soteriology is one of transfer
out of sin's dominion into the sphere of Christ's Lordship, creating
an obedient people who are servants of his righteousness.

It is in Paulinism that Augustine found the antithesis presented
in his *The City of God*[8] as the two loves that create the two societies.
Because he is dealing with the *supreme* love that governs and informs
the heart of *homo adorans,* Augustine is dealing with a radical
orientation at the most fundamental level, directing all of life and
thought in terms of the religious commitment formed with either
the true God or an idol. Accordingly, he sets the religious ground-
motive of the theocentric, theonomic, *theotelic* heart starkly over
against the basic motive informing the rebellious, insurrectionist
sons of Cain who comprise the *civitas terrena* in its enmity to God.
Those of faith are *faithful;* they are covenant-keepers, servants of
the Lord. Those yet in unbelief are covenant-breakers, with apostate
hearts opposed to the kingdom of God and seeking to build the
humanistic Tower of Babel. There is no shared eschatological vision,
no shared value system; two disparate conceptions of the *summum
bonum* separate the two cities. In norms, goals, and motives, there
is no common ground to be found between the two cities. The
antithesis penetrates to the level of the most fundamental religious
orientation and disposition, the existential root-dimension of
absolute presuppositions, basic commitments, and ultimate
concerns.

This Augustinian antithesis presents a different picture of faith
than that which comes to the fore in the Reformation's contract
between faith and works. The antithesis between law and gospel,
though it too claims to be Pauline, does not capture the spiritual
warfare in its global-historic proportions as does Augustine's
philosophy of the two cities. The ultimate question of who shall

rightfully rule over creation and direct its course is not addressed in the introspectively individualist Lutheran antithesis.

Later Reformed theology, as it developed into a *covenant* theology, better comprehended the Augustinian antithesis. The diametric opposition of covenantal response, faithfulness, and obedience versus the apostate stance of the covenant-breaker, was placed in a better position in which to receive due emphasis. Unfortunately, Reformed covenant theology remained bound to the Lutheran law/gospel contrast and thus lapsed into the covenant of works doctrine with its judicially determined concerns and emphases.

The intention of this framework was to undergird the antithesis of law and gospel: works versus grace as two disparate, mutually exclusive and diametrically opposed ways of justification unto life. The way of works defined the prelapsarian Adamic covenantal relationship, but the sin of Adam caused this covenant to be revoked. Its curses were still pronounced upon covenant-breaking humanity, which stood condemned under it because of the representative sin of Adam. No son of Adam, because of imputed guilt, could stand in a positive relation to this covenant. Christ, as the "second [epochal] man" and "last Adam"—a new federal head not of the Adamic race, stood uncondemned by this first covenant, representationally fulfilling its terms with perfect obedience and then vicariously accepting the imputation of its condemnation on behalf of the elect among the Adamic progeny. On the foundation of this keeping of the works-covenant a new covenantal relationship—a covenant of redemptive grace—was established, renewing the offer of justification unto life *in Christ*. By grace through faith, the elect stand in a relationship to Christ which imputes to them the merits of his active obedience, even as their guilt was imputed to him in his curse-bearing death.

Opposed to this plan of salvation was *legalism*. This error may be defined relative to Reformational concerns as the pursuit of justification by the attempt to accrue merit through performance of the law's requirements, reliance on works-righteousness. Legalism was seen as an attempt by postlapsarian man to gain life via the broken covenant of works, and this stood over against the way of faith in Christ's keeping of this covenant, the way of the covenant of grace offered in the gospel and grounded in *Christ's* meritorious works-righteousness.

What this abiding concern with works and grace as the foundational antithesis obscured was a perspective upon legalism as but one form of assault upon the rightful rule of the Lord, an assault that can manifest itself in many forms. Paul's opposition to "works of the law" remained concealed by the imposition of the hermeneutic of Protestant confessional propria upon the texts by Reformed exegetes; thus, the real problem of allegiance could not be comprehended. Legalism was not seen clearly for what it really is as *radical* disobedience: the arrogant self exaltation of self-righteous man in self-sufficient, self reliant assertion of autonomy. Its idolatrous character as human rebellion against its creaturely status in subjection to the Creator was not brought to the forefront. Instead, the Lutheran conception falsely opposed saving faith to obedience and therein made impossible a radical embracing of the Augustinian absolute antithesis.

Evangelical Protestantism still suffers from this gross misconception of the meaning of faith in the Lord Jesus Christ. It has no comprehension of radical repentance, nor of unconditional surrender to the Lord in a pledge of fealty and allegiance. It creates a false dichotomy between Christ as Savior and Lord, between repentance and faith, between faith and obedience, between law and gospel. Because of its easy-believist antinomianism, it has reduced perseverance to a "once-saved, always-saved" eternal security. Accordingly, the masses need only make a punctiliar "decision" and perhaps have some emotionalist experience (called "being *born again*"). Radical discipleship—following Christ in cost-counting, cross-bearing self-denial that seeks first and foremost the kingdom and God's righteousness with all-consuming existential hunger and thirst, that loves God supremely and wholeheartedly—is not the norm, but is merely for the few supersaints as works of supererogation. Narcissism—in the guise of *self-esteem*—infects the rank and file, encouraged by the essentially anthropocentric thrust of evangelical soteriology as it teeters into the religious principle informing the City of Man. Gone is *homo adorns* with his *sensus tremendum*; replaced instead by one who asks, "What can God do for me?" and who thinks that a *sola gratia* salvation is a good deal. The servant thereby arrogates to himself the place of his lord, committing the very sin—the root error of legalism—to which he confidently is sure his appreciation of lawless "grace" immunizes him. We need to rethink the nature of legalism in true covenantal perspective.

The Treaty of the Great King

As is now quite commonly recognized in Biblical scholarship, the Biblical conception of the covenants God has established with humanity are not expressed in the form of bilaterally negotiated contracts between equal parties. Yet is it this bilateralist idea of a *parity covenant* that lies behind the error of legalism, and legalism *cannot* arise within the context of a true understanding of the Biblical covenant form. For the latter type of covenant, a suzerainty treaty-form is inherently suffused with condescending goodness and loving kindness by a sovereign deliverer/provider-king who freely elects, who monergistically, unilaterally, and preveniently comes in grace to administer a relationship.

This covenant is, in its basic intent, a disposition to grant and bestow blessing. That it sets forth both promise and duty, both the possibility of blessing and curse, does not detract from the above. A framework of distinction between conditionality versus unconditionality, while clearly a distinction (of great importance in its proper context) that Paul draws between the redemptive-historical economy of Mosaic *torah* and the Abrahamic blessing-promise fulfilled in Christ (*Gal. 3:18*),[9] does not capture the radical rejection of grace—the absolute contempt for the suzerain-lord's free and sovereign condescension to bestow covenant status—that characterizes legalism. This is true of the discontinuities between the covenant of creation and the covenant of redemption as well as those between old and new covenants, for all of God's covenantal dealings with man have a basic continuity, patterned according to the suzerainty-treaty form[10] as sovereign dispositions of grace[11] that is grounded in the intrinsic structure of the Creator/creature distinction.[12]

The above point is of crucial importance to Biblical religion. For the fundamental disparity between Biblical soteriology and legalism is not due to the difference between law covenant and promise covenant as two species of suzerainty treaties. The former disparity is far more basic than the latter, for it does not comprehend those features common to all of God's suzerainty-form covenants: the identification of the suzerain in his special relationship to the vassal-people by mighty acts of deliverance and protection performed for their benefit, by special favors and privileges granted, and promises of future blessings under his benevolent rule—all of which form the basis for the allegiance of the vassals as a response of love and gratitude.[13] The fundamental disparity between legalism and Biblical-covenantal religion owes rather to the more basic difference between parity covenants and suzerainty treaties. Suzerainty treaties assert lordship, and those who confess Yahweh as covenant Lord, if they truly understand this submission, cannot be legalists. Until this fact is clearly grasped the true nature of legalism, which is always an assault upon the lordship of Yahweh, cannot be revealed in its true depths of perversity, and the legalism/ gospel antithesis will be wrongly equated with an alleged antithesis of covenant law and gospel.

Meredith G. Kline, to his credit, recognizes that the "absolute sovereignty of God in the reciprocal relationship [of the suzerainty law covenant]...prevents the legalistic distortion of the religious-covenantal bond into a mercantile *quid pro quo* contract."[14] Nevertheless, he is vehemently opposed to the implications of John Murray's covenant theology,[15] seeing in it a legalism (salvation by works) that violates the sharp works/grace contrast he posits to distinguish law covenant from promise covenant.[16] This way of viewing legalism in terms of law covenant follows from his whole conception of the priority of law, for he views the covenant of creation as a pure law covenant (in form and content), a covenant bond constituted by vassal oath-swearing. As such, it is a conditional covenant, requiring satisfactory compliance of the suzerain's imposed demands by the subject vassal party.[17] The covenant of redemption, though materially a promise covenant, is, in its formal structure, a law covenant in which the suzerain has unilaterally sworn the oath of self-malediction that sanction-seals the covenant in order to guarantee unconditionally that the blessing aspect of inheritance will surely prevail and all the terms for both parties will be met.[18]

In a law covenant, according to the Klinean view, we can speak of a works-principle imposed upon the vassal. While the covenant is freely and sovereignly initiated according to electing lovingkindness in a unilateral manner that grants covenant status to the vassal people, continuation in the state of covenant blessing is conditioned upon the vassal's faith fulfillment of the stipulations of the treaty opted in the ratifying oath of allegiance. For the covenant itself imposes demands that constitute the basis of ongoing amicable relationship. The covenant sets forth both blessing and curse as the judicial consequences rendered to obedience and disobedience respectively. A promise covenant, on the other hand, assures blessing because the suzerain himself swears the oath of self-malediction that removes the curse-threat from the vassal. The difference between law covenant and promise covenant, between works-principle and grace-principle, is determined by which party—vassal or suzerain—swears the sanction-sealing, self-maledictory oath of ratification, accepting the curse-threat for unfulfillment.[19]

As Kline sees it, the works-principle of the covenant of creation (a principle that is re-expressed in the Mosaic law covenant as a *kingdom-typological overlay* upon the covenant of redemption)[20] makes the nature of this covenant that of a conditional covenant of law, placing the vassal under the curse-threat and demanding vassal compliance. The way of blessing, of justification unto eschatological life and glorification, is by the way of vassal lawkeeping, according to a meritorious works-principle that is based upon pure justice.[21] This covenantal administration stands in starkest contrast to the subsequent covenant of redemption, which operates according to the principle of grace as a promise covenant because Christ has vicariously fulfilled the works-principle inherent in its formal law covenant structure. In this latter covenantal arrangement, the terms of the treaty are wholly and exclusively fulfilled by the suzerain for the vassal (for the Lord himself becomes the Servant of the Lord), guaranteeing to the vassal unconditional blessing apart from any basis in, or judicial consideration of, the vassal's works.[22]

Viewed within this Klinean framework, legalism appears as the treatment of a promise covenant as though it were a law covenant. The vassal therein attempts to construe the covenant relationship as conditional, as maintained by a works-principle that he must fulfil in order to remain in a state of blessedness and ultimately receive the eschatological inheritance promised to the covenant servant who faithfully perseveres in the way of obedience. His faithfulness is the constitutive factor in maintaining the relationship to covenant blessedness. Legalism, if viewed as such, is equaled with covenantal nomism whereby the blessing of eschatological justification is the reward of vassal faithfulness in abiding in the sphere of the covenant by satisfactorily fulfilling the treaty stipulations.[23]

Over against the above portrayal, were we to understand legalism in terms of the more fundamental contrast between suzerainty treaties and parity covenants, as John Murray's view would suggest, we would not understand it as merely a misguided, ill-conceived, and utterly vain effort toward fulfilling the treaty stipulations to the requisite degree of adequacy (for the suzerain—God—demands perfection), an attempt that ignores the exigencies demanded by the postlapsarian situation and consequently fails to appreciate the resultant necessity of redemptive grace in God's subsequent covenant renewal in and through Christ.[24] For legalism is not an attempt to treat the law covenant of creation as though it still offered life and blessing according to a (once valid but now invalid) works-principle of fulfillment—justification by works of law-obedience rendered to the suzerain.[25] It is indeed highly doubtful that we should construe the Adamic covenant of creation as a purely legal covenant based upon a principle of meritorious works-righteousness according to strict justice and to the exclusion of grace, as Kline believes.[26]

As serious as is the error of failing duly to note the discontinuities between the pre- and postlapsarian situations, between the covenants of creation and redemption (for God's covenant is now grounded in and mediated by Christ, in whom alone we can be rightly related to God and stand as legitimate heirs of the blessing-promise), we do not reach the pernicious heart of legalism by this route. Furthermore, it is equally erroneous to ignore the *continuities* between these two covenantal administrations of God's kingly rule as the Lord who requires of man (whether fallen or unfallen) the obedience of faith as covenant response. All who are consecrated unto life in covenant with God must reciprocate in this way of covenant faith-response as existential orientation, and this obligation is never construed in Scripture in terms of meritorious achievement inherently worthy of congratulation and reward (cf. *Lk. 17:7-10*). Because God is the supreme and sovereign Lord, he will not share his glory with another (*Is. 48:11*); there can be no boast or glorying before God (*Rom. 4:2*). The servant's fulfillment of his covenant obligations can never be a ground for boasting (*1 Cor. 1:29, 31; 4:7; Eph. 2:9*), and his receipt of blessing is never the fruit of his own labors (cf. *Dt. 8:17-18*).

Legalism does not express this theocentric and theonomic religious ground-motive, even in the manner of a misguided, misdirected creationist religion that is deficient in hamartialogical and soteriological awareness. For legalism is rather born of the rebellious nature of would-be autonomous man in his covenant-breaking declaration of metaphysical independence from God, in his desire to be as God. It expresses in its depths the very root-essence of sin. In the former conception of the matter, legalism could conceivably be a sincere (if naïve) effort to submit to the lordship of God, an error correctable by greater understanding. In the latter view, however, legalism throws off the yoke of creaturely servitude, renouncing the lordship inherent in the suzerainty treaty-type.

The legalist seeks to approach God as an equal party. This approach is of course with the ultimate intent of gaining advantage over God and subordinating him, but at first the legalist comes to negotiate the terms of a relationship as a bilateral agreement among partners. He bargains with God to hammer out a mutually advantageous and agreeable contract that binds God to terms man helps to set according to an autonomous view of justice and merit. Accordingly, God becomes indebted to man, obliged to reward man's efforts and deeds according to *quid pro quo.*

As such, legalist religion does not simply undermine the idea of redemptive grace in a postlapsarian situation. It strikes at the very heart of the Creator/creature distinction. It assaults the lordship of the lawful suzerain. Proclamation of sin and gracious redemption in Christ is done in a vacuum—often with perverse consequences that distort the very meaning of grace (cf. *Jd. 4*), as we find in many circles of contemporary evangelical religion—if we do not first lay the creationist foundation: "Know that the LORD he is God: it is he that hath made us, and not we ourselves" (*Ps. 100:3*).

The very basis of covenant institution in true legalism is one of merit, and this sharply distinguishes it from any sort of suzerainty treaty-founded concept of religion. In the suzerainty treaty-covenant, the vassal is freely elected unto covenant status, apart from all considerations of prevenient merit and worthiness (cf. *Dt. 7:7-8*), by the condescending lovingkindness of the suzerain. Covenant bestows status, not vice-versa. In legalism, however, man demands to be treated from the outset as an equal, worthy of God's respect and claiming the right to approach God on his own terms. Thus he demands to enter into a contractual relationship based upon *mutual need*—a "symbiotic" arrangement.

In this view, God is perceived as needing man's service, which of course makes the rendering of said service inherently valuable, due a just compensation, and this intrinsic value is the reason why God seeks a covenant with man. Thus, man can bargain on this basis to extract the best deal possible, according to considerations of self-interest. He self-servingly curries favor in order to enhance his value, to attract a better offer from God, so that God will be persuaded to offer him a lucrative contract. Accordingly, the theocentricity of the suzerainty treaty-conception of covenantal piety is exchanged for a self-serving religion of anthropocentrism.[27]

Covenant theology must free itself from the mistaken notion, so prevalent in modern evangelicalism, that the basic religious antithesis can be framed in terms of a law/gospel contrast as an opposition between justification by obedience and justification by grace through faith. The true antithesis is rather that between theonomy and autonomy, between theocentrically oriented, covenant-keeping, faithful devotion, allegiance, and commitment to God and covenant-breaking revolt. It is the Augustinian antithesis between the two fundamental, religious loves constitutive of the City of God and the City of Man. Biblical faith—*saving* faith—is confession of/submission to Jesus as Lord, and this allegiance stands diametrically opposed, not to good works of obedience (which are but the outworkings of a living faith in action), but to the antitheistic desire of would-be autonomous man to assault the kingdom, to usurp this lordship of Yahweh-Christ and exalt himself in *hybris*. Real obedience (which ever issues from the heart and is not the mere role-playing that bears some semblance of external conformity) does not—*cannot*—threaten to overthrow this relation of servant-subject to his Lord and King. It surely does not stand in competition with Christ the Lord, as though it were a rival allegiance-commitment that detracts from Christ the Lord in a way analogous to the nomistic service of the Judaizers in their rival lordship-commitment to covenantal nomism that functioned as an idolatrous devotion to *torah* over Christ, in the Pauline churches of Galatia.[28] The fundamental issue in the truly Biblical covenantal-religious opposition to legalism, Judaizing nomism, antinomianism, and all false gospels and antitheistic ideologies is that of *lordship and service*: "Choose ye this day whom ye will serve."

The kingdom of God has been established in the exaltation of Jesus as Lord and Christ, to whom all who would be saved must bow and swear allegiance. Let us therefore submit in absolute and unconditional surrender to this Lord, seeking first his kingdom as *summum bonum* with whole-hearted and single-minded commitment and devotion, as those who follow Christ bearing the yoke of true discipleship. This—not the cheap grace of antinomian, anthropocentric, easy-believist religion—is the way of life and salvation.

---

[1] *The Epistle to the Romans* (NICNT; Grand Rapids, 1975), 249-50.

[2] See discussion of the aspects of *mythos* and *ethos* in my "'The Blessing of Abraham' versus 'the Curse of the Law': Another Look at Galatians 3:10-13," *Westminster Theological Journal* 53 (1991), 81-83.

[3] I cannot deal with Romans 10:5 in any detail here. A few points, however, are in order. The context deals with *hearing* and *doing* (cf. *vv. 14, 17f.*, and what is said below about the *Kyrios Jesous* confession [*v. 9*] as the "new *Shema*"), returning us to the themes addressed previously in Romans 2 (cf. *2:13*). In that context (on which see my "Lord of Life: The Confession of Lordship and Saving Faith," *Journal of Christian Reconstruction*, Vol. 13, No. 1 [1990-91], 101-102, and D. B. Garlington,

"The Obedience of Faith and Judgment by Works," *Westminster Theological Journal,* 53 [1991], 54-64, esp. 58), Paul opposes a mere *hearing* that does not embrace *doing,* for it is an objective "hearing-stance" that refers to the formal status of membership in a community designated by external covenant identity-markers as the "hearing people": the people who received the *torah.* In Romans 10, however, he refers to an internalized *hearing* that is a *doing:* the "hearing of faith" which is also the "*obedience* of faith: that makes one a doer of the law." For the new covenant community is assembled around the new *Shema* ("*Hear,* O Israel") that Jesus is Lord (cf. my "Lord of Life," 110, n. 30). Paul cites Leviticus 18:5 (a "prooftext" of covenantal nomism used by Paul's Judaizing opponents in the Galatian controversy—see my "Blessing of Abraham," 77, n. 12) to stress the true *doing* principle of covenantal nomism (on which see below, n. 341) that focuses upon the *Shema* as the central tenet of Israel's faith in God as Israel's covenant Lord, demanding exclusive allegiance and devotion. Leviticus 18:5 in context deals with separation from idols and faithful service to the Lord. Israel, however, has Judeocentrically *idolized* the *torah,* setting it in competition to Christ the Lord as a rival allegiance (see Garlington, ÉÅÑÏÓÔ ËÅÉ and the Idolatry of Israel," *NTS,* 36 [1990], 142-151, and my "Blessing of Abraham," 83 and 85, n. 37). By seeking a distinctively *Jewish* righteousness by clinging to the exclusive *torah* identity-markers that serve to separate, she has missed the point of Leviticus 18:5, for she has not really *heard* the law and its witness to its own *redemptive-historical* termination (in the *eschatological* covenant renewal to which the Deuteronomy 30:12-14 citation in Romans 10:6-8 refers—cf. Deuteronomy 30:1-10) upon reaching its end-goal in Christ: the antitypical *law of righteousness* (probably the *Zion-torah* tradition—see Hartmut Gese, "The Law," *Essays on Biblical Theology* [Minneapolis, 1981], 60-92, esp. 81-85 and 89-92. See further C. K. Barrett, "Romans 9:30-10:21: Fall and Responsibility of Israel," in his *Essays on Paul* [Philadelphia, 1982], 144f.) that is the *righteousness of God* to which they ought to submit (*Rom. 9:31-32; 10:3-4*). Here is simply the same point made by Paul in Galatians 3:23-25: Mosaic covenantal nomism was intended merely to protect and preserve Israel as the distinct covenant people through whom God revealed himself until the "fullness of time" of the eschatological revelation of the righteousness of God (the content of the Abrahamic blessing-promise) in the Christ-event (see T. David Gordon," A Note on ÁÉÄÁÁÕÃÏ in Galatians 3:24-25," *NTS,* 35 [1989], 150-154).

[4] *Commentary on Galatians* (NIGTC; Grand Rapids, 1982), 160-161.

[5] Defended in more modern times in the commentaries by Ridderbos

(*The Epistle of Paul to the Churches at Galatia* [NICNT; Grand Rapids, 1953], 1222-1223), Bruce (*Galatians*, 158-161), and Fung (*The Epistle to the Galatians* [NICNT; Grand Rapids, 1988], 141-143).

[6] This, however, is not to deny the exaggerated emphasis upon separation in the Judaism of Paul's day in which the preservation of a holy people set apart from the nations (clearly identifiable by their peculiar *torah*-lifestyle and forbidden to intermarry with, or adopt the customs of, the gentiles) became an end-in-itself, fueled by nationalism and abstracted from the service-aspect of their election as a priest-people. As such, Judaism became a form of *idolatry* that absolutized the Mosaic economy and divorced it from its redemptive-historical context as temporary and subordinated to the Abrahamic promise of universal blessing.

[7] See further the interpretation of Galatians offered in my "Blessing of Abraham."

[8] Book XIV. In Reformed circles, the writings of Cornelius Van Til best capture this framing of the religious antithesis.

[9] Again, see my "Blessing of Abraham," *passim*, esp. 78. Paul's point is that the Mosaic *torah*-covenant was made with Jews, conditioned upon their faithfulness, while the Abrahmanic blessing-promise has direct and immediate reference (*qua* unconditional promise) only to Christ (the singular seed), not the Jews (corporate seed). Participation in the promise is therefore grounded in and mediated through Christ as seed of promise. Conditional/unconditional does not as such distinguish between old and new covenants with reference to corporate participants, for it is Christ alone who has the unconditional guarantee of blessing (and what does this do to the mistaken notion that he was under a covenant of works in our place in order to merit the blessing for us?). There is no reference here as to participation in Christ as blessing-locus to be unconditional. Such participation is clearly conditioned upon the obedience of faith (which is not to deny that, in terms of the eternal elective decree, the elect of God are *unconditionally* elected unto this obedience, nor does it view the covenantal obedience-condition as meritorious). On the conditional/unconditional debate regarding the covenant of grace in Reformed theology, see discussion in Murray, "Covenant Theology," in *The Collected Writings of John Murray*, 4 vols. (Carlysle, PA, 1982), 4. 229-234.

[10] On which see Meredith G. Kline, *By Oath Consigned: A Reinterpretation of the Covenant Signs of Circumcision and Baptism* (Grand Rapids, 1968), 26-38.

[11] See John Murray, *The Covenant of Grace: A Biblico-theological Study* (London, 1954), 30-32.

[12] Cf. *The Westminster Confession of Faith*, 7:1.

[13] Emphasizing here the first two of the six features of the treaty pattern as set forth by Kline (*The Structure of Biblical Authority*, rev. ed. [Grand Rapids, 1972], 121): the preamble and historical prologue.

[14] Kline, *By Oath Consigned*, 37.

[15] Murray, *Covenant of Grace*.

[16] See his "Of Works and Grace," *Presbyterian*, 19 (1983), 86-92.

[17] See discussion of "Oath and Covenant" and "Law Covenant" (chaps. 1-2) in Kline, *By Oath Consigned*, 13-38, esp. 26-35.

[18] *ibid.*, 31-35.

[19] *ibid.*, 16.

[20] Mark W. Karlberg, "Reformed Interpretation of the Mosaic Covenant," *Westminster Theological Journal*, 43 (1980), 46-48, 54-57.

[21] Kline, "Of Works and Grace," 88-90.

[22] *ibid.*, 91; *By Oath Consigned*, 17 (cf. 45), 30-35.

[23] On the concept of covenantal nomism, see E. P. Sanders, *Paul and Palestinian Judaism* (Philadelphia, 1977) *passim*, but esp. 422-423.

[24] *Westminster Confession of Faith*, 7:3.

[25] It is important to bear in mind that the "works-principle" in question is one consistent with the suzerainty covenant-type in terms of the inherent lordship-submission principle of unilateral imposition and nonparity previously referred to.

[26] Kline, in criticizing the traditional nomenclature of 'covenant of works'/ 'covenant of grace' (*By Oath Consigned*, 32, 36), is far more balanced in this regard than he appears to be in his later formulations, as set forth, *e.g.* in his "Of Works and Grace." It is to the stark contrast of works and grace of this more recent piece to which I here refer. Against this sharp contrast (which seems to be but a more consistent development of principles already present in *By Oath Consigned*), see the profitable discussion in G. C. Berouwer, *Studies in Dogmatics: Sin* (Grand Rapids, 1971), 206-208.

[27] See here Socrates' point about Euthyphro's concept of piety in Plato's *Euthyphro*, 12d-15a (Burnet's Oxford text) and the world of thought shared by both Socrates and Euthyphro that views piety as having intrinsic value and goodness as such, being dear to the gods simply and solely because it *is* piety (10d).

[28] See my "Blessing of Abraham," 81-83.

Vol. 4, No. 2, 1977-78
Family Authority vs. Protestant Sacerdotalism
by Gary North

But ye are a chosen generation, a royal priesthood, an holy nation, a peculiar people that ye should shew forth the praises of him who hath called you out of darkness into his marvelous light.

(1 Peter 2:9)

Peter's announcement of the universalization of the Old Testament priesthood was the fulfillment of God's promise to Israel that they, if they were obedient to his commandments, would become a kingdom of priests, a holy nation (*Ex. 19:5-6*). It is this New Testament passage, perhaps more than any other, which has served Protestants as the foundation of their opposition to the Roman Catholic Church's system of sacerdotalism, the doctrine that a priesthood mediates salvation between God and men. The heart of Luther's message, salvation through faith alone, necessarily challenged the sacerdotalism of his day, and it earned him excommunication. He had denied the mediatorial position of the priesthood as the sole agency for the dispensing of personal salvation to church members. In opposition to sacerdotalism, Luther preached that most Protestant of doctrines, the priesthood of all believers.

(Actually, this was not the most Protestant of doctrines. The one doctrine universally held in the seventeenth century by every Protestant church, from the highest of high church Anglicans to the wildest of the Anabaptist of Fifth Monarchy sects, was the identification of the papacy with the antichrist. This doctrine was inserted into the Westminster Confession of Faith, chapter XXV, section 6, to the embarrassment of modern American Presbyterians, who have seen fit to footnote this passage into oblivion, and quite properly so. However, it is interesting to witness the most orthodox of Presbyterians drop the one doctrine which was the touchstone of the Protestant orthodoxy from Luther's day until about 1930. At least they set a most-needed precedent, namely, confessional revision of even the most universally accepted traditions of Protestantism. They recognized that the presence in the Confession of unsubstantiated human opinion, in contrast to clearly revealed Biblical truth, should not be tolerated, once men realize that the traditional opinion is incorrect. It is a precedent that should be honored.)

The problem with the priesthood of all believers, in the eyes of most ecclesiastical authorities, is that one never knows exactly where such a doctrine will lead. From the beginning, Luther and the other orthodox Protestant reformers worried about this theological weapon. It was an ideal tool in their battles against Roman Catholic priests, but it could also be used effectively by revolutionary sects against the authority of ordained Protestant ministers. Since these ministers were usually on the side of the political authorities in the struggle against the revolutionary sects, the leaders of the left-wing sects found it convenient to preach this doctrine to their followers. The doctrine was immediately modified by Lutheran and Calvinist theologians. While the priesthood was not to be understood as the sole means of imparting grace to the faithful, meaning special grace or saving faith, the ordained leaders still had to be respected as ministers of God and as leaders within the congregations. They were more than laymen, possessing the exclusive rights of administering the sacraments, which were reduced from seven to two, baptism and holy communion (the Lord's Supper). The Westminster Confession, after limiting the sacraments to these two, adds: "neither of which may be dispensed by any, but by a minister of the Word lawfully ordained" (XXVII:4). The word "priest" once again became synonymous with "ordained minister."

In what ways, then, have New Testament believers become priests? In what ways are we priests in a new and different sense from Old Testament believers? What did Peter have in mind when he announced this fulfillment of prophecy? The doctrine has to mean more than a merely negative claim that Protestant laymen no longer have to regard as sacraments five of Rome's seven rites. In what active, official ways are all of us priests? For four hundred years, this doctrine has been only a negative argument used by Protestants to challenge the monopolistic claims of Rome. It is not that Protestant churches acknowledge that laymen are priests in any positive, official sense, but only that laymen are freed from five-sevenths of the sacramental claims of a rival priesthood. The two remaining sacraments must be administered by an ordained, exclusive clerical order. Therefore, the priesthood of all believers is still interpreted by Protestant churches as meaning the priesthood of *few* believers, ecclesiastically speaking, and in traditional Christian theology, ecclesiastical authority is what really counts.

The Protestant doctrine of the priesthood has remained dualistic. The offices of the Protestant visible churches have been equated with the office of Old Testament priest and, subsequently, the sacramental offices have been reduced to one, that of minister. On the other hand, the priesthood of all believers has still retained some life as a formal theological concept, though carefully and systematically emptied of content. The priesthood that is now universalized has been limited to the role of family religious leadership. This "universal priest" has authority in his household, but this authority does not extend into the visible church in a formal sense. The "universal priest" is not ordained in any formal church ceremony, nor is he called in any special way into official ecclesiastical service to the flock. In fact, the universal priesthood *is* the flock, to be led by the pastors, and occasionally sheared by the unscrupulous. The Protestant doctrine of the priesthood of all believers is summarized thusly: "There are priests, and then there are *priests.*" This is in stark contrast to the Roman Catholic position, "There are priests, and then there are *priests.*"

Priests in the Old Testament possessed extensive sovereignty. They served as medical officers who had the power of quarantine (*Lev. 14*). They served as direct oracles of God (*Num. 27:21*). They served as judges and civil servants. They offered sacrifices. They were bearers of authority.

The modern Protestant doctrine of the priesthood, meaning church officers, now limits the authority of the priests to strictly ecclesiastical authority. Deacons operate charitable services, elders make judgments in disputes among church members, and ministers (possibly assisted by elders) perform the two sacraments. Rare is the pastor who anoints the sick with oil (*Jas. 5:14-15*). The role of the priest has been drastically reduced institutionally. Ministers preach, administer a pair of sacraments, make decisions with the ruling elders, and cooperate with deacons. They have many unofficial church tasks, such as weddings, funerals, visiting the sick, raising money, and so forth, but these tasks are not defined as being part of the office of priest as such. To make such a claim would be to risk reviving the old Roman Catholic sacerdotalism.

The modern priest is therefore marked by these special features:

1. Ordination of some kind
2. The exclusive right to administer two sacraments
3. The right to execute ecclesiastical discipline

Some Protestant churches also include preaching in the list of exclusively priestly functions. Presbyterians and Episcopalians are fussy in this regard, though some exceptions are allowed some of the time. To gain access to the pulpit on a regular basis, you must be ordained. Since the Calvinist tradition has emphasized the marks of the true church as being the preaching of the word and the administration of the sacraments (and sometimes including the exercise of church discipline), the minister has tended to become the exclusive true priest, since he alone is ordained to perform all of these tasks.

What is the meaning, then, of the priesthood of all believers? *Historically*, the meaning within the orthodox, conservative Protestant churches has been this: a fine weapon to use on Roman Catholics, an illegitimate weapon in the hands of sects—sects being defined as those who use the weapon against others besides Roman Catholics—and a pleasant, painless doctrine which is seldom mentioned any more. *Theologically*, the priesthood of all believers ought to be understood to mean that every believer serves as a *mediator of God's covenantal authority* in the tasks associated with the subduing of the earth. The New Covenant of Jesus Christ announces God's victory, in time and on earth, over Satan's rival claims. If we are priests, then each person should bear the signs of such authority. The Protestant rule should be: "The universalization of *all* priestly functions, unless specifically limited to one group by explicit biblical testimony."

Ordination

There is no question that the Bible limits access to the offices of elder and deacon. The bishop (*episcopase*) must be male, the husband of one wife, sober, patient, and a man who rules well in his own household (*1 Tim. 3:1-5*). Likewise, deacons must be grave, honest, not greedy, husbands of one wife, and good rulers over their children (*1 Tim. 3:8-12*). If we are to believe what we read, at least two unconventional conclusions seem obvious. First, bishops (elders) and deacons must be married men, or at least widowers. Probably a man unlawfully deserted or divorced by his wife would still be eligible. Second, it should be pointed out that bigamists are not eligible, indicating that in the past, churches have been unwise in allowing missionaries to ordain tribal chieftans as church leaders when they were married to several wives. (Forcing them to unload all but one wife was even worse, since the older wives would be forced to go, turning them into social pariahs or even prostitutes.)

If the second conclusion is correct, then we should ask ourselves another question. Is a polygamist forever barred from full church membership? If a pagan from a polygamistic culture is converted, and if he cannot lawfully be compelled to divorce his wives within the framework of the prevailing culture, on what basis can he be excluded from full membership? The early church seems to have faced this problem squarely. Such a man was not permitted to assume the offices of elder or deacon. The New Testament does not exclude the polygamist from membership, however. The coming of Christian culture is not a radically discontinuous event. It must first shape the pagan culture during the period of transition. Christianity is socially conservative, despite the fact that it is radical to the core with respect to the secular foundations of social and political order. Orthodox Christianity acknowledges that Christians have sufficient time, over many generations, to subdue the earth to the glory of God. Christians count the costs of cultural transition, or should, protecting the integrity of the church (no polygamists as officers) while simultaneously refusing to create social chaos (forcing all but one wife out of their home). Even in our own culture, we have no way of coping with the problem of the woman who marries a married man, having been deceived by him. She is given no legal rights with respect to his estate. She is counted as a non-wife. The injured party is penalized and is forced out of a home which she had relied on. There is something wrong here—

something which contemporary Christian social and legal theorists have been content to ignore.

There is another argument which must be considered. Some theologians have concluded that since Paul was a bachelor, the strict interpretation of his language regarding "the husband of one wife" must be abandoned, that is, *if* a man is married, he must be married to only one wife. There are two errors in this approach. First, it assumes that Paul was a bachelor. The Bible nowhere tells us this. He was unmarried, but as to whether he was a bachelor or a widower, the Bible is silent. The one passage that is used to prove that Paul was a bachelor, 1 Corinthians 7:7-8, proves no such thing. It proves only that he was single. He was addressing both single people and widows or widowers: "For I would that all men were even as I myself. . . . I say therefore to the unmarried and widows, It is good for them if they abide even as I." To argue from silence that Paul was in fact a bachelor, and then to conclude that it is lawful to ordain bachelors, since Paul was ordained, is not valid exegesis or logic. The second error in this approach is to conclude that Paul's miraculous conversion and ordination by Christ (*Gal. 1:1*), even if he was a bachelor, is a valid argument to be used against the specific injunctions of this specially ordained apostle. Why should we set aside his stated rules for ordination just because God ordained him in a unique way? God may have set aside this general rule in order to achieve a specific purpose, just as he allowed both Rahab and Ruth to become part of the covenant line of Christ (*Mt. 1:5*), despite the fact that Moabites and other Canaanitic peoples were supposed to be screened for ten generations before they could become full citizens of Israel (*Dt. 23:3*). Paul's apostleship was already unique, whether he was a bachelor or not. When we ordain men to the offices of the church through conventional means, we are not to conduct the ordination in direct opposition to the requirements set forth by God's word. We are not to enact our own miracles or special rules when God's standards are stated clearly. There is nothing unclear about the requirement concerning a man's having to be the husband of one wife before he can seek or accept the office of deacon or elder.

It is very interesting to observe that both deacons and elders have to prove themselves first as husbands and fathers, or at least as husbands, before they are to be ordained. They must have already exercised godly, competent authority. *The family is therefore the primary training ground for church officers*—not seminaries, and not even fully accredited, four-year colleges. It has been the long-standing practice of Reformed churches to substitute proficiency at taking formal academic examinations in place of demonstrated competence in heading a household. The footnote has therefore replaced the family as the preferred screening device for ordination to the teaching eldership, which supposedly must be distinguished from the ruling eldership. (The Presbyterian version of the doctrine of the priesthood of all believers has always been: "There are priests, and then there are priests, but most important there are *priests*.") If a man wants to be a minister, he had better have his footnotes in order, whether or not he has his family in order, or a family at all.

Some readers may think that I am exaggerating. Not at all. Consider the official denominational standards of the church which regards itself, with good evidence, as the most thoroughly Calvinistic Presbyterian church in America, and probably the world.

> Because it is highly reproachful to religion and dangerous to the church to trust the holy ministry to weak and ignorant men, the presbytery shall admit a candidate to licensure only if he has received a bachelor of arts degree, or its academic equivalent, from an accredited college or university. He must also have completed at least two years of study in a theological seminary.[1]

The overcoming of ignorance and weakness is clearly understood to be a direct function of training in some institution of higher education which is accredited, meaning approved by the apostate, godless, rebellious intellectuals who are warring against orthodoxy. An unaccredited Christian college is insufficient; better to be a graduate of a state-financed, officially neutral, apostate university. It indicates that the ministers, as distinguished from ruling elders, will have been compromised with secularism, to one extent or other, in their educational backgrounds, and it also indicates that they will be tempted to set themselves apart from ruling elders on the basis of prior performance of certain academic exercises. After all, as the same book states, "The office of the minister is the first in the church for dignity or usefulness."[2]

Significantly, these same standards do not mention any requirement for godly rule in a household, either for the ruling elder or for the so-called teaching elder. Furthermore, nothing explicit is stated in these standards concerning the absolute requirement that churches remove from high office any man who subsequently loses control over his household. No definition of godly household rule is offered. What *is* specifically mentioned is requirement of formal academic training for the so-called teaching elder. (The requirements were softened somewhat in the post-1968 version of the church's standards: candidates now need only a year and a half of seminary.)

The Bible requires that *all* elders (bishops) be able to teach (*1 Tim. 3:2*). The Bible sets forth *one* set of standards for ordination (*1 Tim. 3:1-7; Tit. 1:5-9*). The official tasks of the elders are always identical (*1 Pet. 5:1-11*). What is the basis for distinguishing teaching elders from ruling elders? Romans 12:6-8 lists these gifts: prophecy, ministry, teaching, exhortation, ruling, mercifulness. Surely these are not separate offices. The other great passage in Scripture which deals with the division of labor within the church, 1 Corinthians 12, also cannot be used successfully to establish multiple elderships: "And God hath set some in the church, first apostles, secondarily prophets, thirdly teachers, after that miracles, then gifts of healings, helps, governments, diversities of tongues" (*1 Cor. 12:28*). Yet attempts are made to single out "governments" or "governings" as the basis of pluralized elderships. What, we might ask, became of teachers as a separate office? Answer: it was a separate office which has been swallowed up, somehow, by teaching elders.

"The office of the minister," the denominational handbook continues, "is the first in the church for dignity and usefulness." But "minister" is defined as teaching elder, and subsequently distinguished from (elevated above) ruling elder. The Biblical citation is 1 Timothy 5:17. This is such a blatant misreading of the Bible that it indicates how weak the theory of the plural eldership really is. What is studiously ignored is 1 Timothy 5:18, which provides the context of Paul's message, namely, remuneration for services rendered:

> Let the elders that rule well be counted worthy of double honour, especially they who labour in the word and doctrine [speech and

teaching]. For the scripture sayeth, Thou shalt not muzzle the
ox that treadeth out the corn. And, The labourer is worthy of his
reward. (*1 Tim. 5:17-18*)

The attempt is made to separate "elders who rule well" from
"they who labor in the word and doctrine."[3] However, as any
Presbyterian, Baptist, or other elder can tell you, the "double
honour" of American Protestantism is not connected with a salary.
The laborers, in this case, are clearly not worthy of their rewards,
if by rewards we have in mind (as Paul did) cash, checks, or money
orders, which are the modern equivalent of corn (grain). Naturally,
the "especially" crowd does receive its financial reward. Somehow,
the magical word "especially" converts "double honour" into cold
cash. Ministers get paid.

What should we conclude? First, all elders deserve salaries,
depending upon the kind of services rendered. Secondly, the only
differences between elders are in terms of personal gifts, and these
gifts are multiple: teaching, helps, governments, etc. The "especially"
refers to greater intensity of service, not a separate office within
the church. He who preaches, teaches, and does public service that
cannot be handled by other elders in a particular local congregation
is entitled to greater pay. It is symbolic of the lack of contribution,
lack of effort, lack of importance, and lack of real power held by
today's so-called ruling elders that they are not reimbursed
financially for their labors. If we accept the principle that the laborer
is worthy of his hire, then we have to conclude that modern
churches rate the value of services provided by ruling elders at just
about zero. Yet this is precisely the opposite of Paul's instructions
in 1 Timothy 5:17. In the modern church, the ruling elder is not
worth double honor, or even single honor. The payment given to
ruling elders indicates the modern church's assessment of the
supposedly separate office: it is strictly ornamental—a kind of
comforting reminder of the first-century church. And if this analysis
is denied, and the ruling elders really are significant, then those
within the present denominations who would defend the office
condemn themselves, for they pay these men nothing. (Of course,
they pay ministers very little. Orthodox Christians want their
religion, but they want it cheap.)

What we have seen in the hierarchical denomination, as well as in a significant number of the congregationally ordered churches, is the continuing elevation of formal academic performance over the requirement that church officers be competent heads of families. The family, which is the training ground of all service and authority, is forgotten. Protestant sacerdotalism has imitated Rome. The self-policing ecclesiastical hierarchies screen candidates in terms of essentially bureaucratic performance standards. *Robert's Rules of Order* is preeminent. The academic degree is supreme. And we find, much to our surprise, that church hierarchies are less like families and more like university faculties or low-level branches of the bureaucratized civil government. Institutionally, the salt has lost its savor. We find the same pettiness, arrogance, and incompetence in making decisions in church assemblies that we find in university life or civil government.

Ordination is a valid concept. It is intimately linked to family authority. When it is separated from the training ground of family life, ordination becomes bureaucratic. So it is with Roman Catholicism, which long ago reversed Paul's dictum and required all priests to be the husbands of no wife. So it has been in modern Protestantism, liberal and conservative. The family has been de-emphasized, and the result, universally, has been the bureaucratization of the churches.

When churches begin to depose ordained men who have not ruled their families well, there will be hope. When churches separate one's elder's tasks from another only in terms of each elder's specific talents and the local church's needs, there will be hope. When all elders are paid in terms of their value to the church, there will be hope. Until then, the best we can do is hope for hope—or, as the case may be, hope against hope. Bureaucrats are almost impossible to dislodge, as is the bureaucratic mentality. The reform will have to come from below, if it comes at all to our existing ecclesiastical structures. In all likelihood, it will take several generations and the creation of competing ecclesiastical organizations. The existing leaders are pledged to their faith in plural elderships, academic degrees, accredited colleges, and zero pay for ruling elders. They had to swear their allegiance to the system in order to get their jobs. The testimony of the Bible has been suppressed too long; the tradition of the formally educated (certified) minister has been with us too long. Crisis will bring change. It is questionable whether voluntary reform will. We can always hope for the best. We can also work to bring reform.

The Administration of the Sacraments

The priesthood in the Old Testament had an almost exclusive monopoly of administering the sacraments. (The exception was the father's role in the family ceremonies during passover.) Only the high priest could enter the holy of holies, and then only once a year (*Lev. 16*). But with the death of Christ, the final high priest, the veil of the temple was rent (*Mt. 27:51*). The holy of holies no longer was separated from the rest of the temple. The kingdom of priests was established.

Who has the authority to perform the sacraments in New Testament times? If we are all priests, does each Christian have the right to administer the sacraments? If not, why not? Is the mark of the priest, meaning the *priest*, his exclusive monopoly of administering the sacraments? In other words, is the administration of the sacraments the exclusive right of ordained church officers?

The answer of virtually all Christian churches is *yes*, the church officers have the exclusive right of administering the sacraments, at least in the normal course of events. Protestants limit the sacraments to baptism and the Lord's Supper (holy communion), and these are the exclusive right of ordained men, or in the case of liberal or pentecostal denominations, ordained men and women.

Before considering the accuracy of this Protestant position with respect to the administration of the sacraments, let us examine the nature of the sacraments.

Baptism

Baptism, argue Christians generally, is the New Testament equivalent of the Hebrew rite of circumcision. It is now administered to both males and females. Baptist groups, who are immersionists, focus on the death and resurrection of Christ and the symbolic link of immersion to this theme. They also baptize only those who have made a profession of faith, arguing that a person's birth into the family of God comes at the time of conversion, and therefore baptism at birth should remain parallel to circumcision in a spiritual sense, not a physical sense. They do not baptize infants because infants have not yet been born into the spiritual family of God. Presbyterian, Lutheran, and Episcopalian churches sprinkle or pour, rather than immerse, focusing on the cleansing symbolism of sprinkling, the cleansing from sin (*Ez. 36:25*). They believe that infants should be baptized, paralleling the rite of circumcision more closely.

Meredith G. Kline's monumental but brief study, *By Oath Consigned* (1968), departs from both positions. He argues that baptism is indeed the Christian replacement of circumcision, but he finds a unique meaning to circumcision that has been ignored by Christian scholars for hundreds of years. Circumcision was the mark of the covenant; specifically, a *law* covenant. This covenant placed a person under the rule of a sovereign God, in the same way that treaties between kings and vassals were made by rulers in the ancient Near East.[4] Circumcision meant that a person was being placed under the two-edged sword of the law covenant: unto blessing for obedience, or unto destruction for disobedience. Circumcision, as a sign of the law covenant, served as a seal of the promise to the elect or as a seal of doom to the cursed. The same rite performed both functions.[5]

Baptism is a testimony to the covenant of redemption in exactly the same way. Its form is that of water. This, argues Kline, refers back to the water ordeals of the Old Testament (and ancient Near East in general) such as Noah's flood, the crossing of the Red Sea and the Jordan, Jonah's three days in the sea, and other symbolic oath signs.[6] Thus, he concludes, immersion is probably the preferable form of baptism for adults, not because it symbolizes the death and resurrection of Christ, but because it is like the water ordeals that were symbolic token of covenant curses and covenant deliverances.[7] On the other hand, Kline also believes in infant baptism, since it has the same meaning as circumcision. It does not affirm the automatic inclusion of the baptized child *into* the covenant; it only affirms his placement *under* the covenant's two-edged promises. Kline is, therefore, a Presbyterian immersionist, though he thinks that infants may be sprinkled.

Those of us who have been convinced by Kline's research and

arguments have a different view of the sacrament of baptism from the views held by traditional churches. The essence of the rite of baptism is therefore *covenantal authority*. The one who baptizes another places that person under the terms of the new covenant. Of course, every man is always under the rule of God's law, but the ceremony of baptism is the way in which the confessing Christian affirms the covenant, either for himself or for his children. He places himself and his children under law. The baptizing person affirms that he, too, is under God's authority. Baptism, therefore, is not the mark of salvation as such; it is the mark of godly subordination and authority. As in the passages of Deuteronomy 8 and 28, adherence to the law brings blessings, and disobedience brings judgment. The Christian announces that he has faith that Jesus Christ fulfilled the terms of the covenant, suffered its curses in place of the Christian, and subsequently brought him to salvation. Christ's obedience to the law covenant is the foundation—the only possible foundation—of the covenant of absolute and unconditional promise. The covenant of law is fulfilled in Christ; the covenant of promise therefore has its legal foundation; the covenant of redemption is delivered to God's elect.

When Shechem sinned with Dinah, the daughter of Jacob, he decided to ask Jacob to allow him to marry her. Jacob's sons promised to allow this if each man in the city became circumcised. Hamor, Shechem's father, was prince of the city. He agreed to the covenant which was proposed by Jacob's sons. All the males of the city were circumcised. Then Levi and Simeon slew every one of them. Jacob criticized them for their action in slaughtering the men (*Gen. 34*).

What was the meaning of this circumcision? The city symbolically placed itself under the rule of God. Not every man was a believer, but every man was circumcised. The prince and his household had been circumcised, and all were under the prince's authority. The men of the city consented to the rite of circumcision. When Levi and Simeon murdered them, they violated the covenantal law, as Jacob realized. The city had placed itself, ritually, under the law of God. The brothers had transgressed the terms of the covenant, and Jacob feared for his life. The people in the land of Canaan would understand the nature of the violation of a covenantal sign between the Hebrews and the city.

The issue was not conversion. The issue was *covenantal authority.* The men of the city had accepted the symbol of covenantal authority. They were subordinate to their prince, and he had placed them under the terms of the covenant, whether to blessing or destruction. By destroying the city's males, the sons of Jacob had executed unlawful judgment, for the men of the city had publicly offered a sacrifice for the sin of Shechem when they submitted to the rite of circumcision. There had been no new crime committed by the ruler or his people that warranted judgment by Jacob's sons. Jacob understood this.

Baptism, since it is an extension of circumcision, should extend to all those under the permanent or covenantal authority of a baptized converted man. An unconverted wife should be baptized when her husband is baptized. Why? Because she is now under the administration of God's law. She vowed to love, honor, and obey him; now that he is under the rule of Christ's law, she is, too. So are the children. If we had permanent servants, or long-term contracts for our servants, they would also be baptized (*Gen. 17:10-13*). The criterion is not personal affirmation of faith in the atoning work of Christ. The criterion is the position of subordination to a ruler who has placed himself under God's law and the ministers of God's judgment. This is why Abraham circumcised his servants (*Gen. 17:27*).

Obviously, a person who professes faith in Christ's covenant of redemption will want to express his acceptance of salvation by placing himself under the rule of God's law. Thus, he will want to be baptized, assuming he understands the rite of baptism. The New Testament makes it ever so clear that it should be an easy matter to get baptized. As soon as a man understands the nature of salvation, he may request and receive the rite of baptism.

We might call this doctrine "the right to a speedy baptism." It is as fundamental to Christianity as an American's right to a speedy trial. And like this latter constitutional right, it is frequently ignored and even resisted by the respective authorities. When Philip explained the Old Testament messianic passage being read by the Ethiopian eunuch, the eunuch asked, "See, here is water; what doth hinder me to be baptized?" Had he been living in the twentieth century, and had Philip been a Presbyterian, the answer would have been, "Well, I'm not an elder, so I can't baptize you. Also, you will have to go through a six-week introductory class. Then, you will have to be examined by the session. If you get through all this, you will be allowed to be baptized." Fortunately for the eunuch, who was going about his business, Philip answered differently: "If thou believest with all thine heart, thou mayest. And he answered and said, I believe that Jesus Christ is the Son of God." Philip immediately baptized him (*Ac. 8:26-38*).

Philip was a lawfully appointed deacon. Indeed, he and Stephen were among the very first deacons ever ordained to the office (*Ac. 6:1-6*). He was not an elder. On what basis, then, do modern churches not accept as valid the baptisms performed independently by a deacon? How is it that the Westminster Confession of Faith states that both sacraments must be dispensed only "By a minister of the Word lawfully ordained" (XXVII:4)? The answer should be clear: *Protestant sacerdotalism*. The plain teaching of Scripture is insufficient to overcome the entrenched tradition of sacerdotalism. Ironically, both the Roman Catholic Church and the Greek Orthodox Church are less sacerdotal, with respect to the validity of baptisms performed by laymen, than most of the Protestant churches. They both acknowledge that while it is improper for laymen, women, or heretics to baptize people, once performed, neither church requires rebaptism. The Lutherans hold the same view. The Reformed churches are silent in their creeds concerning this possibility. Ministers alone may baptize.

The case of the baptism of the Philippian jailer and his household is informative, though not to the modern sacerdotalists. The jailer had been about to commit suicide when he found the cells unlocked, but Paul told him not to fear, since everyone was still in his cell. The jailer was relieved. He came and bowed before Paul and Silas:

> And brought them out, and said, Sirs, what must I do to be saved? And they said, Believe on the Lord Jesus Christ, and thou shalt be saved, and thy house. And they spoke unto him the word of the Lord, and to all that were in his house. And he took them the same hour of the night, and washed their stripes; and was baptized, he and all his, straightway. (*Ac. 16:30-33*)

These observations are in order. First, he was baptized in his own home, or in a place so close to his home that all the household came with him to hear and to be baptized. The next verse reads: "And when he had brought them into his own house, he set meat before them, and rejoiced, believing in God with all his house." Second, there is no indication that they journeyed to a river to be immersed. A reasonable conclusion is that they were poured or sprinkled. Far more important than the mode of baptism was the speed of the baptism.

In contrast to the New Testament, consider the words of Y. Feenstra, in the conservative and Calvinistic *Encyclopedia of Christianity*, on the topic, "Baptism (Reformed View)": "The place of administering baptism should be in the midst of the congregation, in public worship. The church as an organization was intrusted by Christ with its two sacraments, baptism and the Lord's Supper; and it is un-Biblical for individuals to usurp the prerogatives that belong to the church alone."[8] In the next paragraph, he writes, "As to the time of administration, we can only say that it is to be sought for as soon as possible." But "as soon as possible" must be interpreted in terms of "in the midst of the congregation, in public worship." Baptism of schismatics and heretics is lawful, he says, unless those baptizing are not trinitarians. However, such baptism must be "administered in a circle of Christian believers, at the hands of a Christian minister qualified to perform the baptismal act. . . ."[9] Baptism by heretical ministers is tolerable; baptism by laymen is not. This is sacerdotalism.

On the other side of the traditional controversy stands Baptist apologist Paul K. Jewett. He is not concerned about the speed of baptism, but he is also not concerned about the ordination of the baptizer:

> Inasmuch as our Lord did not prescribe it, Baptists have never contended for a precise rubric of administration with reference to external circumstances. It is immaterial whether the candidate be baptized immediately upon conversion or after a period of instruction; whether baptism take place in a river or in a baptistry made for this purpose; whether it be administered on some festival day, as Easter or Pentecost, or on any day; and whether the administrator be duly ordained or a layman.[10]

Nevertheless, his next sentence tells us what is important: "Of course all worship is to be decent and in order, and therefore baptism may not be privately administered at the whim of any individual, but only in the presence of the assembled church and by someone duly appointed thereunto." Busy Ethiopian eunuchs need not apply.

Both Feenstra and Jewett can agree on two points: the assembled church in a worship ceremony is the only proper place of baptism, and the baptism must be administered by someone approved by the church. Feenstra, following the traditional Reformed view, wants only ministers to baptize people; Jewett is willing to allow laymen to do it, if they are church-approved, that is, in some way ordained. But the institutional church, assembled in official worship, is the heart and soul of Protestant baptism. This is also the heart and soul of Protestant sacerdotalism.

For the Philippian jailer, the prime consideration was his own profession of faith. This was also true of the Ethiopian eunuch. A deacon could administer the rite, or an apostle. It could be done in a river, in a house, or perhaps even in a jail. Baptism could be by immersion and (it would seem) by some mode utilizing less water. What was central, administratively, was *speed*, not congregational worship.

Modern churches do not take the circumcision-baptism analogy so seriously that they require infant baptism on the eighth day after birth, as was required for Old Testament circumcision. Some churches, of course, do not baptize infants at all, but no one forces an adult to wait for any specified length of time. But they all require some waiting. The worship service of the church is seen as more important than the rapidity of baptism.

Let us face squarely the explicit testimony of the Book: the presence of the congregation was not required—not for John's baptism, not for the baptisms performed by Christ, not by apostolic baptism. Second, let us face the testimony of Acts 8: deacons may perform lawful baptisms. Third, let us face the testimony of every known baptism in the New Testament: no lengthy screening by elders was practiced. A man was entitled to baptism, at the minimum, immediately after making a profession of faith, if he was in the presence of any church officer. The evidence is overwhelming.

Let us return to our original question. What is the meaning, institutionally, of the doctrine of the priesthood of all believers? The priests of the Old Testament performed the sacrifices and the rituals. In our era, and in fact from the days of the early church, formally ordained people have laid claim to an exclusive monopoly to the administration of the sacraments, however defined. What ecclesiastical manifestation of the universalization of the priesthood can we find?

In some Protestant churches, the election of candidates to the various church positions is made by the congregations, including the votes of women. There is some sharing of the ordination authority. But this is not a priestly function as such, nor was it in the Old Testament. The sacramental function is officially lodged in the office of elder, or more narrowly, the minister. Have we become a kingdom of priests? What is the institutional sign of this transformation?

In the case of baptism, the rite symbolizes subjection to the law of God in a covenant. That covenant is personal (damnation or salvation), but it also has institutional implications, since all authority under God is mediated through duly ordained institutions. Not one single institution, but institutions: family, church, civil governments, voluntary associations, etc. Sacramental authority is lodged in the church, for it was to the church that Christ assigned the responsibility of preaching the word, discipling nations, and baptizing (*Mt. 28:18-20*). Baptism, therefore, is strictly a function of the priesthood. But what constitutes the priesthood?

Any case for the monopoly of baptism in the hands of church officers—not strictly ministers, or elders, but all: minister, elder, and deacon—must be made in terms of a theology of the covenant. Paul warned Christians living in the midst of an apostate civil government that they should take their disputes to wise men in the congregation (*1 Cor. 6:5*). However, he did not specifically say that the judge in the church must be ordained to church office. Given the framework of gifts within a particular church, it may be that some layman has better judgment in certain types of cases than the elders. However, final authority to impose ecclesiastical discipline is in the hands of ordained elders. Therefore, we might conclude that baptism by church elders is required, since they administer the discipline of the covenant, and baptism involves the acknowledgment of the authority of the covenant law structure. There is one overwhelming exegetical problem with this argument: Philip, a deacon, baptized. Deacons are not elders, nor do they participate in the administration of church discipline.

Once it is admitted that New Testament precedents are binding, or if not binding in every case, then at the very least are lawful exceptions to present tradition, then the theologian of the covenant is faced with a most difficult problem. If the diaconate is not properly an office relating to primary church authority—the hierarchical ecclesiastical institution of discipline under God and in terms of his Biblical law structure—then the case for the monopoly of baptism in the hands of church officers must be altered drastically. (Abandoned, preferably.)

Before continuing into more uncharted theological waters, let us recapitulate. It is wholly unwarranted to limit the administration of baptism to elders, and it is especially unwarranted to limit it to "ministers of the Word," a distinctly extrabiblical, sacerdotal caste. Any confession, creed, or church which so limits the administration of baptism is clearly in the wrong. The example of Philip destroys such a position. To be somewhat rationalistic about it, a universal positive is destroyed by a single negative. We cannot say, "Baptism is always administered by elders." Unless we want to say that the example of Philip is somehow irrelevant because of the specific leading of the Holy Spirit—with the Holy Spirit temporarily revoking the "ministerial" monopoly on a one-time-only basis— then we must conclude that the traditional creeds are erroneous when they create a monopoly of baptism for the office of elder, let alone minister.

When we go further, broadening the office of priest, we leave behind a position that is clearly incorrect. We leave behind a position which has explicit Biblical testimony against it. We now face the difficult problem of argument from other principles, an argument which at points faces Biblical silence. All we know is this: what now passes for orthodoxy is incorrect. We may make other incorrect conclusions, but if we stay where we now are, we are sure to be incorrect.

We begin with the principle of the priesthood of all believers

(*1 Pet. 2:9*). We add to this the doctrine of baptism: a rite symbolizing man's life under the law covenant of God, with its two-edged promise of blessing for obedience or cursing for transgression. We see from the examples of Acts that speed of baptism, if not a universal requirement, is nonetheless a universal right of the believer. No man can be refused immediate baptism by a deacon or elder who has witnessed to him, once the man has made a very simple profession of faith. There is not the slightest evidence that Philip, Paul, or Silas recommended any delay. Next, there is strong evidence that speed of baptism takes precedence over any hypothetical requirement that baptism must be performed within a formal church worship service. For that latter position, there is no positive evidence and two very strong cases of New Testament evidence against it: the eunuch and the jailer.

What, then, is my preliminary conclusion? Simply this: he or she who is capable of preaching the gospel to an unbeliever is capable of baptizing that person. If the baptized person is the head of a household, everyone under his or her lawful, covenantal authority should also be baptized. If speed of baptism is primary, as the New Testament evidence certainly indicates, then the person who has brought the message of salvation to the person now professing faith should encourage the other to be baptized. Why? Because the person has just affirmed the sovereignty of God in salvation, and he thereby immediately places himself under the covenant of redemption. If he delays his baptism, he is saying symbolically that he can operate outside the terms of the covenant for as long as the ecclesiastical authorities delay in baptizing him. He is testifying, ritually, that he is in a temporary zone of immunity. There is no such zone of covenantal immunity. The early church taught, in some instances, and in some periods, that the remission of sins provided by baptism could be voided by subsequent sins. Sinners therefore waited until they were dying before asking for the rite or baptism. While not so theologically confused as men were in those days, modern Protestants partake of an analogous error. The error is formal, pertaining to the symbolic meaning of the ritual of baptism, and not substantial—based on a false doctrine of salvation—but it is nonetheless an error. The delay of baptism ritually affirms a temporary suspension of the covenant's authority over the person. It does this for the sake of a theology which is essentially sacerdotal in nature, a theology which in this instance places the doctrine of the institutional church and its officers above the doctrine of the covenant of redemption.

Notice what I am *not* saying. I am not saying that the church, through the officers of the church, should not baptize people. I am not saying that it is always wrong to have the congregation present. I am not saying that women should be allowed to speak, and therefore to baptize, within the worship service of the church, since Paul specifically prohibits women from speaking in the churches (*1 Cor. 14:34-35*). What I *am* saying is that under normal circumstances, the speed of baptism is more important than the consideration of who baptizes or where. If the confessor is hesitant to be baptized until he or she receives further instruction, then it is all right to wait until someone can offer such instruction. But if the confessor acknowledges Christ's position as the Son of God, and acknowledges his reliance upon Christ's substitutionary atonement on the cross, then the person is ready for baptism.

To impress the new convert with the authority of the church, it might be valid to call an elder or minister on the telephone and have him come to the new convert's home for further witness, instruction, and baptism. In an antinomian culture such as ours, the presence of an ordained minister of discipline might be helpful. But it must not be made a requirement, since the testimony of Philip's baptism of the eunuch stands in opposition to the concept of the monopoly of baptism in the hands of an elder-minister. What is *convenient* in any place or time must not be made a universal, formal rule.

What we must get through our heads is that baptism is not universally a mark of justification. It is always a mark of *sanctification*. Sanctification means that a person is *set apart* in a special way under God's authority. Paul tells us that the unregenerate husband or wife is sanctified by the presence of the believing partner in the marriage (*1 Cor. 7:14*). This does not mean that the partner is saved by marriage rather than by grace through faith; it means that the partner is treated in a special way by God, for he or she becomes the beneficiary of living with someone who is formally under God's covenant of salvation, and therefore who is reforming his or her life in terms of God's law. We baptize children because of the position of a believing parent. This is why we should encourage unbelieving wives and children to be baptized, for they are now operating under the authority of a man who is governed by the terms of God's covenant. They are now sanctified by being subordinate to God's law.

Baptism should *not* be understood as a sacrament which symbolizes or authorizes full membership into the church. Children do not vote in church assemblies. In some churches, women who are not widowed may not vote. (Numbers 30:9 indicates a similar distinction between widows and divorced women on the one hand, and married women and unmarried women on the other. A widow's vow is immediately put into operation; a married woman under a husband's authority cannot be held to the performance of her vow if her husband rejects it on the day that he hears of it. The same is true of the unmarried woman: her father can nullify the vow.) Baptism is simply a symbol of God's two-edged covenant, the acknowledging of God's lawful sovereignty over the individual and all those in covenantal subordination to him or her, in the case of the widow.

The concept of democratic voting in a church is a Protestant doctrine of the independents and the Presbyterians. Where laymen vote for officers, an immediate problem appears. How are the less qualified, less educated, less sanctified (in the sense of progressive sanctification) members able to decide between two candidates for office? Will not the "lowest common denominator" principle operate in a church democracy, just as it has operated in political democracy? To mitigate this very real problem, churches have screened candidates for membership. They have required some sort of training before believers are accepted into the church. Only after the completion of such training is the rite of baptism administered. Churches have delayed the rite of baptism for the sake of preserving the integrity of the church, since all baptized people, or at least baptized males, who join the church can vote. Baptism has been linked directly to full voting membership, at least with respect to new converts.

People transferring membership from other churches are not required to be re-baptized, but they normally are interrogated and instructed, if necessary, in the doctrines of the local church before they are allowed to become full voting members. What we should conclude, then, is that there is no automatic relationship between baptism and full church membership, in the sense of voting membership. The screening should indeed take place before full voting membership is granted; what is wrong today is that churches spend time in screening candidates prior to baptizing them. Churches do not seem to comprehend that the same principle applies to the newly baptized convert which applies to the person seeking a transfer of membership: baptism precedes full voting membership; it does not automatically confer such membership. In fact, some churches may feel under pressure to hurry the screening process in order to get the professing convert baptized. The screening process is thereby downgraded, and the "lowest common denominator" principle takes over. The screening process should probably be tightened, but the delay in baptism should be drastically shortened. They are two separate operations, governed by different principles. Screening protects the theological integrity of the church. Baptism symbolizes the covenantal subordination to God and God's covenant by the believer. A believer has a right to baptism; he does not have a right to vote in church elections.

We know that in the parable of the sower, three of the four seeds eventually die. Only one grows to full maturity (*Mt. 13:3-9, 18-23*). This points to the necessity of a far more lengthy screening process. It would not be unwise to wait as long as a year before bringing candidates into full voting membership, though some sort of formal examination process should be used to allow more rapid progress. The Bible required some nationalities to wait three generations, or even ten generations, before they could enter into full membership in the congregation of the Hebrews (*Dt. 23:1-8*). However, the Moabites were in the ten generation classification, yet Ruth was awarded full membership, entering into the covenant line when she married Boaz (*Mt. 1:5*). Her remarkable faith was rewarded, and she and her seed did not have to wait ten generations. Full voting membership in the church should be analogous to full membership in the Hebrew commonwealth. Men should have access to the sacraments and benefits of the church long before they have attained full voting membership. The element of democracy in modern churches makes mandatory a more thorough screening process. A period of probation for new converts helps protect the church's integrity.

The person who is baptized in his own household thereby acknowledges that he is now under God's authority. By having others in his household baptized, he declares that they, being under his authority, are also under God's authority. He simultaneously affirms that he is under God's authority and a person required to exercise godly dominion in terms of that authority. Jesus was under authority and therefore the bearer of authority—the testimony of the Roman centurion which so impressed Jesus (*Lk. 7:2-9*). All men are to exercise dominion (*Gen. 1:27-28; 9:1-7*), but those who acknowledge this responsibility under God are true saints. This is a central fact (probably *the* central fact) of the meaning of the priesthood of all believers.

A priest exercises authority as a sovereign. So does the head of a household, including a widow or divorced woman. If baptism took place today in the households of new converts, the priestly role of the family leader would be symbolized far more effectively. Baptism within the confines of a church worship service does not convey this important meaning nearly so effectively. Church baptisms are not invalid. Unmarried persons living in pagan households or living alone should be baptized in church. People converted in a church meeting may wish to be baptized immediately, or that evening, in the place of their conversions. Nevertheless, the testimony of the Acts is that household baptism is lawful, and in our era, when the family is under fire, and men have abdicated their family responsibilities as heads of households, there would seem to be valid reasons for returning to the precedent of the Acts. Other members of a household might be more likely to understand the nature of the spiritual change which has put them in a newly sanctified (though not justified) position as family members. They are now subordinate to God through the family priest, who will henceforth mediate God's authority, though not salvation. To the extent that Protestant sacerdotalism distorts and clouds this new relationship, it has compromised the integrity, responsibility, and authority of the family. By restricting the location in which baptism is supposedly lawful—an official church worship service—Protestant sacerdotalism has compromised the very institution which is to serve as the training ground of elders and deacons. *Baptism is a meaningful symbol,* and it has not been accidental historically that its administration has been centralized and that the tradition of household baptism has been suppressed. The doctrine of the priesthood of few believers had to be manifested through its own symbolic rituals if it was ever to gain widespread acceptance among laymen—the lawful priests whose authority was steadily being transferred to a far narrower group.

It is significant that Kline refuses to go this far in the extension of the covenant principle. He argues in the final chapter of *By Oath Consigned* that the New Testament does not provide a clear-cut directive with respect to the baptism of servants—children, yes, but not servants. The reason for this hesitancy is Kline's belief that the Old Testament kingdom law structure has no validity in New Testament times. This position has been ably refuted by Greg Bahnsen in the appendix devoted to Kline in Bahnsen's book, *Theonomy in Christian Ethics* (1977). Kline distinguishes the cultural authority which has focus in the covenant family (and, apparently, only in the family) from the "cultic authority focus in the assembled, worshipping congregation with its special officers." The kingdom-cultural focus of the Old Testament kingdom is no longer in existence, Kline argues, since it was a temporary phenomenon. Kline's amillennialism is clearly visible in his explanation of the meaning of the Old Testament kingdom, for that kingdom merely pointed to the final consummation, something which the New Testament structure of Biblical authority does not do, for some reason or other.

> The kingdom of Israel was, of course, not another Caeser-kingdom but, uniquely, the kingdom of God institutionally present among the nations. Its earthly cultural form was symbolic of the ultimate integration of culture and cult in the world of the consummation. The judicial infliction of cultural sanctions by its officers typified the final messianic judgment of men in the totality of their being as cultural creatures. This institutional symbolization of the final judgment and eternal kingdom disappeared from the earthly scene when the Old Covenant gave way to the New.

Why the symbol of final judgment "of men in the totality of their being as cultural creatures" should have been abolished by the New Covenant, Kline does not explain here. He just states that it was. There is an *implicit dispensationalism* in Kline's position—a radical cultural discontinuity between the law-order of the Old Testament and the law-order of the New. There is also an *implicit social antinomianism* in his view of culture, for the civil government is not required to enforce Old Testament civil law, and the officers of the church do not possess such authority. Only Christ possesses such authority to judge, and in our age, this power is not manifested in any earthly institution, despite the fact that the authority of Christ over all the creation was announced clearly only in this age (*Mt. 28:18*). Christ's royal authority is simply a limiting concept until the final judgment, meaning a theory which has no institutional, earthly manifestation. As Kline writes near the end of his book: "In this age of the church, royal theocratic authority with its prerogative of imposing physical-cultural sanctions resides solely in Christ, the heavenly King. The judicial authority of the permanent special officers whom Christ has appointed to serve his church on earth is purely spiritual-cultic. Cultural sanctions have no place, therefore, in the functioning of the central and dominant cultic authority focus of the New Covenant community, and it would violate the spirit of the church's distinctive mission in the present age if such sanctions were to be introduced in connection with the auxiliary family (-household) focus of authority."

It is understandable why Kline, as an amillennialist and a social antinomian, should be hesitant to permit the baptism of unregenerate wives and servants on the basis of the authority conferred by God to the confessing head of the household. The family priest is really not a priest in the ecclesiastical sense, and Kline, like all Protestant sacerdotalists, sees the priesthood only within the framework of the sacramental, monopolistic, cultic institution we call the visible church. In short, there is no meaningful kingdom of priests, so we are still bogged down in the doctrine of the priesthood of few believers. Kline has removed the kingdom in its broad, authoritative, and judicial sense, relegating it to a mere symbol, one which passed into history with Christ's advent, or at least with his resurrection. The only focus worth talking about is the so-called "cultic authority focus in the assembled, worshipping congregation with its special officers." The realm of external legal sanctions is turned over to Satan and his host—sanctions in no way connected with the explicit requirements of Old Testament Biblical law. The new focus is the church, meaning the institutional church. Thus, it should hardly come as a surprise that Kline's amillenialism and his social antinomianism have led him to a truncated concept of the covenantal law-order, and an equally truncated view of all other authority structures apart from the institutional church. That he refuses to extend the circumcision-baptism rite to the entire household, as it was in the Old Testament (*Gen. 17*) is fully in line with his opposition to the reign of Old Testament law in New Testament times. There is no kingdom of priests simply because there is no kingdom, institutionally speaking. Therefore, laymen cannot be priests, institutionally speaking.

In conclusion, baptism is the mark of covenantal subordination. It testifies to God's lawful authority over us and to our acceptance of this cosmic reality. Baptism is the ritual oath symbol of New Testament vassals who affirm their subordination to a sovereign Lord. Therefore, my tentative though strongly felt opinion is this: *the messenger who brings the announcement of our Lord's sovereign authority and sovereign grace has a right to baptize the new convert.* The position of the messenger as a lawful priest indicates this. Second, the principle of a man's right to a speedy baptism indicates this. Third, the symbolism of a delayed baptism—a temporary period of covenant suspension—testifies to this. If this conclusion is absolutely and unquestionably incorrect—which the creeds and traditional practices of most Protestant churches necessarily declare—then it must be shown which principle or principles override those favoring the right of speedy baptism by the person who has brought the message of salvation. Who is the priest?

For reasons of cultural heritage, or geographical circumstances, or a sense of propriety, a particular church in a particular period of time may *recommend* one or another time and place of baptism, though its goal should be speedy baptisms in households as a general rule. It takes time to alter deeply felt and long-honored church traditions. Nevertheless, to insist that "ministers of the Word"—defined narrowly as teaching elders or their equivalent—are alone permitted to baptize, is to go beyond Scripture. A reform of the creeds is mandatory. At the absolute minimum, deacons must be allowed to baptize without prior consultation with elders.

Communion (The Lord's Supper)

Protestants recognize this as the other of the two New Testament sacraments. Like the sacrament of baptism, this one is shared by all believers who are under the authority of God's covenant of redemption. It is open to all of the faithful. It is an ordinance which testifies to the continuing faith in Christ by his people.

Protestants deny that participation in any sacrament automatically confers the blessing of salvation on anyone. Protestants therefore deny baptismal regeneration and regeneration through communion. The sacraments are aids in bringing the message of faith to the attention of both saved and lost, but faith comes by hearing, and hearing by the word of God (*Rom. 10:17*). It is the written and spoken *word* which is the means of communicating faith, not the sacraments. Sacramental symbols illustrate truths that have been revealed to us through the word of God. They have an important purpose, or series of purposes, but the word is primary.

Protestants have usually sought to link holy communion with the Hebrew rite of the passover. The New Testament refers to "Christ our passover" (*1 Cor. 5:7*). The first instance of holy communion occurred during the passover week in Jerusalem, on the first day of the feast of unleavened bread (*Mt. 26:17-30*). Jesus gathered the disciples into the upper room and broke bread with them. Chapters 13-17 of John record his instruction to them during this first communion service. It is not unwarranted to equate communion with the passover, paralleling the equation of baptism and circumcision. But the equation is not, in either case, like a mathematical equation. The two halves are not equal. They are linked over time and across the two testaments, but there are differences.

The passover was the central ritual of the Hebrews. It was an intensely familistic ritual. Each family was to select a lamb, on the tenth day of the first month of the year, separating it from the midst of other sheep and goats (*Ex. 12:3-5*). On the fourteenth day of the first month, the lamb was killed, in the evening hours. It was then roasted and eaten throughout the night, along with unleavened bread and bitter herbs (*12:6-9*). "And thus shall ye eat it; with your loins girded, your shoes on your feet, and your staff in your hand; and ye shall eat it in haste: it is the LORD'S passover" (*12:11*). No leavened bread could be eaten for the next seven days (*12:19*). The father's role in this ceremony was central:

> And ye shall observe this thing for an ordinance to thee and to thy sons for ever. And it shall come to pass, when ye be come to the land which the LORD will give to you, according as he hath promised, that ye shall keep this service. And it shall come to pass, when your children shall say unto you, What mean ye by this service? That ye shall say, It is the sacrifice of the LORD'S passover, who passed over the houses of the children of Israel in Egypt, when he smote the Egyptians, and delivered our houses. (*Ex. 12:24-27*)

The passover in Jesus' day did not involved standing all night, as it had on the first passover night. Jesus sat down with his disciples (*Lk. 22:14*). But he shared his knowledge of the coming events with them, as a father might have shared with his children the story and meaning of the passover. He broke bread with them— presumably unleavened bread—and shared wine from the cup. Then he exhorted them, "this do in remembrance of me" (*Lk. 22:19b*). He then explained his message of victory to them: "And I appoint unto you a kingdom as my Father hath appointed unto me; That ye may eat and drink at my table on thrones judging the twelve tribes of Israel" (*Lk. 22:29-30*). Here was the announcement of a kingdom of priests who will execute judgment. They were meeting together as friends, not in their own homes, indicating that henceforth a man's true family is with his friends in the faith. This does not mean, however, that the household communion service is now revoked.

Early in the Acts we find recorded the practice of the "breaking of bread" (*Ac. 2:42*). Fellowship, breaking of bread, and prayers were practiced at communal meals. "And they, continuing daily with one accord in the temple, and breaking bread from house to house, did eat their meat with gladness and singleness of heart" (*Ac. 2:46*). Later in the Acts, the author records Paul's visits to Troas. "And upon the first day of the week, when the disciples came together to break bread, Paul preached unto them . . ." (*Ac. 20:7a*). There is no doubt that the communion meal had become part of the regular church meeting. They came specifically to break bread. Nevertheless, the practice was not limited to weekly worship services.

Paul's message to the Corinthian church was that it had transgressed in many areas, and among these areas was the communion feast. There were divisions and heresies within the group (*1 Cor. 11:18-19*). In this fragmented setting, each person came to eat his own dinner, with some people going hungry in the midst of the others. Paul asks them if they haven't got homes to eat in? Such divisive behavior is contemptuous of the church and shames the poor (*11:21-22*). Paul reminds them of Christ's words at the last supper, how they should eat the bread and drink the wine in remembrance of his body and blood.

Some came to the meeting drunk. Obviously, this was in violation of good conduct. Paul warns them that a person who partakes of the communion meal unworthily thereby drinks and eats damnation to himself, "not discerning the Lord's body" (*11:29*). This is a central passage, and it has created dissention among the theologians. What does "unworthily" mean? More important, what does "not discerning the Lord's body" mean?

Because this was an official meeting of the church, all things were to be done decently and in order (*1 Cor. 14:40*). Drunken communicants were a contradiction in terms. So were solitary eaters. They were to eat their meal together. If they were hungry before coming to the Lord's table, they were to eat beforehand. There was to be unity in the fellowship of communion, not division, whether theological division or division in the speed and time in which the meal was to be eaten. It was still a ritual meal, although it was more than a wafer and a thimbleful of wine, more than a thumb-size bit of "enriched" white bread. Modern Christianity has reduced the meal to a *symbol of a meal*. In contrast, the

Corinthians had forgotten the symbol of Christ's death and were treating it as if it were nothing more than just another meal. Neither group comes close to either the passover or the last supper.

Those who refused to respect the sensibilities of other brethren, especially the poor, but also the feelings of those who resented drunkenness, were drinking and eating unworthily. They were not taking seriously the sacramental character of worship and fellowship. They had forgotten that they were in church, reenacting a basic historical event in the history of the church. The church of Jesus Christ is referred to by Paul as the Lord's body, and it should come as no surprise that the great chapter dealing with the diversity of gifts within the unity of the body of Christ is 1 Corinthians 12, beginning a few lines after the words, "not discerning the Lord's body." What Paul meant should be clear, but apparently it is not clear to many Christians. *The discernment of the body refers to each participant's awareness of the unity of the church in fellowship during the celebration of the communion meal.* There were divisions in the church, so Paul criticized them (*11:18-19*). They were not meeting and eating together, as one people in fellowship, so Paul criticized them (*11:20-22*). In short, Paul perceived the existence of schism in the church, and he devoted the second half of this chapter and all of 1 Corinthians 12 to a consideration of the need for church unity. There was a great need for healing within the body of Christ, his church.

Those who ate and drank in a disorderly fashion were converting the Lord's Supper into something else. Their actions symbolized their commitment to a divisive interpretation of the symbol of communion. They were testifying to the *disunity of Christ's kingdom*—the kingdom promised by Christ at his last supper. They had converted a symbol of spiritual unity and victory into a symbol of disunity. This was the setting of Paul's warning against eating and drinking unworthily. They had not discerned the Lord's body, meaning the church's presence, in the divided communion feasts of Corinth. This was not mere negligence; it was inevitably a symbolic act, for which damnation was and is a suitable punishment.

Later theologians have misinterpreted the phrase, "not discerning the Lord's body," by focusing attention on the bread which was and is eaten in the communion service. They have argued that the concern of Paul was over the lack of theological understanding within the church, specifically in their inability to understand that the bread which they ate stood for Christ's body, which he sacrificed on the cross. But the verse does not make this mistake: "For he that eateth and drinketh unworthily, eateth and drinketh damnation to himself, not discerning the Lord's body." Had he said "not discerning the Lord's body and blood," then we could conclude that Paul's concern related to their lack of understanding of the meaning of the *elements* of the supper. But their lack of understanding was much deeper than that; they had failed to understand the meaning of the sacrament's role within the church, the body of Christ, of which they were the members. They showed no respect for other members. (The word "members" is applied to parts of the body in the next chapter, and the dual meaning in English—members of a group and members such as fingers—conveys Paul's message quite well.)

This misinterpretation of Paul's phrase, "not discerning the body," has led to a horrendous error on the part of Reformed theologians. They have limited the attendance at the Lord's Supper to adults and young adults. They have feared that young children might fail to understand the *symbolism* of the *elements* of the supper. They have feared that children who eat these elements in ignorance of their symbolic meaning thereby eat and drink damnation unto themselves. But Paul was concerned about the Corinthians' failure to recognize church order. It takes little training to teach a child that church is a special place, that he must behave in an orderly way. Children are alert to special ceremonies, and they can hardly keep from asking what this or that is all about. Modern Protestants have closed the communion table to children because they are afraid that the children will not understand the implications of the elements, and therefore that they will "not discern the Lord's body." The ghastly irony here is that it is the theologians, not the children, who have misunderstood the words of Paul. Paul's concern was with the church, not the elements.

The passover was aimed at the children of the household. It was designed to elicit questions from the children, and the father of the house was to use this opportunity to explain the meaning of the ceremonies. The passover was a means of training children. Its symbols could be passed on to the children more readily because the children participated in the ceremonies. Once again, we see that *the family is the training ground for the faithful.* The father in the Old Testament directed the sacrament of the passover, sharing this responsibility with the high priest, who entered the holy of holies during this special annual festival. In his household, he was indeed a priest, at least for one week each year.

What about the sacrament of the Lord's Supper? The modern churches limit the sacramental character of the feast to operations performed by the elders, or by the minister of the word. If the minister of the word does not direct the eating and drinking of the elements, there is therefore no Lord's Supper, no holy communion. The practice of the modern church has, in theology as well as in practice, removed totally the strong element of family participation and family authority found in the passover. Incredible as it seems, the modern churches have *removed* the element of priesthood possessed by the father in the Old Testament. Despite the doctrine of the priesthood of all believers, the traditional concept of the Lord's Supper has thwarted the exercise of the priestly function by fathers within their households. Modern Christianity has taken away from the father of the house the sacrament which he lawfully administered prior to Christ. The universalization of the priesthood has come to mean the abolition of the lawful administration of a sacrament by laymen which the passover had not only permitted but insisted on. In this sense, modern churches have, in theology and in fact, adopted a new doctrine in direct contradiction to Peter's announcement: "The priesthood of *fewer* believers." Fewer believers, proportionately, perform a sacramental function today than in the Old Testament. Modern Christianity has removed the sacramental privileges from the family in order to strengthen vastly the position of the minister or so-called teaching elder. It has centralized ecclesiastical power and prestige, all in the name of the priesthood of all believers. George Orwell had a good name for this kind of theology. He called it "doublespeak."

Consider the anti-parallels between the sacrament of the passover and today's sacrament of holy communion. In the Old Testament, the sacrament was intensely familistic. In our day, the sacrament has been emptied of all family responsibilities. It is true that the disciples met with Jesus and not their families, but he had called them into apostolic service, away from their families temporarily. The practice of household worship and the breaking of bread immediately returned in the days prior to Pentecost. The sacrament was restored to families, and increased from once a year (in the case of the passover) to possibly several times each week, as converts visited each other's homes and broke bread in fellowship. The church authorities of the next century began to centralize the sacrament of holy communion, and this process has been continued until the present. The church family has sought to replace the household's sacrament.

Another anti-parallel is the element of child training. The passover was designed to rear up godly, informed children who understood the meaning of the ceremonies. In today's setting, children are excluded from the communion service. Again, it represents nothing less than a frontal attack on the family by the ecclesiastical bureaucracy. Out of concern for children's souls, and out of a misinterpretation of Paul's words, the leaders have kept the sacrament from children, who in pre-Christian times would have been full participants.

The passover involved every family, as well as the labors of the ecclesiastical priests. The communion service makes the individual almost wholly passive, and the minister and his helpers wholly active. In some cases, there are no helpers; the minister serves the communion by himself. It is significant that the church has removed the signs of decentralized authority, the institutional buffers between central power and individual action. The minister offers the sacrament, actually creates the sacramental character of the "feast" (a thimbleful of wine or grape juice and a thumb-size bit of bread), and the "universal priests" sit quietly, each one alone in his chair or pew, waiting solemnly to receive the elements. This thin, pale reflection of the celebration of the Lord's Supper in the upper room or in the joyful households of the early church is offered in the name of refined theology—the best that the theologians could come up with.

The supposed parallels between the passover and the modern Lord's Supper are a sham. There are no parallels, except in the rarified atmosphere of shared theological symbols. The blood of the passover lamb was shed and its flesh eaten, and we eat the body of our Lamb when we eat the bread. There is a symbolic carry-over from the passover. But as the sacrament is actually practiced, there is only the shadow of resemblance. Frankly, the so-called shadow of the Old Testament sacrifice and sacrament possessed far more substance than the modern church's version. The modern church has the shadow, institutionally speaking. The modern church has reversed the teaching of the Book of Hebrews, which states clearly that the Old Testament practices were shadows of the New (*8:5; 10:1*). Today's "universal priest" has far less sacramental authority than the Old Testament layman. Modern Protestant orthodoxy has turned upside down the Biblical message concerning the priesthood. The passover served better food to its participants, nutritionally, emotionally, educationally, and in terms of ritual symbolism.

An exceedingly ingenious argument has been used by theologians and church historians to call attention away from the record of the Acts. They have, for well over a thousand years, distinguished the Lord's Supper from something called the *agapé* feast of the New Testament. That is, whenever the breaking of bread in households is mentioned in the Acts, the scholars find nothing except a special feast of the "primitive church" which has long since died out. It was merely transitional, the true rite being the Lord's Supper, that is, the denuded communion practice of whichever church the scholar belongs to. In short, that which is Biblical is relegated to the historically transitional, a local practice of the Jerusalem church; that which is approved by church tradition in any particular denomination is called the Lord's Supper. A typical example of this approach is found in the *Cyclopedia of Biblical, Theological, and Ecclesiastical Literature* (1873), edited by McClintock and Strong, under the topic, "Lord's Supper":

> The Agapé, as belonging to a transient phase of the Christian life, and varying in its effects with changes in national character or forms of civilization, passes through many stages; becomes more and more a merely local custom, is bound to be productive of evil rather than of good, is discouraged by bishops and forbidden by councils, and finally dies out. Traces of it linger in some of the traditional practices of the Western Church.[11]

That is to say, the constant tendencies toward ecclesiastical centralization and sacerdotalism found in the early medieval church finally overcame the familistic and far more household-oriented communion ceremonies of the New Testament church. Unfortunately, this is not the way traditionalistic theologians and scholars say it.

We now come to that passage which, perhaps more than any other passage in the Bible, sends shivers of foreboding down the spines of sacerdotal authorities: "For where two or three are gathered together in my name, there am I in the midst of them" (*Mt. 18:20*). Here was the basis of the early church's so-called *agapé* feasts, meaning the original form of holy communion. This doctrine of Christ's presence is intimately related to the doctrine of the priesthood of all believers. It affirms that when members of the priesthood get together, God is with them in a direct way, just as he was with the priests of the Old Testament. Members of the early church could celebrate the Lord's Supper, breaking bread in fellowship, from house to house, precisely because Christ was present with them.

There is absolutely no evidence in the Scriptures that a church officer was present at every such meeting. In fact, it would be surprising if there had been enough church officers to accompany every feast, since 3,000 converts were added to the assembly on one day alone, a fact revealed to us in the verse immediately preceding the first reference in Acts to the breaking of bread (*Ac. 2:40*). (One thing is certain: with that rate of growth, the early church was not able to wait around for ministers of the word to graduate from an accredited university and attend at least three semesters of seminary.) What the message of the Acts seems to be is that the Lord's Supper was universally celebrated on a decentralized basis, with families visiting families and sharing the meal together. And why not? Christ had promised to be among such groups, and he had not said that an ordained elder had to be present with the group in order to obtain his special presence. Church officers may have been present on many occasions, and they may have then led the ceremonies, but there is no evidence indicating that they were present at every communion service, and there is no evidence that Christ required them to act as officially appointed leaders at every feast.

There is no doubt that sects have abused the doctrine of the special presence of Christ, but this does not deny its validity. Christ honors his word, even in the midst of schismatic assemblies. We must face the fact that there is very little New Testament evidence describing the Lord's Supper as practiced by the early church, especially with respect to what went on in those assemblies. Therefore, to limit the sacrament of the Lord's Supper exclusively and universally to rites directed by a "minister of the Word" is to go far beyond the evidence of Scripture. Once again, we find that the institutional church has monopolized the use and administration of a sacrament on the basis of theological inference—inference based entirely on a doctrine of a priesthood which is sacerdotal and highly centralized. The universalization of the priesthood is denied, for the mark of a priesthood, namely, the lawful administration of the sacraments, has been prohibited. Once again, we see the operation of a different doctrine, the priesthood of few believers. In the case of the Lord's Supper, virtually the whole of the passover tradition had to be abandoned in order to achieve this ecclesiastical concentration of authority. The head of the Hebrew household prior to Christ was permitted to administer a sacrament at least once each year. Two centuries after Christ, the institutional church's authorities were already involved in an effort (one might better say "conspiracy") to abolish even that minimal precedent of the priesthood of all believers.

If Christ is in the midst of two or three Christians when they get together for prayer or celebration, what is unique about the church's weekly worship service? First of all, the worship service is under the care of specially screened elders. These men are supposed to have been screened and tested in terms of a rigorous set of criteria. They serve as heads of the local congregation. They preach, direct the sacraments, and discipline the congregation. The household Old Testament ritual of the passover meal was not intended to replace the sacrifice of the high priest in the temple. The high priest's actions served as the ritual foundation of the household sacrifice. Similarly, the legitimacy of household communion performed by heads of households is not intended to be a substitute for the authorized and required public assembling of the whole congregation (*Heb. 10:25*). The regular and formal worship service of the church is primary; the household feasts are supplementary celebrations. God established regular offices in the church which provide authority (elders) and charity (deacons), indicating the permanent nature of his institutional church. But the permanence of one ecclesiastical institution over time and geography should not be understood as denying the legitimacy of family sovereignty which has sacramental functions within the protecting framework of church discipline and order. The Protestant heritage of multiple authorities—the denial of any final authority on earth, except for the Bible—should be upheld. Sacerdotal tendencies must be removed from Protestantism, and the monopolization of the doctrine of Christ's presence by the institutional church and its corporate worship services is unquestionably an outgrowth of sacerdotalism. We need *plural institutions* and a *unified eldership*, not a plural eldership and a single visible institution in which Christ is allowed to manifest his presence.

Notice what I am *not* saying. I am not saying that officers in the church should never administer the sacrament of the Lord's Supper. I am not saying that the Lord's Supper should not be a basic part of a church's worship services. Indeed, New Testament evidence indicates that the Lord's Supper ought to be at least a weekly affair, as Calvin strenuously maintained, and which is presently maintained by the Church of Christ.[12] I am not saying that women should lead in the church worship services. What I *am* saying is that ecclesiastical authorities have not been given an exclusive right to administer the sacraments. Furthermore, the sacrament is lawful for laymen to administer and enjoy in the absence of a church officer and on any day of the week that seems convenient to them. They are to practice self-examination, just as Paul required (*1 Cor. 11:28*). Self-examination does not require the presence of a church officer. Naturally, the feast should be orderly. Drunkenness is prohibited. But to break bread ritually at the end of a regular meal, or at a special gathering of friends who are members of God's family, is not an infringement on the lawful authority of the institutional church. If these meetings become lawless, or if unbelievers are deliberately allowed to come to the feasts, then church discipline is proper and required, but the universalization of the priesthood involves the universalization of personal responsibility, and a church officer does not need to be present to police each and every gathering at which two or three saints are gathered together. Christ will be there, and this is surely sufficient.

The centralized church, like the centralized civil government, operates on the premise that an officer must be present at important gatherings in order to direct or monitor each decision. Church officers too often operate as if the purpose of church discipline were not fundamentally negative, suppressing that which is unlawful when it becomes a public matter, but leaving men free to work out their own salvations with fear and trembling (*Phil. 2:12b*). Lower assemblies of the church constantly look for guidance from some higher board rather than acting forcefully in good conscience and awaiting any decision which might come on appeal. The result, in church and state, is rather like the story of the two men who were assigned to the task of swatting a fly, with one man using the swatter and the other man giving him directions. The fly finally died of old age. The fly is very much like the problems that are sent up and down the Presbyterian chains of command, with each level asserting the right of the church to intervene, and with nobody ready to take full responsibility for a final, irrevocable decision. They demand authority and then flee responsibility.

Sacraments must be administered by priests. What we must decide is this: Who is the priest? Second, under which conditions does he have lawful authority to perform his duties? Finally, must every instance of every sacramental observance be performed within the confines of the official worship service of an institutional, visible church?

Biblically, there is far less warrant for the ecclesiastical monopoly over the Lord's Supper than there is for a monopoly over baptism. Baptism is a rite based on the acceptance of God's lawful authority over a person's life. An authority structure of some kind is implied by the very nature of the sacrament. But the Lord's Supper, as described by the New Testament, is a time of fellowship, rejoicing, prayer, thanksgiving, and real food. It is a *celebration*. It is linked to households as much as it is linked to church assemblies. The structure of ecclesiastical authority is further in the background than it is in the rite or baptism.

The Lord's Supper is a time to eat. There must be life in the
sacrament, some sense of full participation, some sense of active
involvement. God has given us this rite for positive reasons:
thankfulness, celebration, fellowship, and remembrance of his
liberating sacrifice on the cross. Modern Christians tend to forget
that there is another reason why we need a meaningful, enthusiastic
Lord's Supper. It is the lurking threat of occultism and demonism
close behind or beneath the thin veneer of Western culture.
Christians forget that the rules of the Lord's Supper set forth by
Paul were preceded by Paul's warning against the idolatrous
celebration of demonic sacraments. "Ye cannot drink the cup of
the Lord, and the cup of devils: ye cannot be partakers of the Lord's
table, and of the table of devils" (*1 Cor. 10:21*). In the previous
verse, Paul announced: ". . . I would not that ye should have
fellowship with devils." The tradition of rationalism within
Calvinistic circles has blinded men to the fact that devils exist,
that they have perverse communion festivals, and that man can be
as close to them in such services as they are close to Christ in his.
In fact, Paul never specifically affirms the special presence of Christ
at a communion festival; he *does* affirm the presence of demons at
theirs. The reason why Old Testament law prohibited the drinking
of food was theological, not simply aesthetic (*Lev. 7:26-27*). Blood
drinking, cannibalism, and drunkenness are familiar features of
various occult celebrations. Men need a holy alternative. Christians
need an emotionally satisfying sacramental celebration, not an
austere, rigorously symbolic act devoid of personal interaction and
fellowship. We need something simultaneously sacrificial and
enjoyable, like the "holy wastefulness" of the tithe of celebration
(*Dt. 14:22-27*).

The problem, symbolically speaking, with the modern
communion service is that it is *doubly symbolic*. The passover
symbolized God's deliverance of his people through the shedding
of innocent blood, namely, the blood of an unblemished lamb.
The passover looked forward to the final shedding of blood by
Christ on the cross, but the Hebrews could see this only dimly.
They were to look backward at a real event, their deliverance out
of Egypt, and forward to the shedding of innocent blood. Because
of their place in the history of redemption, they were required to

look backward primarily, to the exodus. They had clearer information about the past than about the future. Similarly, Christians are to look backward, to Christ's work on the cross. Christians are also to look forward, to the day in which we shall eat and drink with Christ in his kingdom, executing judgment (*Lk. 22:30*). Yet it is obvious that the forward-looking kingdom aspect of the original communion service has no part in any modern Protestant denomination's official ritual of communion (so far as I am aware). Christians look backward as much as the Hebrews did during passover. We look back, however, to two events: the original supper in the upper room and to the cross. The early Christians had a real meal, where real bread was broken and real wine was consumed (which was why some men were drunk in the Corinthian church—they were not drinking grape juice). The early Christians therefore had a meal like the one Christ and the apostles shared. The meal was to be a symbolic reminder of Christ's offer of his body and blood on Calvary. But the modern church does not have a real meal. The modern communion service is a symbolic meal which points to a real meal which points to the crucifixion. Modern sacerdotalism has refined the symbolism of the Lord's Supper so that its message must pass through an extra layer of symbolism—the symbol of a meal—to impart its message. Having obscured the original forcefulness of the communion symbol, the modern churchmen then exclude children from the symbolic celebration (which is a time of silence, solitude, and solemnity—a peculiar symbol of original celebration) because children may not "discern the body," meaning they may not understand the symbolism of the elements. The bits of bread are rightly called elements, for they are tiny symbolic scraps representing what once was a real meal.

The great loser in the modern version of the Lord's Supper is the child. The child has no part to play. Compared to the youthful Hebrew of pre-Christian times, he is cut off from the sacrament. We do not give our children the opportunity to celebrate even the pale ritual we have filtered through layers of ecclesiastical tradition. We have neglected the training of our children through ritual participation.

Regarding the sacraments in general, we ought to conclude

that we are still laboring in the shadow of Roman Catholicism. Protestant sacerdotalism has continued the traditions of centralization, monopolization, and the priesthood of few believers. Protestants have officially affirmed the priesthood of all believers, yet the church authorities deny the right of laymen to administer the sacraments—the mark of the priesthood. If we are to overthrow the dead hand of sacerdotalism, we need to expand the role of laymen in the administration of the sacraments and expand the role of the sacraments outside of the narrowly ecclesiastical church worship service. We must heed the warning of the nineteenth-century social philosopher, Lamenais: *Centralization breeds apoplexy at the center and anemia at the extremities.*

Institutional Discipline

A priest exercises godly, lawful discipline within his sphere of authority. He serves as God's representative. A priest who cannot exercise discipline is not a priest. He disciplines (subdues) his portion of the earth to the glory of God.

There is no question that within the confines of the institutional church the elders have the monopoly of imposing sanctions for disobedience to God's law. This is the foundation of the church's ability to cleanse itself from the unrighteous (*1 Cor. 5*). There is a screening process involved in the selection of church elders, namely, prior experience in ruling a family.

Before a man is a priest of the congregation, he must be a priest of his own family. The centrality of the family in church life could not be made any plainer. Bachelors should not be ordained. They have not proven themselves within the priestly confines of the office of family leader. The celibacy requirement imposed by the Roman Catholic Church was imposed for purposes of ecclesiastical centralization. It created a sense of ultimate loyalty and dependence upon the church's ecclesiastical hierarchy. A priest in the Roman Catholic Church is not permitted to have rival institutional claims on his loyalty and energy. The institution of the family helps to remind men of their multiple loyalties in life. A man learns the limits of the possible when he rules over a family. The constraints imposed by reality keep church authorities in their proper place. This sense of reality is not the same as writing term papers.

The fact that every saint is a priest should not blind us to the fact that there are distinctions of authority and honor within the priesthood. Church officers have special authority. Paul affirms this principle (*1 Tim. 5:17-18*). No priest has lawful authority in every area of life. No human institution possesses ultimate and total sovereignty. All authority is limited by Biblical law. This is why the church contains as many priests as it has adult members. When a person can vote in a church meeting, or give advice, or teach a class, or take responsibility for making decisions, he has become a priest. Nevertheless, there are higher and lower priests, greater and lesser priests, within the confines of a single institution. A lesser priest in one institution (the church) may be a supreme priest in another institution (the military). A man may take orders from one person in a particular institution and subsequently give orders to the other person when both are operating in a different institution. This is one good reason why mutual deference and respect should be basic to any higher priest. No one is in high authority in every human institution. *A pastor is a priest, not because he is a pastor, but because he is a Christian.*

The priesthood, like the sacraments, exists beyond the confines of the ecclesiastical offices. The Christian is a priest in principle at all times. He is a priest vested with priestly authority and responsibility only within the confines of a few human institutions. We are a kingdom of priests. A kingdom is wide, and Christ's kingdom is growth-oriented. Its ultimate goal is total domination, under Christ: "For he must reign, till he hath put all enemies under this feet. The last enemy that shall be destroyed is death" (*1 Cor. 15:25-26*). To limit the royal priesthood to the institutional church is to deny the universality of the kingdom of God, equating it instead with the institutional church. This, too, is a theological heritage of Roman Catholicism. The church is equated with the kingdom; the kingdom is then restricted to the spiritual, or else it is understood as the universal external reign of the institutional church; and either conclusion leads to error. The church shrivels under pietism or becomes tyrannical under ecclesiocracy. In any case, the priesthood is narrowly defined and centralized with a vengeance. The idea that a man can be a priest in other spheres of life is ignored. The priesthood is equated with ecclesiastical officeholders.

Romans 13 affirms that God ordains the higher powers. This does not mean that men must always obey the officials of the civil government. If the passage meant this, then Peter could not have uttered his challenge to the state: we must serve God rather than men (*Ac. 5:29*). But there are lawfully ordained higher powers. A plurality of authorities exists, and men are required to obey them. "For rulers are not a terror to good works, but to the evil. Wilt thou then not be afraid of the power? do that which is good, and thou shalt have praise of the same" (*Rom. 13:3*). Paul's language concerning the ruler could not be clearer: "For he is the minister of God to thee for good. But if thou do that which is evil, be afraid; for he beareth not the sword in vain: for he is a minister of God, a revenger to execute wrath upon him that doeth evil" (*13:4*). When the saint finds himself in the role of law enforcer, he is a saint-priest. He is ordained. He executes judgment. He administers discipline. He is fulfilling his tasks as a member of a royal priesthood. Lawful authority, when coupled with personal conversion to Christ, results in a Christian priestly office. The office is not always ecclesiastical, but it is nonetheless priestly. This is why Paul refers to the ruler as a minister of God. All authority is from God; therefore, all officeholders or bearers of authority, in any institution or setting, are ministers. They possess limited sovereignty.

Not every office may have developed special sacraments, although many of them seem to have ritual observances that serve as the equivalent of ecclesiastical sacraments. They have marks of authority, a chain of command, and methods of discipline. But a Christian is doubly a priest, for he always exercises authority somewhere as he subdues his portion of the earth (*Gen. 1:28*), yet he also has the right to administer the sacraments of baptism and the Lord's Supper under some conditions. The word of God therefore makes itself felt in every institution, in every chain of command, as the kingdom expands over time.

What we must guard against is the assertion of absolute monopoly by any person or group of persons within any human institution. No person, no institution, and no lawful authority can ever claim total and final sovereignty. This is why it is necessary to reaffirm the doctrine of the royal priesthood in our own era. *The quest for absolute sovereignty is basic to the institutions of secular humanism.* To the extent that false doctrines of Protestant sacerdotalism complement these centralizing trends, the church is compromised. E. L. Hebden Taylor, an ordained Anglican priest and sociologist, has put it very well:

> Within temporal reality we find a diversity of offices. In order to see the integral unity of these diverse offices it is necessary to turn to the biblical revelation of Jesus Christ as the Supreme Office-bearer in the creation whom we are told is God's Prophet, Priest, and King. All the diversity of offices on earth find their concentration in the office of Christ as Covenant Head of the creation. As such Christ is the full and complete Office bearer, and he is therefore the origin and source of all power exercised on earth. Our Lord has delegated only partial sovereignties to men. In him along all these earthly sovereignties are united in an undivided service of God that involves nothing less than the preservation and redemption of the whole of human life.[13]

Protestant Sacerdotalism

Taylor's observations on the implications of Protestant sacerdotalism are well founded and to the point. The worst implication is the *negative position of the layman* within churches that have adopted centralized sacerdotal tendencies.

> In the New Testament church the "elders" never assumed the authoritative status *vis-à-vis* the laity which they have come to acquire in the Western world. In the New Testament we look in vain for the Western distinction between the *ecclesia docens* and the *ecclesia docta*: between the clergy, whose privilege it is to teach and instruct, and the laity, whose duty it is meekly to attend; the lay theologian was as common in the New Testament Church as he is rare in the Western world. It was not thought necessary in the New Testament to wear a clerical collar in order to speak with authority of the things of God. For modern Western Christianity, on the other hand—both Catholic and Protestant— the very words "layman" and "laity" have been severed from their biblical roots and have acquired a purely negative meaning. The layman is no longer one who through the mysteries of baptism and confirmation has become a member of a priestly body, the

laos or people of God. He is considered only in terms of what he is *not* and cannot do. He is an outsider, a non expert, in short, one who is not a parson or a minister.... Excluded from any active part in the worship services of the church, deprives of his extraliturgical apostolate, the layman is left to his own private devotions. As a result there has been developing over the centuries a rank spiritual individualism leading to religious subjectivism and sentimentalism. Piety, in the modern sense, has become an inadequate substitute for a ministry involving every member of Christ's Body and embracing every legitimate field of human activity. Something has surely gone wrong. The Son of God did not take our human nature upon himself in order that we might be turned some into parsons and presbyters while others are turn[ed] into parishioners and laymen. The apostolic vision of a re-created universe has faded, giving place to a dualistic world, half sacred, half secular. There is no real cure for all this without a recovery of the true sense of the worship services of the church as a corporate action of the whole Body of Christ in any one locality.[14]

There can be little doubt that Taylor's conclusion is correct: "Today's Protestant minister, as to his place and function in the church, differs in actual *practice* very little from his Catholic counterpart." Protestant sacerdotalism has compromised the concept of the universal priesthood, just as Protestant scholasticism compromised the concept of *sola scriptura*—the absolute supremacy of the Bible. Roman Catholic traditions were borrowed heavily by Protestant church officers, and secularism now threatens both with institutional paralysis. The Counter-Reformation of the Roman Catholic Church was more successful, ecclesiastically, than either Roman Catholics or Protestants realized at the time. Most Protestants still have not understood what has happened.

Questions

This essay is a preliminary study of the nature of the New Testament priesthood. It is intended to be a starting point, not a final set of conclusions. There are numerous immediate questions that should be dealt with by churches and Christian scholars. Yet we can rest assured that such a project will be resisted by the established institutional authorities. Some of the traditions of sacerdotalism are over 1,500 years old. It will no doubt take the coming of the realized kingdom to eliminate some of these traditions. Nevertheless, we need to consider these following issues, laboring toward days of institutional reform.

If the mark of the priest is ecclesiastical ordination, in what way are the universal priests of New Testament times ordained? Is there a church ritual which should be added? Why is there no reference to an ordination ceremony for laymen in the New Testament? Or was there one which we do not recognize? If it is baptism, then we face an immediate problem. Should not the baptized (ordained) person gain access to full church membership? If so, then the church would have to screen candidates prior to baptism. But the New Testament does not authorize lengthy screening. If it is the granting of voting membership, an extrabiblical requirement made necessary because of modern practices of church democracy, then a baptized but non-voting church member cannot be a priest. Nevertheless, Peter says that all believers are part of the royal priesthood. Or does he? Is he referring strictly to full church members? Or, finally, is conversion itself the mark of a true priest, the only ordination necessary? This is "ordination by God" comparable to that experienced by Paul on the road to Damascus?

It may be possible that ecclesiastical ordination is not required for lawful priesthood. If so, then the previous questions are unnecessary. My own opinion is that a man can be a priest without visible ordination by another man, and therefore ordination is a function of two events: conversion and lawful access to *any* position of authority. There can be special ordination ceremonies for church officers, but saints are nonetheless priests without such ordination.

What should the mode of baptism be? In churches, adults should probably be immersed, if Kline is correct concerning baptism as a sign of the Old Testament water ordeal-oath. For infants, pouring seems more appropriate. In the home, however, immersion is inconvenient unless the family owns a swimming pool with water in it. Most families are not so blessed. The family shower would be a reasonable compromise, symbolizing the Noachian rains, but somehow the shower does not seem dignified. Showers are reserved in America for fully dressed coaches of victorious athletic teams at the end of a championship season. *Pouring* would probably be preferable, since it involves sufficient water to make it somewhat of an ordeal, or at least a unique experience. No single mode should be universally required.

If laymen are not legitimate baptizers, the church must come up with a reason for their exclusion. What could that reason be? It cannot be that church elders alone have the authority to discipline members, and hence the exclusive right to baptize, because Philip, a deacon, baptized. It cannot be that church officers preside over the worship service, because the New Testament authorizes baptism outside the assembly of worship. Indeed, it was rare in the New Testament to have baptisms specifically confined to a worship service—or explicitly stated to be such. Is ecclesiastical ordination the criterion? If so, there is no explicit evidence to this effect in the New Testament. Is it the preservation of order (*1 Cor. 12:40*)? But baptism need not be administered in a worship service, and Paul was writing about the disruptions of the Corinthians' worship services. To preserve church order outside the worship service, an elder need not be present on every occasion; he needs only to have God's authority behind him as a warning. If mere tradition is the reason, then the church must define rigorously what is meant by the phrase "kingdom of priests," as well as specify just what active role laymen-priests have in the official, Biblically sanctioned structure of the New Testament church. The church must therefore define the negative (what laymen-priests are not Biblically entitled to do) and the positive (what they are Biblically enjoined to do), both inside the institutional church and outside.

In the case of the Lord's Supper, what should the role of the family be? It is quite true that the family of believers is the primary family. Christ told us that genetic families would be split over the confrontation between believing and unbelieving members of these families (*Mt. 10:34-37*). Nevertheless, the link between the symbolism of the passover and the symbolism of the Lord's Supper should be enough to convince us that some elements of family worship should be preserved in the New Testament rite. If we have become a kingdom of priests, it would seem preposterous to eliminate the one element of sacramentalism possessed by laymen in the Old Testament, namely, the administration of the passover rite within the family. There should be some role for fathers in the sacrament of the Lord's Supper. How could it be arranged? In the case of a household celebration, it is easier to perceive. A special after-dinner feast of bread and wine could be shared within the family, or between the family and the visitors. Fathers or household heads of the host family could give the warning to eat and drink in remembrance of Christ. In the church service, it is more difficult to contemplate. The children should not ask the fathers questions here, as they did in the Old Testament, unless it could be done quietly and in good order. But it might be possible for families to sit together at a common table or series of tables set up specifically for the Lord's Supper. The father might break the bread and pour the wine at his family's table, or in that section of the common table devoted to his family. The minister could break loaves, passing them to the fathers, who would in turn break them further. The same would hold true for the wine.

Conclusions

We can list the following clear-cut conclusions with respect to *church officers*:

1. There is no valid formal distinction between elders.
   a. There may be differences of gifts among elders.
   b. Functional differences must not be written into church law.
   c. Requirements for ordination are identical.
2. All elders are entitled to remuneration in terms of services rendered.
3. Deacons do not administer church discipline.
4. All officers must be or have been competent heads of families.
   a. Bachelors must not be ordained.
   b. Bigamists must not be ordained.
5. Ordained officers are not mediators of salvation.
6. Women must not be ordained.

We can list the following clear-cut conclusions with respect to *baptism*:

1. Baptism is a mark of covenantal subordination.

    a. Baptism does not regenerate men.

    b. Baptism is a two-edged sword: blessing or destruction.

    c. Infants of a believer must be baptized.

2. Baptism may be performed by deacons.

3. The authority to administer baptism is not based on the authority to enforce church discipline.

4. Baptism may be administered in households.

    a. The presence of the congregation is not mandatory.

    b. Immersion could not be an absolutely universal requirement.

5. Every believer has the right to an immediate baptism.

We can list the following clear-cut conclusions concerning the *Lord's Supper*:

1. The Lord's Supper is symbolic of Christ's death on the cross.

2. The Lord's Supper is a meal.

3. The Lord's Supper may lawfully take place in households.

4. The Lord's Supper involves the participation of children.

5. The Lord's Supper looks forward to victory and judgment by believers.

6. The Lord's Supper is open to all baptized church members in good standing.

We can list the following *tentative* conclusions concerning *baptism*:

1. Laymen, including women, may sometimes lawfully administer baptism.

2. The unsaved wives and children of believers may be baptized.

3. Immersion is symbolically preferable for adults who are baptized in churches.

4. Baptism does not confer full church membership.

    a. A period of screening is valid.

    b. The right to vote in church elections comes after screening.

5. Delaying baptism symbolizes a temporary period of covenant suspension.

We can list the following *tentative* conclusions concerning the *Lord's Supper*.

1. Heads of households may lawfully administer the Lord's Supper.
2. The Lord's Supper need not be an official ecclesiastical function.
3. Real wine should be served, rather than grape juice.
4. Bread should be broken as part of the ceremony.
5. The Lord's Supper is a celebration.
a. Participants should not be silent.
b. Participants should not be solemn.
6. The family should be integrated into the church's communion service.
7. The Lord's Supper is not sacramentally different from the *agapé* feast.

The rise of Protestant sacerdotalism has paralleled the decline of family sovereignty within the church. The centralization of authority and prestige by the so-called teaching eldership has been at the expense of earlier assignments to officers, such as teacher and evangelist; teaching elders have absorbed these earlier separate functions, not ruling elders. Every movement toward institutional centralization, beyond that set forth in the Scriptures, leads to individualism and fragmentation within the laity. Laymen feel cut off from responsibility within the church and tend to focus their concerns on activities outside the church—activities often unconnected to the concept of a universal kingdom and a universal priesthood of believers.

The family is the authorized training ground of all church officers. The rise of Protestant sacerdotalism was made possible, to a great extent, by the substitution of formal and specifically extrabiblical academic requirements for office. These academic qualifications necessarily limited access to the eldership, making necessary a new, unbiblical division within the eldership, the creation of the office of teaching elder. A *bureaucratic elitism* was and is the inevitable result—an elitism based not on successful performance in a real-life institution, the family, but successful performance in a narrow world of formal scholarship. Presbyterians,

Lutherans, and Episcopalians-Anglicans have been most guilty of this deviation from Biblical standards, along with New England's Congregationalists, but the independent churches—Baptists, Methodists, Friends, Campbellites, etc.—have now adopted the same error, though to a lesser extent.

A disastrous consequence of this Protestant sacerdotalism has been the elevation of the university, and later on the seminary, to a place of uncontested authority. From a historical point of view, we have to say that the university is, in practice, an anti-Christian institution. Its standards of performance are geared to autonomous rationalism. These standards, historically and without exception, have dragged every known Christian university into a compromising secularism within two centuries, and usually within a few decades. Because the university and the seminary are independent of the church, yet attendance at them a requirement of ordination, they have become enemies of the church's independence under God. Protestant scholasticism was a product of the university, and Protestant sacerdotalism is the end result. The lure of Greek speculation, Kantian speculation, or Marxist speculation proved too great for tenured faculties to resist. A rival institution, with different standards and radically different goals, became the training ground of ministers. The result has been the destruction of orthodoxy in every large hierarchical denomination except the Missouri Synod Lutherans, since they alone in this century threw the liberals (invariably referred to in the press as "moderates") out of their main seminary and into the cold, cruel world of non-tenured, non-subsidized teaching in the midst of a Ph.D glut. Protestant orthodoxy committed suicide, in principle, on the day that it abandoned the family and substituted the university as the training ground of church officers.

Find yourself a Christian college. Find a college which adheres exclusively to any historic creed. Find a college which enforces discipline on every faculty member in terms of the creed. Find a college which systematically fires anyone who teaches the content of his discipline in terms of secular standards. Find a college where the administration knows the difference. Find a college which refuses to take a nickel of federal or state financing, so as to maintain its independence. Find a college where the board of trustees enforces anything, ever, in terms of any intellectual principle whatsoever. Find a college without faculty tenure. Find a college out of debt. Such a college does not exist in the twentieth century. (You notice that I did not even mention accreditation. I am not a utopian.)

The whole structure of ecclesiastical authority must be revamped if the churches are to be saved from the continuing curse of Protestant sacerdotalism. They must be restructured from top to bottom. They must return to New Testament standards and scrap the trappings of medieval Roman Catholicism. They must reintegrate the family into the life of the church. They must clean house on the seminaries that supply their ministers, if necessary, and at the very least, see to it that the ministry is equally open to anyone who meets the standards of 1 Timothy 3. The seminary was a jerry-built academic institution which was created to counteract the secularism of the American colleges and universities that had departed, universally, from the Faith, and that was 150 years ago. The churches have not yet learned the lesson of *sola scriptura*. They have preferred to take the accredited short-cut of *scriptura cum academia*. That short-cut has led into the ditch.

You will know that a serious reform has been made when the old ministerial apprentice system is revived, and the seminary is recognized for what it has always been in fact, namely a graduate school of academic theological speculation. We need such institutions, but not to train ministers. You will know that progress has been achieved when the churches stop ordaining bachelors and start revoking the ordinations of those who refuse to marry. You will know that the millennium has arrived when churches systematically remove from office any elder or deacon whose wife or children cannot be restrained by him in their disorderly, long-term rebellion. The likelihood of this is so remote that postmillennialists should consider its probability only after several days of fasting and prayer. It is enough to make an amillennialist out of anyone.

I offer this as a possible sign of the end of the millennium and the imminent return of Christ: when orthodox seminaries stop the practice of raising the salary levels of faculty members who complete Ph.D.'s in atheistic universities (or any university, for that matter). As the great literary critic Edmund Wilson once put it, we missed our opportunity during World War I when we failed to abolish the Ph.D. as a German atrocity.

Then there is that final possible Christian academic reform: orthodox seminaries will cease the revamping of their curriculums and hiring policies in response to the demands of the seminary accrediting agencies, which are universally run by apostates, higher critics, Barthians, and atheists. This reform will be made, I am quite certain, only after the return of Christ, the resurrection, and the Day of Judgment. After that date, most of the officials in the accrediting agencies will be safely in hell. And you can rest assured that every seminary president will send a frantic letter to all donors in order to explain to them the reason why the seminary's accreditation has not yet been renewed by the regional accrediting board, and to assure them that this in no way reflects unfavorably on the overall academic program of the seminary.

----

[1] *The Standards of Government Discipline and Worship of the Orthodox Presbyterian Church* (Philadelphia: Committee on Christian Education of the Orthodox Presbyterian Church, 1965), 19.

[2] *ibid.*, 83.

[3] *ibid.*, 84.

[4] Meredith G. Kline, *By Oath Consigned* (Grand Rapids: Eerdmans, 1968), ch. 1. The essays were first published in the mid-1960s in the *Westminster Theological Journal.*

[5] *ibid.*, ch. 3.

[6] *ibid.*, ch. 4. See, for example, Isaiah 54:9-10.

[7] *ibid.*, 83.

[8] *The Encyclopedia of Christianity*, ed. Edwin H. Palmer (Wilmington, Del.: National Foundation for Christian Education, 1964), vol. I, 536.

[9] *ibid.*, 537.

[10] *ibid.*, I, 518.

[11] *Cyclopedia of Biblical, Theological, and Ecclesiological Literature*, ed. John McClintock and James Strong (New York: Harper & Bros., [1873] 1891), vol. V, 512.

[12] John Calvin, *The Institutes of the Christian Religion*, bk. IV, ch. XVII, sec. 44: "Thus we ought always to provide that no meeting of the Church is held without the word, prayer, the dispensation of the Supper, and alms."

[13] E. L. Hebden Taylor, *Reformation or Revolution* (Nutley, N. J.: The Craig Press, 1970), 413.

[14] *ibid*, 417-18.

Volume 11, No. 2, 1986-87

The Fraud of Educational Reform

by Samuel L. Blumenfeld

The more I read what secular educators write these days, the more convinced I become that their grasp of reality has slipped beyond retrieval. Professors of education are a very special breed, living in a very rarified atmosphere. They tend to discuss the problems of education as if educators had nothing to do with creating them. They pretend to be victims of social forces beyond their control. They are very fuzzy about cause and effect and prefer to speak in broad generalities.

This is particularly true when they write about our illiteracy problem. They write as if they had nothing to do with causing it. Yet the historical record proves beyond a doubt that our reading problem began when the professors of education changed the way reading was taught in our primary schools in the early 1930s. All of that was first exposed by Rudolf Flesch in his well-documented book, *Why Johnny Can't Read* (1955), and further elaborated by Dr. Jeanne Chall in *Learning to Read: The Great Debate* (1967) and by myself in *The New Illiterates (1973)*. In short, there is no lack of knowledge on how we got to where we are today, and any professor of education who sincerely wants to know the truth can find it in any university library.

But in all the recent television coverage of the illiteracy crisis, and in all the interviews with professors of education, I did not hear or see any reference to the information contained in the three books mentioned above, which, by the way, are by no means the only books written on the subject. On television we were shown in the most dramatic and pathetic terms how awful it is to be illiterate in America. But when it came to explaining why so many Americans who have spent from as many as eight to ten to twelve years in public school come out functionally illiterate, no answers were given. If any answer at all was attempted, it tended to indict the home as the source of illiteracy. In other words, if a child came out of an illiterate home, he remained illiterate no matter how many years he spent in school!

No attempt was made to explain why there are so many illiterate homes in a nation that has had compulsory school attendance in virtually every state for almost a hundred years. The media accepts at face value anything they are told by the educators. They cannot imagine that they are being deceived by some of the cleverest con artists who ever earned a doctorate of education.

But what makes matters worse is that there are now many new, relatively young professors, former flower children of the sixties, who see the world through thick Marxist lenses and thereby project a grossly distorted view of education's problems. Their influence is growing within the establishment as their articles appear in more and more educational journals which, of course, are only read by other professors of education.

Professors of education are probably the most useless, parasitic group in American society. They are supposed to teach teachers how to teach while they themselves have never taught a classroom of kids. They teach from theory only, and whatever they write or ruminate about is rarely worth reading, which is why virtually no one outside the profession knows what's going on inside.

Professors of education are a relatively new species. They came into being early in the century when the marriage between education and psychology led to the creation of graduate schools of education. The marriage elevated both subjects to new exalted positions in academe.

Hitherto, teachers were trained in private academies or normal schools. A college degree was not considered necessary to become a teacher. But the marriage of education and psychology made education a "science," a far more complex area of expertise, and so the normal school became a state college which, in time, became a state university conferring doctorates in education.

So now we have thousands of doctors of education who spend most of their time talking to one another and making little sense to the public. If you want to find out what they are saying, you have to read their journals of education, published by the graduate schools of education.

What do they say about the illiteracy problem? Very little that will contribute to its solution. For example, Barbara Ann Scott, Associate Professor of Sociology at the State University of New York (New Paltz) wrote an article for Boston University's *Journal of Education* (Vol. 168, No. 1, 1986) entitled "The Decline of Literacy and Liberal Learning." Writing from a Marxist point of view, she applied class theory to her interpretation. She wrote:

> "Back-to-basics" is basically a demand for functional literacy and, to a degree, cognitive literacy within the bourgeois tradition. It is not an explicit and purposive quest for critical literacy, at least not for the mass of students in the educational system, as has been amply demonstrated by NEH chief, William J. Bennett. The main concern of the mainstream literacy crusade is the short-term, extrinsic payoff, for both the individual and the society, not the intrinsic, long-term pleasure to be found in educational excellence.

> Thus, the literacy crusade currently being mounted by the educational establishment is fundamentally anti-radical and anti-democratic. An authentic (and, consequently, radical) concern for literacy starts with the assumption, in Stanley Aronowitz's (1982) words, that "critical thinking is the fundamental precondition of an autonomous and self-motivated citizenry" (p. 283). This means, in turn, appropriating the bourgeois tradition of liberal learning in order to ultimately transform it in the interest of intellectual and social empowerment. Critical literacy, in short, is the essence of the radical democratic agenda.

> ... Radical educators need to recognize the shortcomings of liberal and conservative approaches to educational reform, take care to avoid co-optation, distinguish short-term from long-term agendas (*i.e.* the progression from cognitive to critical literacy), and be eternally vigilant in defending and extending the liberal arts and sciences curriculum. They need, above all, to remember that the broad tradition of bourgeois culture and liberal learning has often yielded, unintentionally, or otherwise, a radical payoff: namely, the liberation of critical thought and democratic action.

Is it not interesting that the prestigious *Journal of Education* provides Marxists with the means to conduct the class struggle in its pages? But what is even more interesting is the revelation that "critical thinking" is "the essence of the radical democratic agenda." We have noticed in educational journals an increasing preoccupation with "critical thinking" as a new, essential component of the reformed curriculum. We were at a loss to understand what "critical thinking" consisted of until reading Ms. Scott's article. Apparently, "critical thinking" means the application of Marxist dialectical analysis and interpretation to the content of the curriculum. Is it now the intention of our educators to indoctrinate American youngsters in the art of Marxist analysis under the guise of "critical thinking"?

Apparently that is the case. And we get further confirmation of this in a review of Jonathon Kozol's book, *Illiterate America*, by James Paul Gee, in the same issue of the *Journal of Education*. Professor Gee, a specialist in linguistics, teaches in the Program in Applied Psycholinguistics at Boston University. It should be noted that current methods of reading instruction in American schools are based on psycholinguistics, which is, in my view, the chief cause of our learning disability explosion. Dr. Gee writes:

> The physical center of Kozol's book ... is "a plan to mobilize illiterate America." One approach to illiteracy that has worked in this century in such places as Cuba and Nicaragua, Kozol concedes to be impossible for us.... The sole alternative, he argues, is a grass-roots struggle fired from the bottom up. His written call to arms to illiterate America is:
>
> "We need, above all else, to do away with the idea of literacy as training for domestication, contrived to fill existent or imagined lower-level slots and consumer roles, and search instead for instruments of moral leverage strong enough to scrutinize those roles and to examine the political determinants of subjugation: examine, study, stand back, and reflect upon their purpose and, by virtue of reflection and examination, first to denounce and finally transform. Literacy, so conceived, is civil disobedience in pedagogic clothes; a cognitive denunciation of dynastic power, an ethical affront to an imperial injustice. Critical and analytic competence on such a scale is more than 'functional.' It is a literacy for human liberation. It is cultural action: an event, not an idea. It is political; it is endowed with anger; it is not neutral."

What we have here, pure and simple, is a call for revolution on the part of the illiterate masses. Much of Kozol's strategy of using an illiteracy campaign as a means of inciting the masses to revolution is derived from Paulo Freire, the Brazilian Marxist, whose book, *Pedagogy of the Oppressed* (1973), has had a profound influence on radical educators in both North and Latin America. Freire, apparently, is also the source of the "critical thinking" movement. Beverly M. Gordon, professor of education at Ohio State University, writes in an article entitled "The Use of Emancipatory Pedagogy in Teacher Education" (*The Journal of Educational Thought*, Vol. 20, No. 2, August 1986):

> One of the best known advocates of emancipatory pedagogy is Paulo Freire. His writings describe the development of educational pedagogies designed to promote critical consciousness, to enable students to become critical thinkers and active societal participants, and to give people the emancipatory capability of redefining the nature of their own lives.
> Freire's advocacy of education for critical consciousness and his model of emancipatory pedagogy for oppressed groups together heighten our awareness of the inherently and inescapably political nature of curriculum....
> In the emancipatory classroom, students begin to participate as an active citizenry and to overcome their feelings of despair and hopelessness, apathy and alienation.... (E)ducating someone is an awesome responsibility and an unavoidably political act.

Isn't it amazing that there are so many "educated" Americans still roaming the vast Marxist desert, seeking an illusory "liberation"? The failures of applied Marxism never seem to daunt them. The gulags, the starvation, repression, mass murders and religious persecution, which the dictatorships of the proletariat have brought about, never seem to open their minds to question; the stories of defectors, ex-communists, escapees from these Marxist hells make no impression. Why? One can only attribute such blindness to Satanic influences and depraved hearts.

Yet these are the people to whom is entrusted the education of American children.

In sum, we can expect the next phase of educational reform to be dominated by radical ideas disguised in "pedagogic clothes." Such phrases as "critical thinking," "emancipatory pedagogy," and "master teachers" will sound benign to the public but will convey the right message to the radicals.

Volume 10, No. 2, 1984

The Philosophy
of the
Free Market

by Rousas John Rushdoony

In discussing the philosophy of the free market, it is necessary *first* of all to distinguish it from capitalism. All too often, both capital and labor want subsidies, not freedom. They seek statist intervention into the free market on their behalf, as does the farmer, the artist, scientist, beauticians, and many, many others. Lieberman has given us an excellent report on how many occupations are now controlled by state licensing because the practitioners demand a closed shop for their work.[1] Very few capitalists in the 20th century favor the free market; they work, in fact, to hinder its freedom and gain statist protection.

Second, most of the capitalism of our time represents simply a concern for profits, whereas the free market represents a faith in the value of economic freedom. The free market thinkers are no less concerned with profits, but they insist that the good life is a unity. To isolate profits from the worldview of the free market means, in the long run, to destroy profits as well. Profits are but one aspect of a general advantage which accrues from economic freedom, and there is thus a substantial difference between the free market and the capitalism of an interventionist society.

Our concern here, however, is not the advantages of the free market, real as they are, but its undergirding faith and philosophy. The roots of the free market, too seldom appreciated, rest in the doctrine of God. That the church and Christendom have too seldom appreciated this foundation is due to the continuing alien influence of Greek philosophy on Christian theology.

The most commonly used term for God in the Old Testament Hebrew is *Adon, Adonai*, Lord. In the New Testament, the most common term for Christ is in the Greek *Kyrios*, Lord. In both instances, *Lord* means sovereign, absolute property owner of man and the earth, and ruler. This word has a clearly economic as well as

political and religious reference. We are plainly told that "The earth
is the LORD'S (Yahweh's), and the fulness thereof; the world and
they that dwell therein" (*Ps. 24:1*). As the Lord, God is the governor
of all things, including the economic scene, and for another to control
it is a transgression of God's sovereign prerogative.

The necessity of *government* in some form is a presupposition
common to every school of thought. The definitions of that
government can and do vary in terms of the religious premises
involved. The equation of government with the state is a false
one, however popular in pagan antiquity and today. The state is
merely one agency of government among many, and, in the Biblical
perspective, it is emphatically and totally under God.

The economic sphere, like all others, is never lawless. The
question is, whose law governs the economic sphere? The Biblical
Faith sees God as Lord over all things including economics. God's
law covers the economic sphere, and God's created order furthers
certain activities and penalizes others. This order brings inflation
to its sure day of reckoning; it makes transgressions of economic
order catastrophic in the end. The government of the economic
order is thus placed in God's hands. God's law requires certain
things of men: false weights and measures are banned; there must
be a rest and reward even for working animals; God's moral order
must be maintained. God's law does not control activities other
than to punish crimes of fraud, theft, and the like.

In this sense, the market is free from the state but bound by
the law of God. Economic controls and government rest basically
in God's laws for the economic sphere. Supply and demand are
not legislated by the state but constitute a form of given order in
the nature of a God-created reality.

The Greek faith saw the ideas or forms for the structure and
government of life as a part of man's being. Hence, essential and
ultimate government was seen as inherent and potential in man,
and incarnated in the philosopher-kings. The impact of this
Hellenic premise has long prevented Christians from realizing their
theological and governmental potential, because they have trusted
in their own Greek-conceived rationality and ideal rule rather than
in freedom in God's order and government.

In secularized version, this was realized to a degree in Deism and the Enlightenment. The thinkers of that era presupposed God's order with God abstracted from it as an absentee landlord. Because of their mechanistic views of reality, they could assume that a God-created universe could continue working with God removed from it even as a watch, once wound up, goes on ticking for a long time after the watchmaker leaves. It was held that God had transferred his governmental powers to nature, so that nature was now the source of continual and omnipresent law rather than God.

The Enlightenment had two counter-tendencies. On the one hand, the philosopher-king faith of Plato had a profound influence, from the Renaissance on, and led to the divine right of kings and a mercantilist economy. On the other hand, the use of nature to replace the God of Scripture meant an inherent law and order in the very nature of things. Hence, society's need was seen as, not statist controls over the economy, but a free market for nature to enforce her infallible laws on the economy.

The economic consequences of this faith were enormous. While it is true that no fully free market has ever existed, it is also true that this doctrine of the free market led to dramatic economic progress and development.

However, even as this free market development was under way, the rise of Darwinism undermined it. Nature was no longer the source of infallible law. Christians had said nature is fallen; Deism found it infallible ("Whatever is, is right"), but Darwin found it to be a product of chance, mindless, and having no law save survival. This view of the struggle for survival and the survival of the fittest, for a time influenced capitalism, but spelled death for the free market.

Two things had occurred with the triumph of Darwinism. *First*, with God and nature both dismissed as viable sources of government, the economic sphere was now seen as lawless and very much in need of government. *Second*, because the universe was no longer the creation of God, nor the manifestation of a perfect nature, the harmony of interests was replaced with the doctrine of the conflict of interests. Because there was no governing, inherent, or imminent law in the economic sphere, or any other, the economy was a realm of brutal survivalism and lawlessness. It was thus in desperate need of government.

A telling example of the shift from a belief in the free market to state intervention was John Stuart Mill. Under the influence of Darwinism, he moved from a faith in natural liberty to an affirmation of statist intervention.

Because the older governments by God, and then by nature, were seen as gone, men, feeling the necessity and inevitability of government, began, step by step, to introduce state intervention into the economic sphere. The state became the new God, and the new State of Nature. The omnicompetence of the state to govern was assumed as the state took over the functions of God and nature, and socialism, embodying this faith, became an international force and a crusading missionary endeavor. In *1984*, George Orwell depicted the end result of this new faith.

As the Christian faces this new idolatry of the state, he must do so only with a totally Biblical faith in God as Lord over all. No false idols, including the state, are tolerable. Freedom is neither a natural nor a state grant or right, but a possibility only under God's government. The weight of omnicompetent and omnipresent government must be removed from the state and restored to God.

It is *not* an accident that statist intervention into the economic sphere has been followed by intervention into the life of the church. Church and state conflict is dramatically on the increase in the United States. It is logical that this should be so. If the state is *sovereign*, then it is lord over all things within its realm. It is necessary then for it to exercise its supposedly benign oversight over the life of the church.

The framers of the Constitution of the United States refused to use the terms "sovereign" or "sovereignty" in that document. The words were seen as theological, not political. Now we have a sovereign federal government, affirmed to be sovereign by the federal Supreme Court, insisting on the universal jurisdiction of the state.

The battle for the free market is but one facet of a battle against idolatry, against the claims of a false god over us. There can be no compromise in this battle. Elijah's challenge against this new Baal, the state, must be heard: "How long halt ye between two opinions?

If the LORD be God, follow him: but if Baal, then follow him" (*1 Kin. 18:21*)

---

[1] Jethro K. Lieberman, *The Tyranny of the Experts, How Professionals are Closing the Open Society* (New York, NY: Walker & Co., 1970).

Vol. 10, No. 1, 1983

The Artist as Propagandist
by Otto J. Scott

In Greenwich Village twenty years ago, there was a small art store that opened just around the corner from Cornelia Street. It was stocked with plaster statuettes of famous Greek statuary, both male and female. The proprietors proceeded to paint them in lifelike colors. They painted the skin, eyes, nails, and pubes. The effect was startling: passers-by would do a double take and then walk on hurriedly. Finally the police came by, decided the display was pornographic, and ordered the windows cleared. After that the experiment failed, and the shop closed.

But in ancient Greece, the statues were painted. That was how they appeared. They were so realistic that—long after his death— one of Alexander's former generals turned a corner in a palace corridor and came upon a life-sized statue of the conqueror—and fainted. Surfaces of solid white marble are all that remain after centuries of burial: the paint has long since been eaten away.

But there was more to ancient art than the visual, though that was impressive. Ancient plays and poems have been rediscovered, and every scrap is examined. These are unrivaled in their salaciousness and the explicitness of their descriptions—or were unrivaled until the Renaissance. It seems fairly obvious that the open sexuality of the Greek and Roman writers excited the admiration and interest of the Victorian scholars who could satisfy prurience in the name of scholarship with impunity.

The Greeks had a view of life that appeals to the base. They were, for instance, people who believed the gods were cast in their images. In their view, this meant that the gods were motivated in the same way as Greeks. Thus, the Greeks held that the greatest and most dangerous of sins was *hubris*, or pride. Anyone who stood too tall could attract the *envy* of the gods. To the Greeks that was reasonable, for the Greeks were an envious people.

They did not exile criminals in Athens: they executed them or punished them in various ways. They did not exile rebels: these could be considered traitors. They exiled only the successful, whose attributes or attainments could evoke envy.

Their religion mirrored the Greeks'. Being notorious throughout the ancient world for their slyness, they credited their gods with similar methods. Oedipus was tricked into killing his father and sleeping with his mother by being removed from his parents as an infant, raised elsewhere, and told he was an orphan. The truth was disclosed to him only after it was too late. Only the Greeks would consider this heartless injustice clever.

In terms of literature and theater, the Greeks produced much that was witty and glamorous. I recall seeing Alfred Lunt and Lynne Fontanne on Broadway in a play called *Amphitryon 38*. It was based on a Greek legend in which Zeus, desiring a man's wife, had the husband temporarily removed, assumed the husband's form, came to earth and spent the night. In that manner, said the Greeks, Hercules was conceived. I had no idea why it appeared on Broadway in 1938, nor of the significance of a modern audience regaled anew by what the Greeks laughed at in the 5th century B. C.

The greatest possible contrast to the elegant barbarism and cruelty of the Greeks that could be found in the ancient world was the Bible of the Hebrews. Where the Greeks and other ancient peoples dwelled on their kings, queens, and warriors, the Hebrews produced a sacred literature that revealed the sins and tribulations, as well as the triumphs and dreams, of an entire nation. That this work was divinely inspired appears obvious in the examination, for only God could see so deeply into the hearts and motives of people, and lay them so bare.

Time and again we see how the Hebrews rebelled, and turned toward other gods, and time and again were punished. As the rebellions continued, followed by punishments, one begins to wonder at the persistence of the rebels, and their inability to learn from experience—until we recall that every generation of man repeats the follies of its predecessors.

But we cannot regard the Bible as literature: it is far too awesome for that. But we can say that it entered the world stage, as distinct from the culture of a people, with the New Testament. In the Gospel according to St. Mark, we watch Peter—after the arrest of Jesus—go furtively into the courtyard of the High Priest, and stand with the servants around a fire. One of the servant girls recognized him, and he denied his identity. He walked into the outer courtyard, and she followed him to accuse him again. This time his reply revealed his Gallilean accent, but he managed to escape. Auerbach, in his remarkable book, *Mimesis*, took note of the realism of this scene—and especially of the low station of the personae in contrast to the great significance of Peter, who represented "the image of man in the deepest and most tragic sense."[1]

But far more than the detail, the Bible reveals a view of the world at variance with all that appeared before—or since. The multiverse is in the hand of God, and those who find it falling short of their expectations argue that they could correct and edit the achievements of the Higher Power. This is not an uncommon view. There is resentment in our hearts since the Fall. But since the New Testament, there has been hope and understanding. During the Christian ages of faith, the artist—once a despised artisan—has been recognized as conducting an act of worship when he seriously practices his art.

But the world learned this with great difficulty, and recalls it only intermittently. The New Testament appeared at the time of Tacitus and Petronius. Both were men steeped in the world and its virtues and vices, for whom nothing existed beyond the event and its more immediate consequences. They were masters of an enameled art the New Testament rendered instantly obsolete.

But the essence of that obsolescence is difficult to convey. The examples are present, but politicians, for instance, do not seem aware of the example of Judas. Judas, remember, wanted to sell Mary Magdalene's gift to Jesus, in order to distribute alms to the poor. We are now very familiar with this sort of posturing, in which the spiritual descendants of Judas seek to present themselves as better than God.

The overriding difference, however, between the Bible and all the literature of the past was that the Bible was divinely inspired and presented man from the viewpoint of God. To some extent this was not immediately reflected in Christian writing so much as in the Christian attitude toward history. History is a look at the lives of those who preceded us. We can, from the brief eminence upon which we stand in our lives in relation to the past, look back and see someone born, grow to maturity through various experiences, achieve or fail, and finally die. At the moment of death the purpose of that life becomes evident—and not before then. Before death, there is always the possibility that a life, or a person, may utterly change for better or worse. Death writes the last chapter. And suddenly the meaning of that life leaps plainly into view. For a moment we see that life over the shoulder of God, and we are allowed, in the light of that illumination, clear vision.

Through the ages of faith men sought to capture that vision and apply it to life. They did not always succeed, but they tried. They searched for instances of holiness, for lives of sanctity, and for evidences of divine intervention. For all the world was considered God's. He ruled, and men were rewarded as they sought to obey, or to disobey, according to his grace and mercy and retribution.

In time, as we know, the structure began to sag. The art of gilding the lily grew commonplace. It was not enough to discover a saint: it was necessary to paint that saint as too holy to catch cold, too holy to spit or to have weaknesses, or to sin again, even against his own desires. As these incredibilities mounted and the statues of the saints began to proliferate, second-rate art began to have its effect. That effect can be best assessed by regarding the modern works of Hollywood. There second-raters are distinguished by a peculiar and utterly mistaken sense of superiority. They write down, or paint down, or simplify. They do not trust the world to catch the point: they exaggerate to make the point clearer. Then they add a laugh track, so the people will know when to laugh— and what to laugh at. In the process, all credibility is destroyed, because truth is destroyed. But that's the final stage. The early stages are more seductive, like vice itself.

The first great early stage of decline reached the West in the form of the Renaissance. There seems to be a general belief that the Renaissance was limited to Italy, and that it lasted a relatively brief period. We might all be better off if that had been the case.

The fact is that the Renaissance in Italy lasted from the birth of Dante (in 1265) to the death of Michelangelo (in 1564). That's almost 300 years—or roughly the same span of time from John Milton to James Joyce. In the course of those three centuries the influence of the Italian Renaissance seeped across all Europe.

The great commentator on the period was Jacob Burckhardt, a Swiss professor. He had the original intention of writing the history of the Christian period: the Ages of Faith. He wrote the first volume, *The Age of Constantine*. And he wrote the final volume, *The Civilization of the Renaissance in Italy: An Essay*, in 1860.[2] He never got around to the middle volumes, and all the world is poorer as a result.

Burckhardt never received an advance or any royalties from his work on the Renaissance. It took years for the first edition of 1,000 to sell out. Then the Swiss publisher sold the rights— without telling Burckhardt—to a German publisher who printed another 1,650 copies. It took five years to exhaust those, and before a third edition appeared. But the book slowly made Burckhardt famous—though not rich. It shaped some of the ideas of many better-known individuals. But it suffered a peculiar fate at the hands of the scholars.

They first inserted a massive number of notes; sometimes as many as twenty to a page, which made reading the book very tiresome. Then they wrote *about* the book—and in the process of writing about it, they misrepresented it. In the course of this misrepresentation they managed to distort Burckhardt in the general mind from a Christian historian into an art historian. Then they finally interred him from public appreciation by handing these misinterpretations over to educators—who rule the graveyards of truth.

All these efforts were made because the significance of Burckhardt's descriptions of the Renaissance was uncomfortably close to the weaknesses and trends of European society in the 1860s. Burckhardt foresaw the repetition of the rise of tyrants, the decline of liberty—and the looting of the Louvre. He predicted the appearance of what he called "terrible simplifiers" who would reduce learning to formulas and slogans.[3]

This remarkably prescient forecast was based upon a long look backwards at what Burckhardt proves was a period of Christian decline and decadence. Even Dante, acclaimed for his *Paradise Lost and Regained*, used his gifts to place his personal enemies and critics in the deepest pits of hell and had difficulty portraying the superiority of heaven. That obsession with politics was part of a shift away from classic Christianity toward new gods. The Italians began to unearth statues from the dead empire of the Romans and to compete for the honor of being the birthplace of Cicero, of or other Roman celebrities. The visits to the shrines of the saints— once a popular feature of everyday life, declined in popularity. The very idea of a holy life began to fade, and was replaced by the old pagan idea of fame.

To become famous was to achieve a place in the memory of society; to become a historical figure was to be transformed into the equivalent of a god. Then legends would be created, to adorn the figure in the Pantheon. Thus the pagan empires rose again in the world of imagination. Italy became transformed into a commercial center where the discovery of double-entry bookkeeping was a marvelous step forward, where merchant bankers began to operate on an international level, and where demagogues arose to seize power.

Burckhardt has left us unforgettable portraits of the essence of a tyrant. He is not the unpleasant ogre of legend: he is Prince Charming. He is affable and friendly and walks in the midst of an adoring crowd. He knows the people—and he takes care of them. Men who do not want another man to take care of them are the only ones who do not find this situation attractive. The political situation of Italy was too complicated to describe: let it suffice to say that the persecutions of Christians by Emperor Frederick II on one end and the papacy on the other created a situation where Italy could not be united. The states were in the hands of despots. These little courts, supported by taxation, were ruled by usurpers. The only means the despot had of achieving legitimacy was by surrounding himself with men of talent: poets and scholars, painters and musicians.

Petrarch, a favorite at such courts, advised these rulers to be the fathers of the people. The Princes then proceeded to take charge of everything: "to restore buildings and churches, keep the police, drain marshes, watch the food supplies and the distribution of liquor, support the sick and helpless, protect distinguished scholars."[4] Anyone who protested against all this diligence and concern could be sure that those who felt benefited would lead the charge against them.

There were uncertainties in such regimes, however, and as time passed, conventional limits in the exercise of powers began to fade even from memory. The possibility of attaining supreme power by a coup excited every range of imagination—like the possibility of becoming a Castro or a Mao Tse-tung or a Stalin or even a Hitler today excites the impressionable young.

Meanwhile every sort of crime spread from the top: murder, incest, rape, robbery, deceit, torture. Burckhardt described Lodovico Sforza, nicknamed the Moor because of his dark complexion as "the most perfect type of despot of that age." He surrounded himself with scholars, poets, artists, and musicians. Leonardo da Vinci worked for him and later served Cesare Borgia. They gilded the image of the Court.

Art, in the Renaissance, played a crucial role. The ruler of Verona specialized in entertaining men of letters, who were expected to make him famous in return for lavish gifts. The list of these men and their patronage can be found in any art history of the period, but these are volumes that expurgate the dark side of that period.

Cesare Borgia prowled the streets at night, dagger in hand, surrounded by guards, murdering innocent pedestrians for the sheer pleasures of sadism. Lodovico Sforza was a mass murderer in the most personal sense, and also ruler of Milan. An earlier tyrant of Milan—Barnabo—kept hunting dogs that he released upon people.

The list is nearly endless and the corruption spread through all levels of Italy. Poison became popular; adultery commonplace; murders were ordered even from the Papal Court. The mixture of splendor and misery was as striking as in the days of Imperial Rome in the times of Nero or Caligula; it was those times restored.

In that period artists were commissioned to create wonderful works. The themes were, as before, taken from the Bible, but the artists were working from a different sort of social environment. It's no use saying that an artist can surmount his environment: the fact is that all men are shaped in large measure by the tides and forces of their time.

Those who resist still reflect these fashions, modes, attitudes, and styles. Look at an old daguerreotype taken, for instance, in 1860: General Grant and his men, say, sitting or lounging around

one of their camps. There are always trees, and only a few of the
officers have anything to sit upon. Grant is leaning against a tree:
like his senior men he is in shapeless clothes that reflect the heavily
rural background of the period; his posture is careless because the
United States had not yet achieved its enamel period where a public
image had to be carefully fashioned and artfully projected. There
is no mistaking the period of the daguerreotype, just as there is an
eerie similarity in the men and women snapped by a photographer
in the 1890s, or the 1920s—or today.

So the people of the Renaissance come to seem alike. They
built cathedrals and their artists painted so wonderfully that
perspective and color and theme seem almost supernaturally
blended. Some proof of their high quality can be seen by the fact
that those remaining works that appear on the market are purchased
for millions of dollars—sometimes by persons who sneer at history
and the past, and Christianity, and the West.

Yet when we look at these artists and writers personally, we
wonder at the strange mixture of talent and cowardice that we so
often see. Da Vinci's first commissions were to design dresses for
the ladies of the court of Florence; later he worked for Sforza, the
"Moor," tyrant of Milan, whom he depicted in gigantic statue.
Raphael as a boy witnessed scenes of butchery in the public square
of Perugia, and Burckhardt speculated that these memories may
be responsible for the small, early pictures he painted of St. George
and the dragon.

The atmosphere by which these great artists were surrounded
is nearly beyond the powers of imagination to visualize. The
Renaissance witnessed the rise of men like Werner von Urslingen,
whose hauberk bore the inscription, "the enemy of God, of pity
and mercy."

At a time when torture, witchcraft, devil-worship, divination,
and sorcery reappeared, the masters of the visual arts portrayed
celestial scenes of heavenly bliss; clouds harboring cherubs and
angels; saints praying for the intercession of the Almighty. They
became the propagandists of the Vatican and of the dukes and
princes and despots of the city-states. A careful observer might
note, in this development, that there came a subtle change in the
graphic arts. In addition to discoveries in perspective and an

increasing expertise in musculature and anatomy, there came a far more earthy and sensual style of representation. The unworldly aspect of Christian art, once notable, became progressively less visible—and the world grew proportionately larger.

But painters and musicians deal in mediums that do not openly address people in languages understandable to everyone. That could not be said of poets and writers. These men called themselves "humanists." They were the experts who could revive antiquity and its personalities and customs. They could create reputations— and they could destroy them. Their disputes, their scrambles for the favor of one or another prince; their vituperations, were bloodless but lethal.

On the surface they produced elegant productions; underneath the surface they created obscene poems and parodies, satires and vilifications. The printing press enlarged their arena and extended their audiences. They led truly dreadful lives: uncertain, chancy, filled with receptions in palaces and private worries about money on which to live. They struggled for professorships, jobs as tutors in princely families, secretaryships. They enjoyed luxury and privation simultaneously, and attracted both admiration and boundless contempt. They had to move constantly from one court to another as people demanded new faces, new styles, new stories.

All this led to licentious excess and "a total indifference to the moral laws recognized by others." "Such men," Burckhardt observed, "can hardly be conceived to exist without an inordinate pride. They needed it, if only to keep their heads above water, and were confirmed in it by the admiration which alternated with hatred in the treatment they received from others. They are the most striking examples and victims of an unbridled subjectivity."[5]

Does this sound familiar? It should. Think of our professors, running alternately to Washington and to large corporations, telling the bureaucrats in each what they most want to hear; sandwiching in applications for foundation grants between books compiled by their graduate students, to which they affix their own names and demand royalties. Think of the television and Hollywood film writers, anxious to share in coke parties at the homes of large producers, as willing to write pornography as a letter home. Think of Norman Lear, whose productions mock the family and all moral values, and who is outraged that Christians dare attempt to be heard on public issues—as though they had rights. Think of Lear and his many contemporaries as described by Ben Stein in "The View from Sunset Boulevard"—and you have the humanists, updated—and riding for a fall.

For of course the Italian Renaissance fell. It had to fall. It was too rotten to stand. In 1527 the robbing, looting Spaniards of Charles V were allowed to sack Rome, and for the next nearly four hundred years the Italians lived under foreign domination. Those who do not understand what that means are fortunate; in the case of Italy it broke the back of the nation, seemingly forever. To this day it remains a region where people a mile apart in separate villages speak different dialects and hate each other. In Italy proper, nobody is from Italy. They are from Roma, or Genova, or Sicily, or some other town, city or village; hardly ever from Italy.

This is the sort of punishment described in the Bible for those who abandon God. Nor can it be said that the ancient Hebrews were the only people upon whom such punishments fell, or can fall. Their history can serve as an illustration, but it is by no means the only one. The fall of the Italians—the most advanced in their day, the wealthiest, the possessors of the great villas and art treasures and banking houses and theaters and cathedrals and churches and schools and printing presses and all the other artifacts, services and glories of civilization—sent a shudder through all western Europe.

The Reformation was advanced by the fall of Italy and the Sack of Rome; all the predictions of disaster for vice were verified in awesome fashion. The Vatican, in later years, conducted a reform of its own, and it not only rid itself of the loathsome practices that had so long darkened its pretensions, but it launched a great propaganda program to lure the Protestants back to the Church. The Baroque period was one result.

More to the point is the belief of the Reformers of the North that beauty is a worldly snare; and that art is an instrument of the devil. That belief was not total, of course— the Dutch masters are proof that painting survived and flourished, and Germany is crammed with beautiful works produced under Protestant regimes. Portrait painting, like many other novelties, moved north to England and France and enjoyed a high status.

Much the same can be said of music and literature and other aspects of the arts: they continued. But so, to a large extent, did the Renaissance outside Italy. Shakespeare can be counted as a Renaissance writer. The Tudor courts were Renaissance in their conduct of popular tyranny, their executions of fallen favorites, their insouciance regarding Christian principles. But Henry VIII and Elizabeth I led the English monarchy toward the edge: so did James I. Charles I lost it to the Puritans and the Presbyterians: reformers both.

Since then, we have seen the cycle repeated several times in several places. France became the great glitterer after Rome, Florence and Milan and the rest of Italy fell into the shade. Luxury mounted concurrently with vice. Its famous Enlightenment, however, seems to have its seeds in England, in the period from 1660 to 1750. There, with the Restoration, a wave of ridicule was launched at religion with devastating effect.[6]

It caught, with its wit and cruel exaggerations, a young Frenchman who later called himself Voltaire. He never forgot that impression, nor did he ever abandon that weapon. Of course, art flourished during the Enlightenment, but it was an art completely caught, like the Greeks, in a world where vice was held to be attractive and interesting, and virtue dull and stupid. Homosexuality—that Greek specialty of Plato and Company— emerged from the shadows to enjoy transvestite dances and masques. Pornography reappeared and so did the prototypical "humanists"—the men of letters struggling desperately for a secure niche in the world; available to any who could pay the price. Peter Gay subtitled his book on the period: *The Rise of Modern Paganism.*

You know the results. I wrote a book about the French Revolution and I can still recall my surprise and even fear when I realized that it is as contemporary as today's newspapers. Radical lawyers like Robespierre, revolutionary journalists, idealistic rich radicals, and radical intellectuals socializing with pornographers and courtesans and dishonest politicians are familiar to us today.

Of course, the Terror took people aback. Terror, followed by a war that lasts twenty years is not easy from which to recover. In the end France was broken. The largest nation in Europe. The richest. The most populous. The land with the greatest number of palaces and chateaux, of art treasures and newspapers, of learned doctors and men of letters—all crashed. To this day France is divided between those whose forebears suffered and those who think their forebears benefited. Its greatest treasures remain those left over from the *ancien regime*; it has never—and will never—have another time of glory.

But the lesson remained unlearned. The teaching of religion dropped downward; educators turned from the Bible to lesser productions to teach about life and the world, and the meaning of history. In that turning, those lessons dropped utterly from sight. People were left with propaganda, with slogans and stereotypes and doctored legends and falsified narratives.

A new Enlightenment, of sorts, appeared in the late Victorian period. It was accompanied, in Britain, by the usual turning toward the ancient Greeks. I have two books in my library on the subject, and they make fascinating reading. The English modeled their boarding schools for boys on Sparta. Later the fashion switched to Athens, where there was less austerity and more sensuality, including homosexuality—which became known in Europe as the "English disease," distinguished from flagellation.

When Kipling went to London as a rising young author, his reaction was like that of Luther to Rome. He was horrified by the fact that persons like Oscar Wilde were drawing-room rulers. That spurred a desperate sort of poetic effort to establish a different more virile sort of Empire, but the slide was far too steep for even a great poet to stem.

The European equivalent of the Sack of Rome turned out to be World War I: mass suicide. The leaders of Europe had, by that time, retained the façade and lost the essence of a Christian civilization. Their fratricidal conflict proved the point beyond words.

After that came the rise of Burckhardt's terrible simplifiers, and the new tyrants. Like their predecessors in the Renaissance, they offered great lures to artists. Royalties from massive printings, ovations in the theater, and crowds to welcome you at railroad stations, medals, interviews, and parties with the mighty—Paul Hollander describes these lures in his work, *Political Pilgrims*.[7]

Hollander names a long list of western artists, and journalists who succumbed to these lures. In his conclusions, he blames a loss of religious faith and a rise of belief in—of all things—a sort of magic. Nothing really dangerous can happen to us, say these modern humanists; nothing will ever really change. But, of course, it will.

Inevitably these illusions amid complete license, amid a collapse of traditional values, create their own reaction. Christians, as appalled as Luther and armed with much more information, are actually appearing in public once again to argue their beliefs and to stand up. Norman Lear may not like it; the United States Supreme Court may not like it – but so what? Lear is simply another little man with a megaphone; the Court can rule, but it cannot determine beliefs or events.

Today I write with a computer. A software program called—believe it or not—Perfect Writer enables me to type, correct, and print my own material. This is like bringing a printing press within the grasp of every individual. And that spells the end of the information monopoly; the media menace. The rule of those who allow only one side of every argument to be heard will end with this decade.

As a Calvinist I do not believe in any ladder of earthly progress, and I will not ascribe these developments to any effort of men alone. But I recall doing an essay earlier this year on the way that Luther's protest was spread all over Europe. He pinned his arguments—or the points he wanted to make—to a church door because that was the way scholarly debates were then conducted. What happened next was that a printer received a copy—not from Luther, by the way—and tens of thousands of copies then began to alert all Christendom.

We can say, therefore, that God provides the instruments—including people—to accomplish his purposes. New instruments are now at hand, and the people are rising. The great examples before us, and the lessons we need to understand, can be found in our traditional Christian literature, in our Bible, in our forebears, in our history, and in our hearts.

I am astonished, in looking at the history of France, of Italy, of the English empire, at how closely it follows the patterns explained in the Bible—at how repetitive these lessons are. Yet the seasons of man repeat, from infancy to old age; the seasons of the year recur and will continue to do so—and follies repeat themselves when the wisdom of the past is hidden from general view. If we were properly educated regarding the nature of this civilization, its origins, and its experiences, it would, in my opinion, provide the same sort of mingled grandeur and meanness that the Bible illustrates. For the world remains essentially the same. Christians survived Rome, they survived the Renaissance, they survived the French and Russian Revolutions, and they survived global wars.

We did not survive by accident. Unlike the Greeks, we know that we do not live in a world of chance. In this world everything that happens shows the hand of God. And of all men, it is the artist who is blessed by the talent to convey that sense of purpose to others. The failed artist becomes a propagandist; the true artist serves God.

---

[1] Erich Auerbach, *Mimesis* (New York: Doubleday, 1955).

[2] Jacob Burckhardt, *The Civilization of the Renaissance in Italy: An Essay* (Connecticut: Phaidon Publishers, 1955).

[3] Jacob Burckhardt, *Force and Freedom: Reflections on History* (New York: Random House, 1943).

[4] *Renaissance op. cit.*, 5, 6.

[5] *ibid.*, 164, 165.

[6] John Redwood, *Reason, Ridicule and Religion: The Enlightenment in England 1660-1750* (Harvard University Press, 1976).

[7] *Political Pilgrims: Travels of Western Intellectuals to the Soviet Union, China and Cuba 1928-1978* (New York: Oxford University Press, 1981).

Volume 4, No. 1, 1977
The Failure of
Seminary Education
by Rousas John Rushdoony

In the modern era, the church, while numerically strong, has grown less and less influential and more and more peripheral to everyday life, to politics, economics, the arts and sciences, and all else. For most people, the church is irrelevant to the "real world" of human affairs. It provides a limited moral training for children, a social focus for the family, and not much more. Churches have numbers, not strength. Both in membership and in leadership, the churches are radically weak.

Our concern here is with the leadership, and with those who train them, the seminaries. In analyzing the failure of the seminaries, it is necessary to point out, *first*, that the modern seminary is a rootless institution in many respects. At one time, the entire focus of education was theological; all life and education had, more or less, as its function man's better ability to serve, enjoy, and glorify God. The university was a product of the Christian Faith. Only Biblical faith, with its affirmation of *one Lord, one faith* (*Eph. 4:4*), could create a university. For paganism then and now, the universe is really a multiverse, not a single realm of one law under one God, but a multiverse of many possibilities, potentialities, and diverse law systems and life styles. Biblical faith made the birth and rise of the university possible. The essential education of man, when school and university were, more or less, Christian, made everything in life relevant to Christian faith. While education has never in the past approximated the ideal or standard of Biblically oriented instruction, it has all the same made, in Christian eras, the Faith basic to all things, so that a Christian world and life view of sorts dominated the scene.

Now the seminary student comes to his seminary usually with a long background of humanistic education. His seminary training barely scratches the surface of his deeply ingrained humanism. Within ten years, because most pastors do little serious or "heavy" theological, philosophical, and Biblical reading, their underlying humanism has reshaped their ministry. It is commonplace to encounter Arminian and Calvinistic pastors who are zealous contenders for the Faith in their churches but whose theology is so interfaced with humanism that their ministry is radically compromised.

At this point, the failure of seminary education rests, not in the seminary, but in the absence of Christian schools and colleges as the necessary prelude to seminary. It is, of course, necessary that these schools and colleges be essentially rather than nominally Christian. Thus, one of the best hopes for seminaries today is the rapid growth of the Christian school.

Second, we must recognize, on the other hand, that seminaries too often have a false orientation. They represent a denomination, an ecclesiastical body, rather than the Faith. The difference is an important one. If the seminary is created by an institution, its basic loyalty will be to that institution. So many new denominations, rebelling against what apostate seminaries have done to their old church, all the same reproduce the same pattern of control that leads to an institutional rather than a theological seminary.

In an institutional seminary, the financing comes from the denomination, whereas in an independent seminary, it comes directly from those who stand for the Faith. The difference is an important one: the wayward denominational seminary is less responsive to popular protests, and more remote from the people it serves. Everything is done through channels.

Third, this does not mean that independent seminaries have the answer. They, together with the denominational schools, are too often oriented more to academic respectability and to scholarship than to the pastorate and the Faith. The preferred student is the academically oriented student, not the student whose goal is the pastorate.

Moreover, scholarship, in the modern era, is too often scholarship for the sake of scholarship. Scholars think and write for their peer group, not for the people of God. With the rise of seminaries, scholarship has left the pulpit for the seminary, and, in the process, become less and less mindful of the pastoral responsibilities. Calvin, Luther, Knox, the translators of the King James Version, and others were better scholars than today's seminary professors, and they spoke and wrote for the people in the pew. Their scholarship had a theological, not academic, orientation, and it was therefore more popular.

On top of that, most seminary scholars write with the modernist scholar in mind. They are endlessly answering learned fools who need no answering, and who never read what the evangelical and Reformed scholars write anyway. To waste time and study on such an enterprise is intellectual folly, and is contrary to Scripture (*Mt. 7:6*). All too much of evangelical and Reformed scholarship is an exercise in irrelevance. There is little profit or meaning in it for God's people. It speaks, not to the problems of life, but to the problems of academic scholarship.

The seminary graduate should be a scholar in the word of God, trained to continue his studies and to apply the word to every area of life. The academic rather than pastoral scholarship of seminary life does not prepare the student to do this. It is better oriented to graduate studies than to pastoral studies, to academic questions rather than pastoral ones. The result is that much of the student's education has a minimal value.

Fourth, when the seminary seeks to become "practical" in its instruction, the result is a series of "junk courses" for pastoral training. The best and only sound pastoral training should come directly out of theology, Bible studies, and church history. By separating "pastoral psychology and counseling" from theology, both subjects are impoverished. By divorcing church administration, church law, church organization, etc., from church history, both are again made impractical. Luther and Calvin, we should remember, were scholars who derived their churchmanship from theological, Biblical, and historical studies.

The so-called "practical" courses, moreover, are taught by the worst possible men—big-city, big-church pastors who are hired as professors. In the past few years, I have encountered this same situation several times, one of a suburban church, newly begun; in other cases, of country churches. The small congregation is scattered over a farming community; the pastor lives next door to the church. The custodial work is parceled out: the minister is to clean the church weekly; the men come in to do painting and repairing on the manse and church; the women take care of kitchen needs, planting shrubs, and the like. But a problem develops: the young minister rebels, saying it is wrong for him to "wait on tables" (*Ac. 6:2*). The apostles dropped that task only when the church grew beyond their ability to cope with all needs, so that some "widows were neglected in the daily ministration" (*Ac. 6:1*). Paul did not hesitate to work to avoid burdening churches he wanted to feel freer in authority to instruct. The point is that seminary graduates are imbued with a false sense of their own dignity by the academic community. On the foreign mission field, Bible school graduates are more successful very often than are seminary graduates, because they are not as self-important. (One seminary graduate was dropped by his church's mission board when he said that he and other missionaries were living on too high a level to have any close contact with the people they sought to reach. Although dropped by the board, he continued as a missionary and was rated by a native scholar as the most influential missionary in that country.)

However, a central problem in the inadequacy of seminaries is eschatological. An eschatology of defeat (amillennialism) or rapture (premillennialism) does not need a world and life view, because it has surrendered much of history to the devil. Christianity is, however, inescapably a world and life faith because the God of Scripture is the sovereign God. He is Lord of all things, and Biblical faith speaks to every area of life, without exception. An eschatology of retreat and withdrawal will not concern itself with Christ's lordship over every realm. In American history from its earliest years, it has been very clear that any decline in postmillennial thought in theology has also been marked by a radical decline in the power and relevance of theology in American life.

An eschatology of withdrawal will not concern itself with what Scripture has to teach concerning politics, economics, conservation, marriage and the family, the arts and sciences, and other like subjects. The Bible is reduced to an ecclesiastical manual, whereas the Bible is in fact God's word for all of life. John Witherspoon's pupils exercised a determinative influence in the writing of the U. S. Constitution because Witherspoon's theology, however defective in some of its apologetic approaches, still represented an older and more catholic interpretation of the Reformed faith. Witherspoon saw the relevance of God's law to economic and political concerns.

Some years ago, I asked a seminary student about his theology courses. He described them as "about as dry as corn flakes." This is too often the case. Theology, where man should see the relevance of God's word to the totality of life, is too often marked by an abstraction from life, and by a barren, rationalistic logic. It views life from the study, and with the logic of the study. Calvin's *Institutes* smells of the battleground. (I am reminded of the criticism of Dr. Cornelius Van Til by an ostensibly Reformed scholar; he described Van Til's apologetics as "always too controversial" to be sound apologetics! This is a good illustration of the contemporary love of barrenness.)

This rationalistic sterility manifests itself in the seminary's neglect of music. At best, music has a minor place in the seminary curriculum. The Bible, however, has a major and central section— the Psalms—which is a songbook. Music appears in other parts of the Bible, and its links to theology and faith are strong. Whatever the theological problems of the medieval church, it deserved the name *Catholic*, because its approach to life was catholic, and it gave music a very central position. A living faith is a triumphant, singing faith, and the seminary today gives us nothing to sing about. We are told by some historians that there has never been a popular war without fresh and popular songs. The modern church has no "new song" for the Lord of any vitality, character, or joy. An eschatology of retreat, together with an abstract theology, cannot give birth to music. It is hardly worth a funeral dirge.

Contributors

R. J. Rushdoony is chairman of the board of Chalcedon and a leading theologian, church/state expert, and author of numerous works on the application of Biblical Law to society. Contact Chalcedon to learn more about the author's life, ministry, and writings.

P. Andrew Sandlin is executive vice president of Chalcedon and editor-in-chief of the *Chalcedon Report* and other Chalcedon publications. He holds undergraduate or graduate degrees or concentrations in English, history, and political science. His essays have appeared in numerous scholarly and popular publications, and he has written or edited several monographs.

Samuel L. Blumenfeld is a leader in U.S. homeschooling and phonics, and he has lectured on these subjects from coast to coast and abroad. State school authorities once called him statist education's "public enemy number 1."

Cornelius Van Til was the leading Reformed philosopher of religion of this century, the author of many books, a professor at Westminster Seminary, and a thinker of international influence.

When these articles were published, Gary North was editor of the *Journal of Reconstruction*. He has written scores of books. He is president of the Institute of Christian Economics.

Otto J. Scott, a Christian social critic and writer, edits *Compass*. Among his numerous books are *The Secret Six, James I, Robespierre: The Voice of Virtue, The Professional — A Biography of J.B. Saunders*, and *The Other End of the Life Boat*.

At the time this article was written, James Jordan was finishing his seminary education at Westminster Seminary in Philadelphia. He has written a number of books. He is president of Biblical Horizons.

J. A. Wermser was a bailiff in Amsterdam, Holland from 1842 until he died in 1862.

The late Joseph Braswell did undergraduate and graduate work in philosophy at the University of South Florida, but his real interest was in theology and Biblical studies. He published several articles in various journals.

CPSIA information can be obtained
at www.ICGtesting.com
Printed in the USA
FSHW011130051121
85970FS

9 781891 375040